Advance Praise

"Roselee Blooston's beautifully written, brutally honest memoir of endurance and ultimate acceptance of the cataclysmic sudden death of her life's partner rings truer than any of the many I have read and more movingly than any I could have written. Writing has been a catharsis for Roselee, as it was for me. Here is a helpful and, yes, healthy lesson for surviving the trials and tribulations of widowhood and the essential task of becoming a 'new you.' As Roselee put it at the book's end: 'Facing loss opened me up, and I like who I've become.'"

—Jane Brody, New York Times columnist & bestselling author of *Jane Brody's Guide to the Great Beyond*

"A gorgeously written, and gripping account of loss and love. Blooston brings to life the glittering city of Dubai, while at the same time letting you into her heart and her marriage. Uplifting and resonant, this book offers solace to anyone who has walked in a loved one's absence."

—Claire Bidwell Smith, author of *The Rules of Inheritance*

"After her husband suffers a life-threatening aneurysm halfway across the globe, Blooston finds herself navigating far more than the emotional dislocations of imminent, then actual, loss. From the moment she lands in Dubai, she must contend with the social dislocations of a country where women—newly bereaved widows included—have no standing. Riveting from start to finish, Blooston's beautifully written memoir is a truly original contribution to the grief literature."

—Jill Smolowe, author of *Four Funerals and a Wedding*

"This intimate, vigorous memoir of a contemporary marriage, an extended family, and the immense strains of sudden, unforeseen widowhood is an absorbing book, well worth reading. Moving back and forth between the chronicle of unfolding events and remembrance of the whole span of her marriage, Blooston's dramatic narrative joins the important new genre of widows' own stories. Blooston's memoir of her life with and without her exciting, loving, difficult husband captures the ache of an empty bed, the way that a newly bereaved person simply cannot imagine how they will ever again be able to feel peace or happiness again, and how, nevertheless, we slowly do find comfort, and even joy."

—Lise Menn, Professor Emerita of Linguistics, University of Colorado/Boulder, co-editor, *The Widows' Handbook*

"A timely, honest, heart-wrenching marriage memoir, from love at first sight to sudden widowhood in a foreign culture. As she struggles with grief, panic, family conflicts, misogynist bureaucrats, financial insecurity and disturbing revelations, Roselee Blooston stands up for herself—and emerges transformed."

—Jacqueline Lapidus, co-editor, *The Widows' Handbook: Poetic Reflections on Grief and Survival*

"Incredibly clear-eyed and composed, yet candid account of a life, a marriage, a love, a family, and a tragic death and its aftermath."

—Eric Levin, deputy editor, *New Jersey Monthly Magazine*

Dying in Dubai

Dying in Dubai

*a memoir of marriage, mourning,
and the Middle East*

Roselee Blooston

Apprentice House
Loyola University Maryland
Baltimore, Maryland

First Edition

Printed in the United States of America

Paperback ISBN: 978-1-62720-115-5
E-book ISBN: 978-1-62720-116-2

Design: Ashley Chestina Nicholson
Editorial Development: Lorena Perez
Author photograph taken by Maureen Gates.

Author's Note: Some names have been changed.
Brief excerpts from this book appeared in different forms in
The Widows' Handbook, Jacqueline Lapidus & Lise Menn, eds,
Kent State University Press 2014, and in *The Vital Force*, Vol.27,
No.3, August 2010, Good Karma Publishing.

Apprentice House
Loyola University Maryland
4501 N. Charles Street
Baltimore, MD 21210
410.617.5265 • 410.617.2198 (fax)
www.ApprenticeHouse.com
info@ApprenticeHouse.com

In memory of Jerry
For Oliver

And ever has it been known
that love knows not its own depth
until the hour of separation.
—Khalil Gibran

PART ONE

Coming Apart

1

I lay in a suspended state, barely breathing, reclining in the plush Emirates Airline seats next to my son as we hurtled over the Atlantic. Though the plane was traveling at unimaginable speed, with a force beyond my comprehension, my body resisted the inexorable movement, as if all five feet of me could stop the inevitable. If we never arrived, we would never have to know.

I couldn't eat or sleep, watch a movie or read. The flight to Dubai would take nearly fourteen hours, but time meant nothing. It had lost its reliable rhythm. Fourteen hours, fourteen minutes, or fourteen seconds, every increment equal to every other, every moment excruciating. We would arrive the next evening, an entire day gone. *And with it, what else?* I closed my eyes and tried to still my mind, and slow my wildly beating heart. I couldn't look ahead to what we might find, or back on what we might have already lost: our security, our family life together, my identity—w*as I still a wife?*

Every so often, I touched Ollie's arm. My almost-grown young man was the very image of his father, with his strong nose, expressive mouth and thick wavy hair, though without its salt and pepper. He sat up most of the night, and watched whatever the screen in front of him offered. As we descended, I held his hand. I wanted to scream, cry, let loose my fear and rage. *How could this be happening?* Instead, I remained quiet, steeling myself for what was to come. I looked into my son's sorrowful eyes—my eyes—their deep blue piercing me, begging *Make it all right, Mom*. I wanted to protect him, but that wasn't possible now. He was too old, and it was already too late. It killed me that Ollie had received the first call, which had set in motion a reality out of our control. He was in this horror with me. There was nothing from which I could spare my child, or myself. Agony.

This would be my third trip to Dubai and my son's second. Jerry, Ollie's father and my husband of twenty-four years, might die in a land none of us had any love for, a land I never wanted to set foot in again. But here we were, in torment, heading towards…

We could not have known then what the next two weeks would bring.

I stared in front of me, and watched the elegant flight attendants in their trim tan suits and veiled red fezzes as they leaned over other passengers, offering them anything they wanted. When they walked past me, I averted my eyes, closed them, and pretended to sleep. There was nothing they could offer me. I was beyond help. *What did I want?* Not to think the next thought that pushed towards the surface of my consciousness. Each time it threatened to rise, I forced it down. I knew what it was, but I could not allow myself to think it. If I did, it could be true: *He might already be dead.*

2

Two days earlier, Sunday, January 20, 2008 – Day One

8:45 a.m. I was outside in the backyard of our Montclair, New Jersey home, throwing tennis balls to our black and yellow Labrador retrievers—Edgar, aged ten and a bit arthritic, and Tizzie, an eight-month-old pup. I tossed one ball after another directly into Eddie's opened mouth, a game he loved as much as he used to love chasing them. Tizzie, of course, could run, though she still hadn't gotten the hang of dropping the round fuzzy thing at my feet so we could do it all over again. I threw a second ball. Surprise; she scooped it up and brought both back to me, releasing the last one onto the bare ground and keeping the original to soothe her teething gums. Edgar had retreated to his favorite spot under a barren azalea bush, watching us serenely, making no demands.

I came back into the kitchen, and put the dogs' water bowls on the floor. As they slurped eagerly, I noticed the flashing red light on the answering machine indicating a message. It was from Jerry. *Oh good.* For the past three and a half years, the high point of my day, the moment I looked forward to, was the iChat with my husband. I lived for my daily dose of Jerry. He was supposed to have been home two days earlier, but had had a last minute change of plans. I had been so disappointed. I longed to see him, to touch him.

I played the message. Jerry said he had to cancel our talk, because he had "the worst headache of his life," and he needed to lie down. I looked at the clock, and quickly calculated that since it was nine hours ahead of Eastern Standard Time in Dubai, the time there was now 5:45 p.m. I didn't want to wake him, but I was worried; I had to reach him, and I knew the best way was by email. He kept his iPhone by his bed and checked messages at all hours, whenever he heard the beep. I wrote: *If it's really the worst headache of your life, get medical attention immediately.* I don't know what prompted me to send that message—something I had read once about headaches.

He didn't answer. I told myself it was probably not so bad, probably his sinuses. Jerry had always had allergies and sinus headaches, and like me, he tended to be dramatic. He'll feel better in the morning, I thought. Of course, he will.

Then I put it out of my mind and went about my day.

5 p.m. EST. I had just come back from walking the dogs when I got a call from Ollie, who was a senior at the University of Chicago. Raine, Jerry's personal assistant in Dubai, had found Ollie's number on Jerry's phone, and had called to say that Jerry was brought to the hospital unconscious. *What?* I shuddered. *Jerry in the hospital?* I tried to picture him lying on a gurney, and couldn't. I couldn't take in the news—Jerry in extremis—nor the messenger. Raine. That woman. I felt my fingertips go numb as I gripped the phone. Then I wondered why she called Ollie, why she hadn't called *me.*

I called Shari, my best friend, who lived not five minutes away. She immediately came over. I was more upset that Jerry still had Raine in his life, after I had told him to stay away from her and he had agreed, than I was about the possibility, which I couldn't absorb, that my husband was in serious physical trouble.

"You can kill him later," Shari said. Only that afternoon, we had been having one of our endless discussions about our husbands—hers a disappointing breadwinner, and mine an errant traveler.

"He's got to come home for good," I told her. "I can't stand this anymore."

I swallowed, though my mouth was rapidly going dry, and called Raine. I had never spoken to her before. In her vaguely European accent she told me, "It's bad, very bad," then gave me the number of the emergency room. *Bad.* The word hit me like a slap. How could such a little word hurt so much?

Everything around and within me began to slow down, as if my entire nervous system had short-circuited—the air, the dogs' obliviously wagging tails, my mind. I walked into my study, sat in front of the computer, and stared at the screen. Shari sat opposite me on the couch, but even her warm, enveloping presence could not stop the chill that shot threw me. I willed myself to call the emergency room doctor.

"I'm Jerry Mosier's wife," I said, enunciating too carefully, my tongue thick with terror.

I could hardly understand him, but his rudimentary English did not prevent me from hearing this: "The prognosis is poor. The brain is filled with blood from a massive hemorrhage." Each word—*prognosis, poor, brain, filled, blood, massive, hemorrhage*—looped through my mind, skating on the surface of my consciousness, as if to avoid sinking in, while my body constricted in a vise of tension meant only to keep me from breaking into a thousand pieces.

The doctor wanted to know what drugs Jerry took. I said maybe Ambien, Prozac, Tylenol, asthma medication. I told him what Jerry said about the headache, and asked what they thought was wrong. He said the bleeding came from one of three things: a stroke, an aneurysm, or a drug overdose. Then he told me they had transferred Jerry to the ICU, that he was on a life support system including a ventilator, and that he was not expected to live. *No. No, no, no, no, no.* Each statement, a punch in the gut.

The doctor wanted to know how soon I could get there. I mumbled, "As soon as possible." *Possible?* What was possible now that the unthinkable had come to pass?

When I put down the phone, the muscles in the middle of my back seized up; my mouth went completely dry; my body froze. I placed my left hand on my heart, and kept it there. I could feel the relentless beating against my ribs, but I couldn't feel anything else. *This must be shock*, I told myself. I had never been in shock before.

I called Raine back, and found out that all of Jerry's friends and colleagues had come to the hospital as soon as they heard. Everyone wanted to know when I was coming to Dubai. I had to go, but how could I? *If I went, it would mean that this was happening.*

Shari said, "This is what you were always worried about."

I nodded slowly. She was right. Three and a half years earlier, when Jerry started working in the Middle East as a media consultant, this was my greatest fear, that one day I would get a call, have to cross the ocean only to find him in a hospital. It was a fear that stemmed partly from the location, and partly from my husband's frailties.

Eventually, Jerry too, sensed something amiss. All through the previous year, he had said often and at random, "My head's going to explode." I chalked the statement up to stress. Now the words resounded within me like a premonition.

I looked into Shari's sad brown eyes, grateful that my friend was there. If she hadn't been sitting across the room and propping me up with her love as I made the calls, I wouldn't have been able to function at all. Even so, it took twenty minutes for my fingers to tap in the correct numbers for Emirates Airlines. My half-shut brain couldn't connect the number on the screen with the keypad on the phone.

Finally, I managed to make reservations for the next night. I knew it might be too late, but Ollie had to come home first. I couldn't go without our boy. I wouldn't. When he asked me if Dad was going to be okay, I had said I didn't know. It was the truth. I promised him that we would fly together—the only promise I could make. We would see him together.

I called Jerry's brother Scott, with whom we were closest, and asked him to pass the word to the rest of the family. Scott's low, throaty assent mirrored my shock.

Then I called George. Next to my husband and son, he was my dearest relative, three years my junior, more like a twin than a little brother. I needed him now like no one else. Our parents had died; I was estranged from our younger sister. Unlike the rest of my family, my relationship with George was blissfully untroubled. We always stood by each other. I had introduced him to Jerry the weekend of Simon & Garfunkel's Central Park concert in September, 1981. The three of us had staked out a tiny patch of ground on the periphery, and spread a blanket. What a treat, even without sightlines, listening together to "Bridge Over Troubled Water" and other favorites. From that day forward, George had unconditionally accepted Jerry, called him brother.

There wasn't much George could say when I told him, but hearing his soft, gravelly voice mumbling his concern kept me from dissolving completely.

By then it was late. I hadn't eaten dinner. No appetite, only a heartsick nausea. I opened up the foldout couch for Shari. She stayed all night. I went to bed, eyes open, body rigid with pain, Edgar snoring beside me. Over and over I replayed how, four years earlier, my husband had wound up in Dubai in the first place.

"You're not going to like it," Jerry said, squinting through his wire-rims at the computer screen in front of him. He wore black-framed glasses, which made him look like Elvis Costello's twin.

We were downstairs in his basement office. The walls touted AdFactory, his company's logo—an industrial building with smokestack that Ollie and I had painted orange, while putting footprints and dog paws up the side of the opposite wall, and covering the uneven cement floor in a deep blue. Instead of giving himself the title of director or president, his business cards said, "Plant Manager," an example of the wit and outside-the-box thinking that had given my husband a colorful, if rollercoaster, career in advertising. Before striking out on his own, he'd had real successes while working as a copywriter at New York agencies in the '80s and '90s. He'd come up with the Air Force's "Aim High" campaign, which lasted decades and was recently revived, as well as the "candy bar with the cookie crunch" tag for Twix. Jerry, Ollie, and I had screamed with delight when George Costanza spouted the line on *Seinfeld*. Along the way, Jerry won an Addy, the advertising world's highest accolade.

But for the past year and a half, work had been evaporating, and we grew more and more desperate. We took out an equity line on the house to pay our basic expenses, and cut everything to the bone. In March, Jerry broke down. I'd never seen him so low, and it scared me. He would go back to bed at 11 o'clock in the morning with a pillow over his head to block the light. *Where was his irrepressible energy?* Jerry was the kind of guy whose sense of self-worth depended on his worldly success. How much money he earned, how much recognition he received in the form of praise or better yet, awards, set his inner level of contentment. He wasn't superficial, just very old-fashioned, very male in the primal, provider sense of the word. When he couldn't provide, he came apart.

One particularly dark evening he came home in despair. "I'm worth more dead than alive," he said, pursing his lips at the grim assessment.

My mouth opened. Nothing came out. I feared he would hurt himself. I couldn't imagine life without the man who had been the very definition of alive.

"I'd never leave you and Ollie," he said under the glare of the emergency room's lights, where he stayed until morning. Antidepressants leveled him off, pulled him back from the edge. Or maybe it was simply the regularity of everyday life: the meals, the dog walks, watching baseball on TV, holding hands over scones at Starbucks. I didn't care. I wanted more than anything to have my man back, the one who made me laugh, who was so vigorous and full of ideas, the one who always landed on his feet. The dread in the pit of my stomach never left me. I was afraid he wouldn't get well, we wouldn't survive financially. Most of all, I was afraid life would never be stable again.

Like many women, my biggest fear was ending up on the street. The sense of insecurity was traceable to the time my attorney father expressed his disappointment that after receiving a Vassar education and an MFA—a terminal performing arts degree, equal to a PhD—I couldn't find a job. "She could go on welfare," he had said. I remember sitting at the kitchen table with him, and feeling baffled and ashamed at having let him down so much that he could make such an outrageous statement.

My mother, who had been standing at the stove, shot back, "That's ridiculous. She was raised to marry a millionaire." My mouth dropped, this time more out of anger than shame. It was 1973, not 1953. Where was the woman who had raised me to be strong, independent, a go-getter? Resist as I tried, the message from both parents—a matched set of diametrically opposed views—sunk in. They agreed on one thing: that I wasn't fit to support myself. I felt defeated, a failure before I had even begun.

Though I proceeded to land a fulltime tenure-track teaching position at a respected university, the "welfare to millionaire" split emerged repeatedly throughout the years, as I tried in vain to make a decent living as an actress, teacher, and writer. My financial dependence on Jerry contributed to my sense of incompetence no matter what my accomplishments were. We both believed that raising Ollie was the most important full-time job, but my feelings of inadequacy and shame never quite abated.

Still, I sent out résumés to every university, community college, and private school within driving distance. Before the downturn in Jerry's work, I had left my adjunct position at Montclair State University, with my husband's blessing, to run full-time the non-profit writers' organization that I had founded. But as with most of my artistic and educational career, I put in a lot more than I got back. Drained, I reached a point where I couldn't work only for love; there had to be money, too. And though I lacked confidence, I was determined to do whatever was necessary.

Meanwhile, Jerry had been interviewing for a high-level media consultancy at an international broadcasting network.

"What do you mean I'm not going to like it? If it's a job that pays well, why wouldn't I?" Suddenly, the possibility that we were going to make it out of this crisis dangled in front of me, and I felt a surge of hope.

"Oh, it pays. Mega bucks," Jerry said. "That's the good news. The bad news is that I'm going to have to be away quite a bit."

"Oh." My shoulders sank. The longest Jerry and I had been apart in our twenty-three years together—over twenty as a married couple—had been a ten-day stint he had spent in Brataslava years earlier. It had been very hard on both of us. I realized he would never have considered such a job if Ollie were still in high school; Jerry treasured every day with his only child. But our son would be graduating soon, and then off to college. It was just me my husband had to consider. Yes, I was an adult, but the prospect of being separated from my partner for long periods of time rendered me childlike, vulnerable. Early in our courtship, Jerry had turned down a job offer in Chicago because I wasn't ready to uproot myself for someone I was just getting to know. But now, despite my fear, I couldn't and wouldn't stand in his way. It was too important to him and to our family. "Where?" I asked.

"The station is in Dubai. The United Arab Emirates." I couldn't picture where that was. I knew next to nothing about the Middle East. What I did know alarmed me. We'd all been shaken deeply by 9/11. Ollie had watched the towers fall from the front lawn of his high school. We could see the smoke from all over Montclair for weeks. A close friend of Jerry's had barely escaped from the south tower. My husband's office in the city was only twelve blocks away; he had happened to be home with a cold that morning. Sheer luck.

"Don't worry," Jerry went on. "It's very Western there, very safe. All they care about is building skyscrapers and making tons of money."

"Um." I was skeptical. It seemed unreal, too far from our current lives to make sense to me.

"Al Arabiya is new, so I'd be there to help them get the word out, position themselves as a moderate voice in the Arab media scene, something to counter Al Jazeera."

I sighed, confused. I asked why him, why not someone who's more familiar with the culture?

He reminded me of Advocacy Communications, the public interest advertising agency he'd started in the '80s, and the 1995 public relations campaign he had worked on for *Desert Warrior—A Personal View of the Gulf War*, a book by Saudi prince Khalid bin Sultan. I nodded, but had only a vague recollection. "The Saudis own the station. It seems once you've entered their world, they never forget you, so my name came up. They're convinced Americans know advertising, PR, and media better than anyone."

I shook my head in disbelief. "Wow. Talk about timing."

Jerry smiled his Kermit the Frog smile, which never failed to charm me with its goofiness. Then he got serious, swiveling his chair to face me. "I won't do this unless you are okay with it."

I moved closer, studied his gray-green eyes glowing with expectation, and kissed him on the forehead. I didn't know what I was going to say until the words came out of my mouth. "I think it's a huge opportunity—the opportunity of a lifetime. You've worked so hard for so long to get to a place where you can do something on a grand scale. Now here it is. And we sure as hell could use a way out of this hole we're in, but…" I paused, not sure I wanted to go there, feeling that I had to.

He pulled himself up straight. "Here it comes."

"But you're still you, with your challenges. So this could be the best thing that ever happened to you, or the worst. It could go either way." I put my hand on his. "I don't want to have to fly over there and see you in a hospital room."

He stroked the back of my hand with his free one. "Don't worry, I'm not going to drink. I'm not stupid. It's illegal except in hotel bars."

I folded my arms and stepped back. Jerry had many years of sobriety behind him, thankfully throughout our son's childhood—a long stable period, which had lulled us both into believing it would last forever—but his recent depression put him at serious risk of relapse. I was afraid neither of us could go through it again.

I took a deep breath. "I want you to have the career you've always dreamed of," I said, "to fulfill your destiny, and I do believe that this is it. So though the prospect makes me nervous, I don't think there's a choice. You have to do it. But you also have to understand, there's got to be a time limit." I paused. I'd always had a strong sense of my inner clock, and my limits. "Four years. As long as Ollie's in college. That's it. That's all I can do." He nodded, and kissed me. We had made the decision together, as we always did. I was excited, relieved, and unsure how we would navigate this new future together and apart.

Ollie graduated from high school in June, and over the summer Jerry took a couple of brief trips to Dubai to get oriented. The station put him up in five star hotels, a luxury he relished along with the first class flights on Emirates Airlines. "You wouldn't believe the amenities—a private cabin to sleep in, along with incredible food, and impeccable service." He sounded like he was writing their ad copy. "I can't wait for you to come."

There it was. He missed me already. And I missed him. I ached for my husband like a newlywed. When Jerry first took the job, I thought fleetingly of joining him, but I couldn't live with the idea of leaving Ollie during his freshman year and moving thousands of miles away. "One of us has to be stateside," I said. Jerry, though disappointed, agreed. Our son's welfare was our top priority.

And then there was the fact that I was Jewish. During the interview process, Jerry was asked if he was. The UAE had no formal diplomatic relations with Israel, and being Jewish might have put him at "a disadvantage." This assessment churned inside me. Even if I could have gone, I did not belong where my husband would be, a truth I found tough to accept.

At the end of September, Jerry and I drove our only child to the University of Chicago, a thirteen-hour trip from our New Jersey home with the car packed to the gills. At the campus gate, through which we could not follow our son, seniors stood holding boxes of tissue. I didn't cry until we got back to the hotel room. Then I let out a torrent, pacing back and forth, while Jerry wept on the bed. We tried to cheer ourselves up by going to a Mexican restaurant, but Jerry's mind had already turned to his new career, while mine was stuck on the impending upheaval. I felt a gnawing, anticipatory loneliness, because I knew that as soon as we got home, Jerry would be leaving—this time for two whole weeks.

All at once my nest emptied and my spouse went away. Then menopause; the night sweats began almost immediately after Jerry left. And my work life went into free fall. The non-profit was in its last days—my choice—but that didn't make it any easier. Four changes at once: my son, my husband, my childbearing self, my work. Any one of them would have been enough to handle. Together, I felt overwhelmed.

The markers of my world had dissolved and I was profoundly disoriented. I hardly knew who I was.

3

Day Two

5 a.m. A second doctor called, waking me out of the stupor into which I'd fallen only an hour earlier. I wouldn't have called it sleep. Raine and Kamilla, a station colleague of Jerry's, had arranged for a consult with this outside neurologist. His assessment was as clear as the first one was opaque. The toxicology screen came back negative for drugs and alcohol. I exhaled.

Thank goodness that in this crisis there was no alcohol in Jerry's system. I was afraid that had there been, the hospital staff would have treated him with less concern, that they would have written him off. Public drunkenness in the UAE wasn't tolerated. I used to worry that he'd end up in jail after a bender, which was why I didn't tell the emergency room doctor what one of his New Jersey friends said when he'd heard of my husband's plight.

"I don't know if you knew, or if this will help, but Jerry told me he couldn't stop drinking over there." I nodded, though the caller couldn't see me.

"I know," I said, and thanked him.

My husband's face flashed on the computer screen—one of our iChats, when it was afternoon in New Jersey and evening in Dubai. "Hiii." His pale face loomed; he was leaning too close to the screen.

"You've been drinking," I said, instantly seething. *How could he?* He knew how dangerous it was. Common sense, though, had nothing to do with it. He couldn't help himself, and I couldn't help him. I hated feeling so powerless.

"Noooo," Jerry said, his smile as broad as his denial. He was leading a double life: one here, one there, one sober, one not.

A rehab counselor had told him he had to "learn to reconcile his two lives." I knew he needed to go back for more treatment. We had talked about it often, but he wouldn't consider returning. Watching him juggle and avoid set off all my alarm bells.

"I'm fine," he said, believing his high functionality meant exactly that. I desperately wanted to believe, too, but the constant knot in my stomach said otherwise.

Now it was blood filling his brain that threatened him, an exponentially more perilous threat than a drunk-driving accident or a run-in with the police. I listened as the second-opinion doctor told me the test results were better than expected. It was possible my husband could recover. I thanked him and got off the phone. I began panting as if I had just run around the block. The doctor's words instantly became my mantra: *It was possible Jerry could recover. It was possible.* Now we had some hope to carry with us on the plane.

Then I went into automatic pilot mode. I recognized, dimly, that my feeling self had gone underground, submerged by the necessities of this emergency. There was no time, no energy, no way to *be* other than to *do* what had to be done. There was no choice. I had to function. I had to move.

First I packed, remembering to include a scarf, shawl, long-sleeved tops—even in "liberal" Dubai, it was best to bring modest options. Then I wrote out instructions so Shari could take care of the house and the dogs. I opened our safe and retrieved our passports—Ollie's, mine, and a copy of Jerry's, as well as one thousand dollars in cash. The money had been stashed there since 9/11. Somehow, my emergency felt as earth-shattering as the nation's had years earlier. I was about to close the safe's door when I stopped, and pulled out the legal file. Better take copies of our marriage certificate, Jerry's will, the medical and legal powers of attorney. Not a conscious acknowledgment my husband might die—I couldn't let the words form in my mind—but the repressed thought directed me to be prepared. *Just in case.*

Then Shari went home to change; she would return in the evening, before we left. I called Kate, a dear friend who had been the maid of honor at my wedding, as well as members of my writers' group, and asked them to phone others. So deep was my inner paralysis, I could hardly register their gasps of shock, their words of support—*he'll be all right...Jerry's a fighter...he always bounces back.* I could walk, talk, ready myself for the trip abroad, but not think beyond it. They spoke of the future, a future I couldn't picture.

I waited for Ollie to arrive. I had arranged for a car to pick him up at the airport, because I didn't trust myself to drive. I tried to settle myself by practicing T'ai Chi Chih, the non-martial, westernized version of T'ai Chi I had taken up a year earlier to help ground me while my life frayed. But I was not in my body. As I shifted from one foot to the other, I couldn't feel my own weight. I repeated the T'ai Chi Chih refrain: *focus on the souls of your feet.* It didn't work. My head floated high above the rest of me, a disconnected balloon.

When Ollie finally walked through the door, he was pale, exhausted, unshaven, with his long, brown hair uncombed, though none of this obscured his beauty. As a child, his looks had won him representation as a print model, but since I had no interest in being a stage mom, his career was brief. Ollie had Jerry's slender frame, and his mannerisms—the quizzical head tilt, the shoulder hunch—a striking resemblance friends and family never failed to note. I saw myself in our son as well, in his big blue eyes, even features, loud scratchy voice, and levelheaded perceptions. But on that day there was nothing level about me.

We hugged. For a moment, I reentered my body, my mothering self. The sheer size of my boy still had the power to surprise me; I was hugging my baby, not an almost-grown young man. I drank in his smell, the familiar sweetness mixed with the airplane's stale scent. When we let go, I offered to make him some lunch. Ollie said that he wasn't hungry, and went immediately to his room to re-pack for the trip overseas. All at once, the house seemed too vast, too empty, too much a reminder of all we might be about to lose.

For the rest of the afternoon we hardly talked. There was too much to say.

That night Ollie's best friend Keith, a reliable young man who knew what was important, came to the house to see us off. He and Shari embraced us, and stood inside our garage waving as the car pulled away. In the back seat of the Emirates limo, Ollie and I waved to our receding friends, our receding life, falling away behind us. Whatever we were about to face in Dubai, we both knew nothing would be the same again.

The car service to JFK came with the business class tickets that I had purchased. I knew when I booked them that I would never feel free to spend that kind of money again, but I didn't think either of us could get through the long flight any other way. Indulgent? Yes. Foolish? Perhaps. But I was in survival mode. No price was too high.

I turned around, faced forward, then looked out the window opposite Ollie's at the cold, sparkling Manhattan skyline. I was motionless, locked within myself, steeling myself for the moment when we arrived at the airport and had to surrender to our unwelcome journey.

4

Day Three, Dubai

When we left the plane and proceeded through customs, Ollie was stopped by Dubai security. *Oh no. Not now. Not this.* The official, dressed in long white robes—a dishdasha, the full-length shirtdress traditional for Emirati men—took one look at my son and pulled him into a room, just beyond baggage claim. The door closed. I inhaled sharply, as if they had ripped him from my arms.

Immediately, I told a second guard in a suit uniform, "I am his mother. His father is in the Rashid General Hospital ICU. We don't know if he is alive or dead." I forced myself to speak calmly, but inside I was frantic. We were losing precious time. I didn't have an international phone; we were supposed to get Jerry's iPhone later from Raine. Wali, his director friend, was waiting outside to take us to the hospital, but I had no way to contact him to tell him about the delay. I wanted to magically vanish and reappear at Jerry's bedside, but I was trapped in the airport along with my son.

"Don't worry, Mama," the guard said. "Come sit here." *I'm not your Mama.* I felt patronized, handled. He directed me to a bench across from the closed door behind which they were doing God knows what to Ollie. "This is routine. For your security, too." *Was he serious?* My security was lying prostrate in a hospital bed.

The door opened. I saw Ollie standing in front of a table, his face ashen, his body taut. He was trying to hold himself together. I looked down and saw that he was barefoot. I wanted to rush in, grab him, run for the exit. The door closed again. I couldn't believe that this—this violation, this interrogation, on top of the reason we were here in this foreign country—was actually occurring.

After what seemed like an eternity, Ollie was led from the room. I stood, desperate to reach out to him, knowing I couldn't. The guard who had questioned Ollie placed his suitcase on another table and unzipped it. He opened vitamin bottles, unrolled socks, removed the top of Ollie's deodorant. Meanwhile, time was passing. I pictured Jerry lying inert on a hospital gurney, and I lurched toward the mental image, then righted myself, slapped back by the presence of the guard and the harsh lights. I opened my mouth, gulped air, and slowly exhaled a silent hiss in a panicked version of labor breathing.

When the interrogator was done riffling through Ollie's belongings, he smiled at us both. "Follow me," he said, and then walked us outside to Wali, as if courtesy could erase what had just happened. Ollie jumped into the backseat of Wali's SUV, and I slid into the front passenger seat. *Go, go,* I thought, *Get us out of here.*

I had met Wali, a short, balding Jordanian with soulful eyes, one year earlier, while visiting Jerry in Dubai. As soon as the guard handed us over, Wali smiled and said, "Good news. Jerry's blood pressure is down. He's stable, and I am taking you straight to the hospital to see him." All I could think was, *Thank God he's still alive.*

In the car, Ollie poured out the interrogation. They had asked him repeatedly, "Do you do drugs? Have you ever done drugs?" Then he was told, "You do drugs. Yes, you do," to trip him up, to confuse him into an admission. Shades of Jerry's experience.

Every time my husband reentered the United States from the Middle East, US Security detained him for questioning. Wali said the procedure was triggered because Ollie had long hair. Profiling. They assumed an American "hippie" had drugs.

Rashid General was the government hospital of Dubai. As with all government buildings and many private ones, its sliding front entrance displayed huge painted faces of Dubai's sheikhs— Sheikh Mohammed bin Rashid Al Maktoum, the current ruler, and Sheikh Zayed bin Sultan Al Nahyan, who founded the United Arab Emirates, and for whom the city's main highway was named. Their mural portraits seemed especially ominous in the night's shadowy half-light. The hospital lobby was deserted, except for workers polishing the gray linoleum floors, and one woman behind the reception desk in a black abaya, which covered her from neck to toe and was accompanied by a hijab, or headscarf. After Wali addressed her in Arabic, she waved us in. We went through two more security checkpoints, past beret-wearing policemen. Now that I was in the building where I knew my husband was, I had to restrain my urge to skip the checkpoints and to race up the stairs. I wanted nothing more between us.

At the ICU, yet another policeman had us don gowns over our clothes, and scrub our hands with disinfectant. Then he allowed us through the swinging doors, and into the ward. Jerry's bed was directly in front of the main door. I gasped and grabbed Ollie's hand.

There he was, behind a curtain, ventilator tube in his mouth, with more tubes running all around his body. Jerry. My man. My husband. My best friend. My partner. The one person in the world who defined life for me. He looked so fragile, so vulnerable, smaller prone than standing. Sweat dotted his brow. His expressive face, now immobile, seemed more delicate. His long, beautiful eyelashes, which I had dubbed, "Liz Taylor lashes"—an admiring tease he had protested, but secretly enjoyed—stood out in ghoulish contrast against his yellow skin. *Wake up*, I thought. *Wake up. Tell me this is all a mistake, that it isn't real.*

Seeing him this way—quiet, motionless, struck down—was worse than the vision I had conjured since the call, because it was *real*. My husband was in peril in this strange land. The weight of that truth bowed my shoulders, crushed my chest.

I told myself to breathe, then leaned in, saying, "Jerry, Jerry, Jerry," over and over and over again.

Jerry Michael Mosier was born with a congenitally blocked bile duct, spending the first six weeks of his life in an incubator, hooked up to tubes, after enduring a very dangerous operation to unblock it. Big stuff in 1955. Very few of these operations had ever been done; it was miraculous that he survived. When I first heard the story, early in our courtship, I thought about how feisty he was. I could easily imagine, while looking at the scrawny, energetic twenty-six year old, the frail infant fighting with all his might to live. Jerry was so full of life, and so driven to achieve, to experience, to connect.

He was a runner then, preparing for marathon after marathon. In 1984, when we'd been married just over a year, he ran in the hottest New York City Marathon on record. Only ten percent of the runners crossed the finish line, and Jerry was among them. I was so proud.

Over time though, the incubator story came to mean something else to me. I began to see that Jerry's fragility never left him. Underneath all the accomplishment, creativity, and sheer vitality was the same baby, alone, separated from his mother, crying out to be held—to be safe and at home, not only in the world, but more importantly, in his own skin. This was the Jerry whom I loved, and who drove me to distraction with his extremes.

Not many people knew this about Jerry. He seemed so strong

and capable, and he was, but he was also a tender spirit trying desperately to get out of the bubble in which fate and his body had placed him. After the incubator, he created bubbles of his own, some safe—our family of three—some not: the drinking world, the world of Middle Eastern conflict. He was playing out his initial struggle on a larger and larger stage.

My father had called him "restless" when Jerry changed jobs once too often for his liking. He didn't understand that my husband was searching for more than satisfying work. The frenzied activity, the schemes and demons came from an unsettled soul, which couldn't recognize its own intrinsic wholeness. Over three years into the latest journey, he had grown weary. His face looked more haggard every time he returned from Dubai. We both knew the grueling schedule couldn't continue.

Bending over his hospital bed, seeing my husband's restlessness stilled, I wanted it back, all of it, the good and the bad, the joy and the struggles, the crazed life, during which at least we were moving. Together. There, then, was when everything stopped. And though I stood next to his bed, we were separated by more than the miles that had kept us apart. It struck me, as I watched the ventilator force Jerry's hairless chest up and down, that he had come full circle, back to the helpless baby in the incubator, separated from those who loved him most, and I hated that this was so.

I had trouble reaching over the railing to touch him, but I managed to stroke his arm and his long, tapered fingers. I picked up Jerry's cool, limp hand. I kissed his cheek, and whispered in his ear, "Sweetheart, we are here now. Please come back to us. We love you." I imagined his voice echoing mine, *I love you, too*, but there was no sound other than the machines monitoring his tenuous hold on life.

Then Ollie spoke, bending as well. I could hardly see his face for the tumbling locks. "Dad, I need you." We held each other and cried. Wali turned away.

The ICU night supervisor, a Pakistani doctor, motioned us into his office, asked us to sit on a blue vinyl couch under a flickering fluorescent light, and explained the dire nature of Jerry's condition. I heard fragments. *Big bleed, not stable enough to operate on. The next few days will tell. Most patients in this condition don't make it. Prognosis poor.* Same as the phone report. The doctor's words seemed to transform the room from spare and plain to brutal and ugly.

Ollie looked at the floor. I realized this was the first time he had heard how serious his father's situation was. I cupped his hands in mine. Then the doctor said, "I don't know what your religion is…" and fixed his eyes on mine. I let my response—silence—linger. I wasn't about to tell him.

On our first family trip to Dubai a little over two years earlier, from the moment we stepped onto the tarmac, I had the distinct sensation that not only was I in foreign territory, but also that I was a true alien. I didn't want anyone to know I was Jewish, or that Ollie was, either.

It wasn't as if I had spent my life as a practicing Jew. My parents' most fervent wish was for our family to fully assimilate. Being American had been more important than being Jewish; we even celebrated Christmas. My mother called it "a pagan holiday," an excuse to shop, decorate, and eat. And of course, I had married outside my ethnicity. But I had an immediate visceral reaction to setting foot in a land that was technically at odds with Israel. I knew this was a minor factor, something I had wrestled with and put aside when Jerry first proposed the job. But breathing the air, being there again under such terrible circumstances, was an altogether different experience. My body, simultaneously shut down and on high alert, seemed to know that it didn't belong here. Perhaps jet lag had peeled back my defenses. I couldn't shake a profound sense of isolation in a hostile land.

The doctor continued, "…But here we say, *Inshallah*, God

willing, he will recover. Now you pray." His tone angered me. The doctor's job was to save my husband, not to tell us to pray.

Jerry, ever a man of action, always jumped in to do what was necessary. As a fifteen year-old Boy Scout, he received their Award of Merit for administering mouth-to-mouth resuscitation to a man who had collapsed on the street. Years later, Ollie and I watched in awe when, at a turnpike rest stop, Jerry performed CPR on a fallen stranger until the ambulance arrived, while passersby remained oblivious. And as a kayaker accompanying swimmers on a nine-hour marathon around Manhattan, Jerry had rescued one who'd become trapped in the pilings. *Who would rescue him now?*

When we left the hospital, I was suddenly aware of my exhaustion. I'd been awake all night. We had left on Monday; now it was Tuesday night. The cumulative effect of the long flight, of Ollie's interrogation, of seeing Jerry in a hospital ward, hit hard. As Wali drove us to Jerry's apartment, I sank into grogginess one minute, then startled into vigilance the next. Ollie sat silently next to me, lost in himself.

I looked out the car window at block after block of building cranes. When we had visited, Jerry had told us, rather proudly, that Dubai, in its manic race to create itself over night, used ten percent of the world's total construction equipment. The stark silhouettes of half-completed skyscrapers set against the night sky chilled me. The strange up-from-the-desert modern city gave me nothing to hold on to except mile after mile of crude strip malls, luxury car dealerships, and massive office towers meant to signal Dubai's arrival as a player on the world stage. Titillated as he was by the possibilities, Jerry used to complain, "There's no *there* there."

The city, originally a tiny fishing village that was home to pearl divers, had, in forty years, transformed itself through a flurry of building projects and an open-arms approach to business people from all over the world into a twenty-first century power center.

Ninety percent of its population were ex-pats, including my husband, who as a survival technique, must have decided it was real enough for him. He seemed to have gotten used to the artifice, and to have found a way of accepting, or at least tolerating, the false front of this new Arab metropolis. For me, though, so alienating and otherworldly was its landscape and culture that Dubai might as well have been the moon.

We arrived at the apartment building in the desirable Marina district. I looked up at the two huge banner portraits of the sheikhs hanging from its glass walls, so similar to the hospital's renderings, only many stories larger. They seemed to say, "Never forget where you are, and who rules." *As if I could.* Wali told us that he would pick us up in the morning to return to the hospital. Inside the building's revolving door, in the dark marble and glass lobby, the night clerk handed me the apartment key and the iPhone that Raine had left for us, and then gave us a lingering, mournful look. I looked away. I couldn't acknowledge his concern with more than an over-the-shoulder nod. A stranger's pity. Too painful.

Although Jerry returned to the states every two or three weeks and stayed about as long, his time at home wasn't nearly enough for me. It took almost a full week for him to get over the jet lag and then, before we knew it, he was preparing to leave again. The schedule ate up our life together. Out of his usual three weeks in Montclair, only the middle week had any semblance of normalcy. I never really adjusted, and neither did he. Our daily phone calls or iChats helped, but I found myself storing up the minutia of everyday life to tell him when we talked—stories about the dogs, my writing, our neighbors and friends, news about Ollie. Five minutes or fifty, our conversations were never long enough. My husband wasn't a foreign correspondent or a soldier in harm's way, but his job strained us nevertheless. We were living outside each other's realms, and it felt totally wrong.

In the spring of 2006, when Jerry stopped staying in expensive hotels and rented the apartment—he had used the British term "flat," yet another confirmation that he was adapting to a new life without me—I was distraught. I interpreted the move as a sign that he wasn't coming home for good anytime soon. The logic of his explanation, that it was so much more economical, not to mention more relaxing, to have a place of his own, did nothing to calm me. I became despondent. I saw him slipping further and further away from me and our life together, and more and more enmeshed in the artificial world of a sandcastle city.

I tried to convince myself that this was temporary, a necessary though uncomfortable glitch in our long partnership. I tried to look at the benefits, the fact that his job had radically improved our financial situation. But money and mantras didn't assuage me. In addition to putting down roots, Jerry had just applied for residency—the only way, he explained, to sign a lease—and had formed a documentary film company, an outgrowth of the contacts he had made while at the station. The more entrenched in the United Arab Emirates my husband became, the more I despaired of our future.

By the time Jerry had been in his Dubai apartment for ten months, I was long overdue for a visit to see it. Summer in the UAE was far too hot—up to 130 degrees during the day—and the fall was not much better. The only time to travel was winter. My first trip there had been the family vacation fourteen months earlier, when we stayed with Ollie at a hotel on the beach. The trip would be my second time in the country, and my first in Jerry's apartment. I had seen pictures of the place, of course, with its floor to ceiling windows, the hotel beaches visible below, the Arabian Sea, the marble bathrooms—three and a half of them—and the ultra-modern vibe. Jerry worked with a designer for window treatments and basic furniture, but he said that he wanted my touch to warm up the space's marble and glass, to make it "more homey." After much resistance on my part—I didn't want him to think of home as any place but our house in New Jersey—I relented, and flew with him to Dubai.

As soon as I entered the apartment, I said, "You need some rugs, lots of them, and pillows, and a nice bedspread. It's too cold in here." I didn't mean the temperature.

Jerry beamed with excitement that I was finally involved. Standing there, the fact of the apartment, and all that its existence meant for us, made me loathe it even more.

The next day we went to the Mall of the Emirates, one of Dubai's many shopping centers, and certainly the most well-known. It housed a 400-meter indoor ski slope. Jerry and I watched through floor to ceiling glass windows on the second level as families tumbled, slid and yes, skied, down the 6000 tons of artificial snow. The desire to import a season the country could never know seemed to me an exercise in absolute control, however frivolous. Dubai had a lot to prove to the world, that it could compete, be anything to anyone—for a price.

Afterwards, we went shopping. As we walked through the mall, I noticed three women dressed in burkas, the traditional head to toe black covering favored by Muslims in the UAE. I heard clicking and looked down. On one woman's feet were the unmistakable red soles of Christian Louboutin pumps, and on the other two, Manolo Blahniks. Their swishing gowns revealed pastel chiffon knee-length dresses underneath. Then I spotted the designer handbags. "Money," Jerry said. "Lots of it." I found the contrast between repression and luxury disorienting, to say the least.

At the carpet store, my husband haggled with a couple of dealers over stunning Persian and Afghan rugs large and small. The prices were incredibly low. We purchased a gorgeous blue and cream rug for our bedroom in Montclair, and another ten, on his expense account, for the apartment. Then we picked up towels, his and hers terry cloth robes, duvets for the three bedrooms, pillows, throws, and a few framed posters for the walls. Jerry already had put up some of his photographs, but there was so much wall space, he needed more.

On the way back, we stopped at Spinney's. The small, British-style market carried "biscuits," or cookies, more tea than coffee, and had a separate area for Haram meats—pork products that Muslims and observant Jews were not allowed to eat. But of course, there were no Jews there. The store had an aisle of basic kitchenware with lovely blue and white bowls Jerry could use in his foyer to hold keys and change, and as ashtrays. He was smoking again; everyone smoked in Dubai. His pattern had been to substitute one addiction for the other. The dormant habit had reasserted itself, much to my dismay, though I told myself it was better for him than drinking.

When we got back to the apartment, we laid the rugs on the polished marble floors. They looked spectacular, but didn't entirely eliminate the bachelor pad atmosphere. Then I put my new robe, and, at his insistence, a few of my clothes—a swimsuit, a beach cover, a pair of linen pants, a top, some sandals—in his closet to keep there. "So you'll feel at home when you come back," Jerry said hopefully. I sighed. I knew I could never feel at home there, despite the truth that *he* was my home.

That night, after dinner, we stood on the bedroom balcony and watched the sun set over the Arabian Sea. Jerry pointed out a faint mountain silhouette—Iran—in the distance. "It's so close," I said, as disturbed by the proximity as my husband was thrilled. Danger excited him.

Lying in bed that night, he held me and said, "Thank you so much for doing this. It means everything to me that you have helped me make this place livable."

I took a deep breath. "You're welcome," I said, not sure if I meant it.

Jerry fell asleep, his head on my chest. I stared at the ceiling, and back to the black bedroom windowpane. I knew everything I did to help him stay more comfortably, and potentially longer, was undermining what I wanted: for him to come back home once and for all. I had stamped my taste on his generic luxury apartment, only further confusing the issues between us. I didn't want to disappoint him. I was trying to be a good wife by supporting my husband's job of a lifetime, but I was acting against myself. *What good would it have done to resist?* I couldn't risk creating even more distance between us. He couldn't handle it, and neither could I. No, I resolved. I needed to stand with him, even if it meant pushing aside my own needs.

As Ollie and I entered the apartment, flashes of Jerry flooded me as if I had been there when it happened, and seen the devastation myself. My husband covered in vomit on the floor in the front hall, the kitchen floor strewn with glass from the stove top—Raine had vividly described what she found when the apartment staff called her to check on him. The second opinion neurologist had explained that the hemorrhage had caused a brainstorm, which in turn caused the destructive behavior. Before Jerry lost consciousness, two apartment workers had found him wandering the halls, incoherent. Instead of calling an ambulance, they had put him to bed. A wave of guilt washed over me. *I should have been there.* Not them. Not her.

Raine had made sure the place had been cleared before we arrived, and it crushed me to see the clean, empty floors covered in the lush oriental rugs Jerry and I had chosen together. *How could I be here without him?* But for Ollie, the experience was entirely different; he had never been to his father's place before. I could see how overwhelmed by it he was, the polished minimalism nothing like our home in New Jersey. I put my hand on his back and steered him down the long hall towards the guest rooms. "Take your pick," I said, attempting lightness. Ollie shrugged and put his suitcase in the room closest to the master.

I plugged in the iPhone. My husband had been a first adopter when it came to any new Apple gizmo. He had stood in line for this one, and proudly displayed it to curious strangers while drinking his morning coffee at our local Starbucks; it gave him yet another excuse to engage in lively discussions. Jerry loved to talk. I, too, had thought the phone was cool. Now it seemed both a lifeline and another disturbing reminder of the complicated, fast-paced life that had brought us to the brink of disaster.

I climbed into Jerry's bed, and pulled the dark green velvet spread I had chosen for him around me. At four o'clock in the morning, I woke up shrieking. Ollie ran into the room. We clung to each other, shaking. Then, without asking permission, without needing to ask, he took his father's side of the bed, and stayed there until dawn. Not since he was a little boy with a fever had my son slept next to me. We were alone, together, still hurtling into the unknown.

5

Day Four, The Hospital

Three hours later, light poured through the bedroom windows. Feeling more drugged than rested, I forced myself to eat a few spoonfuls of oatmeal and drink a sip or two of weak coffee. I knew I couldn't keep going on fumes. Ollie nibbled on toast. I was concerned; he looked so drained. Neither of us had had any real sleep.

We went downstairs and outside the apartment building to wait for Wali. The Dubai sun, strong even in January, startled us. Ollie shielded his sunglasses with his hand and said, "It's too damn bright." Yes. The desert sunlight hit me like another assault. Wali's car pulled up and he greeted us with, "No change. He's stable." *Thank God*. Wali had taken it upon himself to call the hospital for us. I was grateful. I couldn't have made that call myself. It was all I could do to simply *be* there.

In the car, Ollie and I took in the city's daytime skyline and the hundreds of immigrant laborers at each building location in jumpsuits color-coded by job site or migrant camp—blue, green, yellow, white. During our 2005 visit, Jerry had told us that the workers were likely from Pakistan or India, indentured to the city's construction companies, sending most of their meager pay home to their families. They couldn't leave, even if they wanted to. I understood that whatever my husband and I had been going through, ours was a privileged separation, but I still felt a kinship with their situation. Trapped. We were all trapped.

Palm trees lined Sheik Zayed Road, along with out-of-place grass, too green for the desert. I wondered how much water it took to maintain such golf-course luster. The city was one huge, glitzy building site aiming for a cross between Las Vegas and Rodeo Drive. Revulsion swept through me.

We entered the ICU. The room was ten times brighter than the night before. The hospital's head of neurosurgery, a stocky doctor originally from Iraq, stood next to Jerry's bed, surrounded by a group of visitors. He held out his hand, unusual for men in this part of the world. I shook it. "Where were you?" he asked. No greeting, just the question, and its indictment: *Why weren't you with your husband?*

There it was. My guilt voiced by this stranger. I was too stunned to answer.

Then he introduced the group. "Neurosurgeons from Houston, Texas," he said with pride. This reassured me. He must have been competent to earn such a following. One of two woman doctors locked eyes with me, bit her lip, and looked down—a silent message that turned my stomach.

The neurosurgeon continued. "Your husband has suffered a ruptured brain aneurysm. In order to operate we must find the source. The CAT scans show too much bleeding to see where the problem is. We are going to do an MRI this morning, to see more. I will call you later." He nodded and left the ward.

A brain aneurysm? I didn't know exactly what that was, and I was so intimidated by the setting I couldn't ask. Later I would learn that an aneurysm is a ballooning of the vascular arterial wall, sometimes congenital, sometimes developing over time, often diagnosed only after it bursts. I would also learn that smoking and drinking are risk factors, but of course, not every smoker or drinker develops an aneurysm. Of all my fears for Jerry, this wasn't on the list.

The other woman doctor and a man, both quite tall, approached me. "This is a very good hospital," the woman said. "State-of-the-art. The neurology department is world-class. If anyone can help your husband, they can." I thanked them. Their high opinion meant something. I could see in the slight release of my son's shoulders that what she'd said had given Ollie what he needed to hear, but I couldn't seem to absorb her words in the way they were intended. I couldn't escape how desperate the situation was. I was afraid to hope.

The group moved on to other patients. Ollie, who had been shadowing me, sat in a folding chair next to Jerry and took his hand. I stroked my husband's brow. His skin was cooler than the previous night, his face more relaxed. *Or was it my imagination?* I whispered in his ear, "We are here. We are with you."

Then I began to panic. Money. *How would we pay for this?* ICU, neurosurgery, hospitalization for who knows how long. I went to the ward desk, directly across from Jerry's bed—there was no privacy at all. A young woman in a black abaya sat in front of a computer. I asked if she spoke English.

"Everyone speaks English here," she said.

"I am Mr. Mosier's wife. I need to know what the charges for his care are so far."

She opened a folder with Jerry's name on it. "First I must ask you a question. How old is your husband?"

"Fifty-three."

"Oh." She glanced at his inert body. "He looks so young. We thought he was forty." I smiled. Jerry would have loved that.

"According to his identification, your husband is a legal resident of Dubai. This is a government hospital. There is no charge." In this worst of circumstances, Jerry's formal commitment here—our sore spot—had become a saving grace. This horror wouldn't bankrupt us. I gave the young woman the iPhone number, and asked her to call me and no one else from now on with any news. I didn't want Raine, or Wali, for that matter, in the middle.

Then two gray-haired women, one with a short no nonsense haircut, the other in a loose bun, entered the ward. They wore long multi-colored skirts—Indian, perhaps—and no headscarves. We smiled at each other. The one with short hair came over to me. "My son has been here for weeks. He works for the State Department. He has a brain infection. My sister and I are hoping to take him home soon. What about you?" I told her that my husband's condition was very serious. "This is an excellent hospital, " she said and turned to a man in a black polo shirt and black pants, who stood a few feet away. She waved him over.

"Your husband is an American?" he asked.

I nodded, begging him with my eyes to help us, *please help us*.

"This is where we would have taken President Bush if anything had happened during his visit." Bush had been to Dubai only a week or so earlier. "Your husband is in good hands." It wasn't help exactly, simply another assurance from a reliable source. I wanted to believe that the medical expertise this man and the Texas doctors touted meant Jerry would make it. But I didn't know how to channel that optimism when I was overcome with terror. His head had exploded, just as he had said it would, an awful irony after the real world danger he had faced traveling for shoots in Lebanon during February 2005.

"I'm okay." Jerry sounded strange, his usually resonant voice too thin.

"What?" I propped myself up on my elbow while pulling my body over to my husband's side of the bed. I looked at the clock: 6:50 a.m. I was so sleepy that I didn't remember picking up the phone.

"I'm all right. I wanted you to know immediately. I wanted to get to you before you turned on the news."

I sat up and rubbed my eyes. I knew he was traveling, I just couldn't remember where. "What happened?"

"Rafik Hariri, the Prime Minister, was just assassinated."

Then it came to me. Jerry was in Beirut to meet with a production company for his upcoming documentary on the region.

"I just landed. I was on my way to the hotel. A car bomb took out his motorcade. They're saying one thousand tons of TNT. The hotel, too. All its windows were blown out. I've found another smaller inn, in a safer area."

I took a deep breath. "My God," I said. This was exactly the kind of thing I had worried about when Jerry started traveling in the Middle East—random violence, Jerry caught in the crossfire. "Please be careful. Please. I love you."

"I love you, too," he said. "Oh, and happy Valentine's Day."

I shook my head. "Yes, really happy."

Attendants surrounded Jerry's bed. I jumped. *What was wrong?* They told me that they had to bring him downstairs for an MRI. We followed, and sat in the waiting room. The walls of the MRI room were glass. We would see everything: Jerry being transferred to the machine and slowly sucked under it down to his stomach. Part of me didn't believe that this inert person was Jerry, my whirling dervish of a man. While I stared at my husband's legs, the iPhone rang. It was Raine. She was in the hospital. Whether I was ready or not, she was coming to meet us. I held my breath.

A few minutes later, a tall, willowy redhead entered. She had a perfect complexion, hair in a high ponytail, and was dressed in designer jeans, shoes, and top. Jerry had described Raine to me, but I'd never met her before, and was not prepared for how drop-dead gorgeous she was. I felt like a troll, a middle-aged frump, but when I saw her, prancing down the hospital corridor, eyes glued to her cell phone, long perfect nails tapping out a message, her glossy beauty made a kind of infuriating sense. Of course he would have been taken with her. What man wouldn't have been?

She embraced me and then Ollie, while rattling on about what she'd be happy to do for us: cancel and return Jerry's rental car, handle the apartment utility bills, which she did whenever Jerry was away, arrange lunch with Wali's wife, Sabeen. I thanked her. At this point, I was so undone, so exhausted, that I would gladly take any help offered. Even from Raine.

The attendants wheeled Jerry's gurney out of the MRI room. A nurse said the results wouldn't be available for a few hours. The doctor would call us.

We left with Raine to go to lunch. Outside, in the hospital parking lot, she couldn't find her car. Ollie rolled his eyes, as we followed her up and down the rows of cars, sweating in the noon sun. In the middle of our search, she made a call. "Can I get a *mas*-sage this afternoon? Four? Brilliant. Thanks." I suppressed a smirk at her blatant insensitivity. *She* needed a massage?

After ten more minutes of wandering, we found the car.

Sabeen was waiting for us near the hotel lobby buffet. I didn't know which hotel it was, and didn't care. I had met Wali's wife once before, with Jerry. Though as fashionable as Raine, there was nothing superficial about her. She radiated strength. This was both her television news presenter—we would call her an anchor—persona, and her true character. And she beamed with post-partum glow. She and Wali had recently become the parents of a baby boy.

Sabeen hugged each of us, and urged Ollie and me to eat.

Neither of us had eaten a real meal since getting the phone call, three days earlier. I still had no appetite, but knew I had to feed my body, or I would collapse. The buffet was massive. I heaped my plate with hummus, pita, salad, chicken, and then picked at it, every once in a while putting fork to mouth, tasting nothing, forcing myself to swallow.

Sabeen painted an upbeat scenario of Jerry's long recuperation from this brush with death. "Of course, he won't be able to fly for months, so you will move here." I stopped mid-bite. "Wali and I will help you in any way possible. We'll make sure you have what you need—breaks, exercise classes, friends to have lunch with…" *As if it would be an extended vacation.* I almost choked.

Raine chimed in that since her boyfriend's recent motorcycle accident, she knew all the best physical therapists in Dubai. Oh. She had a boyfriend. Then I remembered Jerry telling me about her various romantic adventures. Maybe I had been over-reacting all along.

I began to hyperventilate. Ollie stopped eating. I hated this city. I hated its shallow façade concealing a total lack of culture: no art, no museums, no bookstores—well, one inadequate shop selling only romances and thrillers that Jerry had found near the marina—no history, just shiny buildings, over-the-top resorts, consumption on display. I couldn't imagine having to live here, even if it was to take care of Jerry.

I remembered Shari's response right after the call when I asked, "What if he's a vegetable?"

"That would be the worst thing," she had said.

I pictured our comfortable home in New Jersey, the lawn covered in snow, and Ollie in college many time zones away, our dogs, our tree-lined neighborhood, our friends. Even if I could work all that out, I wouldn't be able to handle the suffocating lack of real freedom. On our family trip to Dubai, I had asked Jerry who the tall men in the long white robes were, standing around the lobby of our posh hotel; to my Western eyes, they added to the captivating exoticism of the place. "Police," he said. "They're everywhere."

I shuddered at the memory. I considered myself a strong person, but if I had to live here, I knew I would crack.

Back in the ICU waiting room, we met Kamilla, Jerry's station colleague, the one who had arranged for the second opinion doctor. She was thinner than I remembered from my visit a year earlier. And blonder. She took my hand, looked me in the eye. "Jerry is tough. He has already beaten the odds. He wasn't supposed to make it through Sunday night. It's a miracle he's still alive. There's hope." I nodded out of rote politeness. Her well-meaning vision of my husband's possible recovery, just like those that had come before hers, didn't penetrate. Her words sat on the surface of my consciousness like a vaccination that didn't take.

She continued, "You are not alone. We are your family here. We will see you through this." She paused. "Oh, I wanted to ask you, have you found Jerry's other mobile and his SIM card?"

Huh? I shook my head. *What was she taking about?*

"His local *mobile*?" Accent on the *i*. "We can't keep calling you on the international phone. It's too expensive." She sat back, waiting for my response.

Oh. The iPhone. I couldn't believe she was tallying expenses when Jerry's life was on the line. Another sign that Ollie and I were there without a net. No matter how supportive his friends and colleagues were, they weren't *our* friends. Friends didn't make petty demands during a crisis.

When I didn't answer, she went on, "If you can't find the card, you can stop in any phone store in Dubai and get another one. You can even replenish it at any gas station." She smiled at her own helpfulness.

I stared at her. This was utterly beyond me, and I was in no shape to argue. I could barely move from one moment to the next, and she wanted me to go out and buy a phone? I didn't have a car, and even if I did, the last thing I could do was drive. All I *could* do, all I *wanted* to do was what I had to—be here for Jerry—and try to cope with whatever came. But I couldn't say any of this to her.

Kamilla must have seen it on my face. "Well, you can take care of it tomorrow." She retreated, and quickly changed the subject. "Do you have food in the flat?" Without waiting for my answer, she said, "I will take you to Spinney's." This I could do. Had to do. There wasn't much to eat in the apartment.

Kamilla waited in the car, while Ollie and I went inside the store. Memories flooded me. I pushed a narrow wire cart past the aisle, where a year earlier I had picked out pretty Moroccan dishware for the apartment. Ollie plodded behind me. We were both too drained to make sensible choices. We threw some wan bananas, yellow-green broccoli, and mottled potatoes into the cart, and then cruised down the bread, cereal, and pasta—labeled "noodles"—aisle. I couldn't imagine cooking, but I put a box of spaghetti in the cart, along with milk, juice, and cookies. We walked down the soft drink aisle, and Ollie grabbed a carton of Coca-Cola, Jerry's favorite. "For when Dad gets better," he said, his eyes pleading with me not to contradict him. He was holding on to the threads of hope thrown to us by the outside doctor, the Texans, Wali, Sabeen, and Kamilla, none of which I could seem to grasp.

"Sure," I said, giving my son what I couldn't give myself.

In the apartment, no sooner had we shelved our purchases than the hospital called. The neurosurgeon wanted to see us immediately.

We didn't say a word in the taxi. The hospital was on the other side of town, about twenty-five minutes away. I missed Wali. It felt further with a stranger driving. The endless vista of skyscrapers, empty and full, the hot-cold light, and the commercial signs we couldn't read offered no relief.

In the hospital, a young woman dressed in the standard black abaya—she'd probably be a candy-stripper back home—led us through the long, gray basement halls to the neurosurgeon's office. This was the man who thought I was a bad wife, whose question that morning had indicted me. Now he seemed more neutral, all business. He motioned us to sit opposite him on a beat-up leather couch.

"The MRI did not reveal the source of the bleed. It did show that your husband's brain is experiencing vaso-spasms from all the blood. Normal for this condition, but we cannot operate until the spasms stop."

I inhaled deeply. "When it stops, what will you do?"

"*If* it stops," he corrected, "and we can see the aneurysm, I will insert a coil to repair it. For now, though, all we can do is wait. I'm sorry. You understand that your husband is in very serious condition?"

I wouldn't have called my state of mind *understanding.* I understood the gravity of Jerry's situation on only the simplest level; my deeper self could not comprehend *this* happening *here.* But I nodded, and asked, afraid of the answer, needing to know, "Is it possible that he can live through this?"

The surgeon paused. "It's possible."

He had said what I wanted to hear, but still didn't quite believe. Ollie let out a huge sigh. I took his hand. We stood, thanked the doctor, and left.

That afternoon we met Ashar at Jerry's bedside. He was a businessman with whom Jerry had begun a side project, which if it came to fruition would be worth millions. All I knew about this man was that Jerry liked him, that he was highly educated and reputed to be a billionaire. Ashar appeared to be in his early fifties, like my husband, and wore a long linen robe with no head wrap. He spoke to Ollie about losing his own father when he was in his twenties. *As if Jerry were already dead.* But he made Ollie laugh, for which I was grateful. Then he walked us outside the building. We had called a taxi, but no car came. After a while, Ashar asked, "You'll be all right, won't you?"

The only possible answer was "Yes, we will," though I was far from sure. We watched Ashar get into the back seat of his chauffeur-driven limousine and pull away. I later wondered if he didn't offer us a ride because I was a woman. Would it have been improper for us to be in his car together? Thus stranded, we crossed the busy circle outside the hospital grounds and found a storekeeper who gave us another taxi number to call. After we waited forty minutes, alone and bereft, the cab arrived.

6

Ollie

On the burnt orange leather coach in Jerry's living room, Ollie and I sat and nibbled on cookies, yoghurt, and some apricots we had found in the refrigerator. Ollie stared at the blank flat-screen television on the opposite wall.

"I need distraction," he said. He turned on the television. As I had discovered the previous year, CNN was the only familiar station available.

"Heath Ledger dead at twenty-eight," the anchor announced.

"Mom!"

We were both transfixed by the news of such a young, gifted person's death. The celebrity tragedy momentarily trumped our own, and seemed somehow related. I remembered my mother's death in 1994. There weren't enough limousines available to take our small family to the cemetery because Jackie Onassis' funeral had taken every car in the DC area. Anything could happen, any time, to anyone. We watched the coverage until, as if it were a junk food splurge, we'd had enough.

Then we looked through the wall of windows at the sun setting over the Arabian Sea, and in the distance, the foggy outline of land. I pointed and told Ollie what his father had told me. "That's Iran," I said, with none of Jerry's enthusiasm. Ollie stared and said nothing. Thousands of miles away from home, in fear of losing everything, the bay and the border served as two more measures of our lost state. *Where were we?*

Ollie hung his head. Brown strands shaded his eyes. "Mom, is Dad going to die?"

Oliver Blooston Mosier was born on September 8, 1986, ten minutes to midnight, two weeks before my due date, and the night before our third wedding anniversary. On the way from Brooklyn to St. Vincent's Medical Center in Greenwich Village, Jerry was so rattled he drove south on First Avenue—the wrong way—with me squatting in the back, shouting directions between labor pains.

When the nurse brought Ollie to me, swaddled and clean, and laid his peacefully sleeping self beside me in the hospital bed, I had a sure sense that this tiny person had more wisdom and clarity—new as he was—than his parents would ever achieve, no matter how long we lived. I also understood, although this baby was closer to me than any other human being, that he wasn't *mine*. Before he was conceived, I addressed my fears concerning motherhood in my fourth solo comedy, *Mad Moms*. As soon as the initial New York run ended, I became pregnant. Now, with my son in my arms, my vague anxieties subsided. The knowledge that my job would be to shepherd him along his path, to help him become his full self, hit me viscerally. And just as I imagined in those first few hours, he became a mature and confident little boy and young man. He always knew who he was.

After tending to our Springer Spaniel at home, Jerry returned to my hospital room the next morning with champagne and cake to celebrate our anniversary and the birth of our son. We toasted,

"To us, to baby Ollie." We laughed. "At least he has his own day," Jerry said, but we were both overjoyed that the two most meaningful dates in our lives would be forever linked.

On our first Valentine's Day as parents, Jerry gave me *A Mother's Work* by James Fallows, and inscribed it, "Together we'll find the balance."

My husband knew how concerned I was about keeping my creativity alive. He was a true partner, sensitive to my needs even as we focused on our baby. We were in it together.

Jerry threw himself into fatherhood, coaching Little League, starting a father's group at Ollie's elementary school, helping with homework, attending every cello concert, fencing tournament, and school play, and sharing with Ollie his passion for dogs, cars, history, architecture, and the Yankees. From toddlerhood on, Ollie accompanied Jerry on long city walks, soaking up New York lore. When Ollie was older, they would discuss at length the work of George Carlin, PJ O'Rourke, and Christopher Hitchens.

Jerry taught Ollie to cook, starting when he was old enough to sit up in a backpack, lean over Jerry's shoulder, and observe his father chopping and stirring. At the tender age of five, Ollie progressed to knife skills, and by ten was designated "sous chef," a role that continued throughout his high school years. On Sundays, my guys spent all day creating Bolognese sauce and pasta from scratch, while screaming at the Jets on TV. One evening a couple years later, after throwing a dinner party for his college friends, Ollie called his father to say that Jerry's cassoulet recipe had been a hit.

Jerry surprised Ollie with a full page picture in his high school yearbook; it showed our two-year-old son striding confidently across Martha's Vineyard's dunes above the caption, "Proudly Marching to a Different Drummer since 1986." On a poster-sized version of the same picture, mounted for signing at Ollie's graduation party, Jerry wrote, "Never follow." My husband gave our son what he had spent his own life seeking: complete love, guidance, and acceptance.

I stroked Ollie's back in widening circles. Again, he asked me if his father was going to die. "I don't know, sweetheart. I don't know." I didn't, but my foreboding was contagious.

"I need Dad," Ollie's voice cracked, "to show me how to be a man." Only the night before, I had heard him tell a friend, "It's so important to be a father."

Both the plea and the declaration broke my heart, and made me proud. I had always thought Jerry was at his very best in that role. "He already has," I said.

I could not relax, lying alone in my husband's bedroom under the covers we had purchased together. When I finally fell asleep, I dreamed our house tumbled through space—an ink sky, thousands of stars—and shattered as it fell. Bolting upright, breathing hard, I screamed.

Ollie came running. "Call George," he said.

It was dinnertime in Princeton. I heard the sound of running water and the clank of pots and pans. I visualized George in his kitchen with his gentle wife, Jeanne, and their twelve-year-old twins, and longed to be with them, surrounded by their warmth. Then my brother asked me what was happening. "It's awful, so awful," I said. "We are entirely alone here. Jerry's friends are trying, but they don't know us. We have no one."

George said he wished he could come, but he had let his passport lapse, and it could take days to get a new one, days we didn't have. "I'm so sorry. I want to help."

I told him that just hearing his voice was enough, and for a moment, it was true.

7

Day Five

In the hospital ward, Ollie and I waited for the outside consultant to arrive. He was the doctor I had spoken to on the phone, while I was still in New Jersey, the one who had offered hope. After talking with the surgeon yesterday, I badly needed a second opinion.

I held Jerry's hand. It was cool, dry. Though I didn't want to, I was getting used to the tubes, his stillness. This alarmed me. He was so active—the kind of guy who was always in motion. *How could this be the same person?* The answer: it wasn't. This man lying in front of me, quiet and unreachable, wasn't my Jerry. Not really. Ollie stood on the other side of his father's bed. My son's eyes roamed up and down Jerry's body, searching for signs of life, willing him to move.

"I looked at all the test results, and examined your husband," the consulting doctor said. We had gone out into the hallway for more privacy. How strange that the public hallway of a hospital was more private than the ward; it was true in US hospitals as well. This doctor, a Palestinian, spoke with a perfect English accent.

His full head of curly light brown hair indicated he was decades younger than the hospital's neurosurgeon. "I concur with the doctor here. We must wait for the blood to absorb and the spasms to subside before operating. This could take anywhere between four days and two weeks."

Two weeks? I couldn't fathom such a wait.

The consultant turned to leave. "I trained under your surgeon. He is the best." Another vote of confidence, which only partially registered in my stalled brain.

When he was gone, I hugged Ollie and said, "We'll hold on to that," but I wasn't holding on to anything. I was falling in slow motion, woozy, and afraid I might pass out. Ollie looked exhausted as well. We had yet to sleep through the night. "I have to go back to the apartment to lie down," I said.

But we didn't lie down. Ollie and I sat in front of Jerry's computer and poured over emails from friends. *Oh, Roselee, how is Jerry? What can we do? Am thinking of you constantly. He'll be okay, I just know it. We are with you.* The longing and emotion on the screen contrasted with my growing numbness. I didn't have the energy to answer them all. To a few I wrote that the news was grim, but there was still a chance he would survive. Writing the words, I almost believed them. Almost, but not quite.

We found the local phone in Jerry's desk drawer. Luckily the numbers for all his contacts were in it. I called Kamilla. She was happy we could communicate more easily. And more cheaply.

I called the hospital ward to give them the new number. I was operating by rote.

Then I called Shari. It was early morning in New Jersey. I could hear the yearning in her voice. She wanted me to tell her Jerry would make it. I was afraid to say it, afraid it wouldn't be true. She told me the dogs were fine. It was good to speak with her, but no one, not even my best friend, could reach me. I was on another planet.

George called. He hoped it was okay with me that he'd told Vicky what was going on. She was our younger sister from whom I had been estranged for almost four years. He apologized again for not being able to come because of the passport lapse. "It's fine," I told him, though he was the person I most wanted to be with us, adding, "We will need you after." *After what?* I was projecting the unthinkable, my words ahead of my thoughts.

"Vicky is going to call you. I think she will come. I promise she won't be a burden to you." *Burden.* George, a writer, chose his words carefully.

My sister and I had had a rocky relationship ever since my teen years. Unlike my brother, the middle child, who could listen and empathize with anything I told him, my sister, six years younger, couldn't be trusted. I had to tread very carefully with Vicky. I didn't want confidences to be used against me. Vicky lived alone in the house we grew up in, which she had inherited. Because she had never married or had children, and because she was emotionally shaky, our parents feared for her future to such an extent that they put her before my brother and me, an action I tried to accept, in spite of my hurt. It was my nature to open up, to talk about my life, my feelings, but she didn't know what to do with the inevitably difficult, messy stuff, and ended up lashing out. We went through two estrangements: one in 1994, immediately after our mother died, that lasted five years, and another ten years after the first.

When Ollie was about to graduate high school in 2004, Vicky was the first person I invited. We had been in a good period, and I really wanted her with me. Our parents were both gone, and Ollie needed his whole remaining family to celebrate with him; so did I. Vicky accepted the invitation, and got time off from her work as a news producer. Then, a few days before the graduation, Ronald Reagan died. The public funeral was to be held the week after, but Vicky insisted that she had to stay in Washington in case the station needed her. I begged her to come. George got her to admit that the bureau had not asked her to cut her vacation short, that they didn't actually *need* her. I blew up. I pleaded: *I* needed her more than her workplace. She refused. Even in my fury and pain, I understood I had broken my own rule: *never ask anything of Vicky.*

A few minutes after I spoke to George, Vicky emailed Ollie asking if I would take her call. I told him yes.

"Roselee, it's Vicky. Do you want me to come to Dubai?" This was the first time I'd heard her voice since election night 2004, a voice exactly like my own, only with more edge. After our post-graduation argument, she had taken a three-month "break" from me, which I had found torturous. I didn't know what to do with the silence. That evening she had wanted to talk about Bush and Gore. I wanted to talk about our problems. After a tense conversation, I wrote her a letter suggesting we go to counseling together to work on our long-standing issues. I never got a response. This devastated me. How could she walk away *again*? George attempted to intercede with a pointed email, addressed to us both, though aimed squarely at our stubborn younger sister: *I don't want you two meeting over a hospital bed.* The next silence had lasted over three years.

"Yes," I said, "come." My response was automatic. I was desperate for someone, anyone, to be here with Ollie and me. We were under such duress that even a sister who had rejected me felt like a lifeline.

Vicky would fly out of Washington that night and arrive Friday morning. "We'll be at the hospital. Come straight there." I gave her the address.

After we hung up, I thought, *How surreal that she should be the one to rush to my side.* The split over her not attending Ollie's graduation was part of a larger family pattern of not showing up, beginning with my wedding. For my family of origin, sad times exerted a stronger sense of obligation than happy ones.

It was late. Ollie had gone to bed. I didn't know what to do with myself. I hadn't practiced T'ai Chi Chih since the day we left for Dubai. So I began, facing Jerry's bed—slowly, deliberately, moving softly, trying to stay present, not succeeding. About two-thirds of the way through the nineteen movements, I came to one I had never really "gotten" called Light at the Top of the Head, Light at the Temple. It had always seemed awkward, out of flow with what came before and after. But something changed.

When I cupped my hands above my head, opening and closing them the requisite three times, a bolt of energy—benign lightning—shot through my being, from the top of my head to the soles of my feet. It seemed to come from far above, and was undeniably power-ful. The charge quite literally grounded me. I had never experienced anything like it. The ICU doctor had told me to pray. I did not, not in the conventional sense. Instead, barely hanging on, I went through the motions of my practice, and channeled something stronger than myself—the vital force, chi, that the practice sought to circulate. The sensory experience shocked me. It had happened, instantly, at my moment of greatest need. A prayer answered after all.

8

Day Six, Turning Point

Ollie and I entered the ICU, and were met at Jerry's bedside by the head of the critical care unit and two nurses, young women in white headdresses.

"I'm sorry," the doctor began. A bottomless well opened inside me. "Your husband took a turn for the worse overnight." My stomach tightened, my breath became shallow. *Why hadn't they called me?* "The neurosurgeon will be here shortly to explain to you." He walked away from us. I felt Ollie's hands on my shoulders, keeping me from disintegrating.

One nurse tucked in Jerry's bedding. The other adjusted a bag of fluids hanging from a pole above his head. Neither one looked at me or at Ollie. Jerry seemed more unreachable than yesterday. Or was that my unnerved imagination?

Beads of sweat dotted Ollie's forehead. "Mom, Mom, what's going on?"

"I don't know, honey," I said. But I did. I knew Jerry was not coming back to us. I could feel it in the emptiness within and without, a weightless absence that took the place of my heart, lungs, stomach, and bowels, and that removed all depth from our surroundings, as if we and the room around us had been flattened into two-dimensionality. This was what I had been steeling myself for, ever since the first phone call. This was what I had dreaded. Then I thought of last night's T'ai Chi Chih experience. *Was that the moment? Was that Jerry shooting through me?*

As the neurosurgeon approached us, Ollie put one hand in mine and kept the other on my shoulder. He automatically assumed his father's protective role. "I'm sorry to have to tell you that the most recent tests on your husband show he has no neurological functioning." The cold terms froze like icicles in front of me.

I took a short breath in and held it. Ollie squeezed my hand. "You mean he's brain dead?" I began to breathe faster. I was afraid I would hyperventilate, faint. Ollie looked up at the ceiling, straight into the glaring lights.

"Yes. I am sorry. There was nothing to be done. Too much bleeding." He went on. "In our country, a person cannot be declared dead until the heart stops beating. We do not turn off the machines keeping a patient alive. We have, however, in the past, for patients from *other* countries, in situations like yours, turned them down to minimal levels." *Minimal levels*. My mind repeated his words without fully comprehending them.

"And if you do that, how long before he...?" I couldn't say the word.

"Three days at most."

I felt my body swaying. "My brothers-in-law will arrive Sunday night. I do not want to do anything until then." Scott and Ross had to be here before...

"Very well. I will arrange a meeting with the ICU doctors for Monday morning."

Automatically, I reached into my purse and retrieved copies of

Jerry's living will and his medical power of attorney, both naming me executor, along with our marriage certificate. I held the documents out to the doctor.

He shook his head. "That won't be necessary. You are the wife. We will do what you want." I wondered how he *knew* that I was the wife. He didn't. He simply believed it. After all, who else would have stood there, having this deathbed conversation with him? In the US, all the paperwork would have to have been in legal order, no matter what the hospital staff believed. But in a quasi-dictatorship, the doctor accepted my status on faith. Strange, but in this dire instance, a relief.

The surgeon bowed, backing away. "Again, I am so sorry."

Oliver and I stood in the middle of the ward and sobbed into each other's arms.

"Dad has to die?"

"Yes, yes," I said, squeezing him tightly.

We were still holding each other when a woman with gray hair and dark clothing entered the ward. She scanned the room, then walked rapidly toward us. *Who was this?* I didn't know her.

Oh. My. God. It was Vicky.

Only six months earlier, I had overheard Jerry in his basement office talking to Vicky on the phone. I knew it was my sister, because he said, "Please call her. She needs to hear from you." This threw me. He had never interceded before. At that point, three years after I had begged her to work it out with me and gotten no response, I had let go of my desire for reconciliation. Or so I thought. I was afraid to open myself up to her. I didn't think I could handle the possibility of being hurt again. Jerry had had plenty of experience with my sister's volatility. He'd witnessed her on more than one occasion storming out of our house or a restaurant after something had offended or upset her. He must have been very worried about me, and how alone I was with him away, to have reached out.

After Jerry guiltily hung up, I asked him what Vicky had said. He didn't want to tell me. When I pressed him, he revealed she wasn't ready, that she said she didn't have to deal with me if she didn't want to. "I'm not married to her," she said.

"See," I told my husband, "it can't be fixed."

Then there we were—Vicky having flown half way across the world to be with me, because of him. We hugged lightly. She air-kissed my cheek and embraced Ollie. "Tall, and look at this hair," she said, twirling a spiral strand on my son's head. I told her what had just transpired, that Jerry was brain-dead. She walked over to my husband's bed and touched his arm. Then we sat on folding chairs in the corner of the ICU. I began to cry. She put her hand on mine without pressure. How bizarre to have gone from no contact to togetherness in such a situation.

The two women I had met earlier in the week entered the ward. I remembered that they, too, were sisters, one the mother, the other the aunt of the stricken young man. They approached us, and knelt down beside me. I was undone. "How will I go on without him?"

"You will," they said in unison. Their gray heads, along with my sister's, created an odd picture: the women in their sixties next to my forty-nine-year-old sister, her salt and pepper hair giving her unlined baby face a kind of eerie pre-maturity.

I nodded as the women kept talking to me, their words less important than their compassionate concern. These sisters, both strangers, both genuine and kind, gave me a nanosecond of comfort, even as a dark pit widened inside me. The aunt patted my shoulder. Then she and her sister rose to go down the hall to their nephew/son, who was recovering, who would finally be able to go home to the United States. Their hopeful scenario seemed as foreign to me as Dubai itself. I didn't know what was next for me, for

Ollie. All I could focus on was the limbo of Jerry's body kept alive in this stark setting. I was in an alternate universe where I did not know how to breathe, how to think, how to take the next step. My feeling self seemed both shut down and hyperalert.

I jumped to my feet. "Let's get out of here." As I fled the ICU, fled the impending death sentence, guilt passed through me, but it didn't stop my flight. I could no longer sit there holding Jerry's hand. I was abandoning my husband; it seemed to me at that moment that there was no other way. Sadness threatened to engulf me, though I could no longer feel it, only act on it. I had to do whatever was necessary to survive. Jerry was a vital, brilliant mind, a restless spirit, a passionate man with whom I had fallen in love at first sight. Already I thought of my husband in the past tense. No amount of whispering in his ear would bring that mind or spirit back. I couldn't bear it. I had to go.

9

The Bus Stop

It was nearly twenty-seven years earlier, on May 11, 1981, shortly before midnight, when I stood alone at the bus stop at Eighty-Second Street and Second Avenue on the Upper Eastside of Manhattan, dressed in a black cowboy shirt with blue embroidered pockets, black culottes, authentic tooled cowboy boots, and a cowboy hat adorned with a huge yellow silk rose. I held a hobbyhorse with a sock and button head attached to a long red pole. It was raining, and I couldn't get a cab.

I had just performed part of my solo act, *Intensity Jane in New York*, at the Comic Strip across the street. Though it went well, I didn't quite belong in the comedy club world. My dream was to act. I'd spent a good part of the '70s in Texas, first in graduate school at the Dallas Theater Center, and then teaching at the University of Texas at Austin. When I resigned that job, I willingly foreclosed a safe tenure track life. I got my Actors' Equity card by playing the title character's grieving widow in the Austin Dinner Theater production of *Goodbye Charlie*. In my only scene, which opened the show, I ran onstage and threw myself onto the casket. The casting director had been impressed with my wail. Thus armed with professional credentials, original material, and a passionate belief in my destiny, my twenty-six-year-old self hit the Off-Off Broadway theater and club scene, and spent the next two years intent on making it in New York.

A few minutes went by with no bus in sight. Then a bespectacled young man in a yellow slicker joined me. "Been waiting long?" he asked.

I had no sense of how tall this young man was—my height is five feet and a significant quarter-inch—but I felt instant ease in his presence, even though his energy exuded anything but calm. He radiated an intense, nervous vitality that matched my own. He was smart—I could see the sharpness in his eyes, which he trained on me with undivided attention. Usually my attractions registered physically first, then through personality, as I got to know a guy. But this was different. Cute as he was with his open grin, sparkling eyes, and wavy dark hair, I had a strong sense of his entire being, inside and out. I didn't think: *man.* I thought: *person.* In a single moment, I experienced him whole, and found him irresistible.

His question, my answer—"not long"—and the ride down Second Avenue was all it took for both of us to be smitten. We introduced ourselves, talked about what we had done that evening—he'd been working on a film with some college friends—but were too shy or too well brought up to exchange phone numbers, or even last names. So when Jerry got off the bus across from the United Nations at Tudor City, where he had a tiny studio apartment, I feared I had missed my chance.

The next day I called a restaurant he'd told me about that some friends of his ran. The person who answered the phone didn't know him. I hung up, kicking myself. *Damn, that was the best guy I'd ever met.* Ten minutes later, the phone rang. It was Jerry. "I called the comedy club and asked for the cowgirl's number," he said. They gave it to him, something that would never happen today. "If I hadn't gotten the number, I was going to show up at that theater gig you mentioned." His determination thrilled me.

Two days after meeting Jerry at the bus stop and one day after speaking with him on the telephone, we had our first date. He came to my apartment to take me to lunch. Jerry appeared a bit older than the young man in the yellow slicker, but adorable in his blue blazer, pink button down shirt, and khakis. This time he was wearing contacts instead of glasses, and his green-gray eyes looked huge. I lived in a building at Fifteenth Street and Third Avenue, so he suggested that we go to Pete's Tavern, the famous writers' haunt on Irving Place only a few blocks away.

The restaurant was packed and the food wasn't much, but that didn't matter. We were totally focused on each other. We talked about the history of Pete's, which Jerry knew a lot about, and careers. "I'm an advertising copywriter, currently unemployed, and driving a cab," he said with incongruous bluster, barely hiding his concern about my reaction.

I smiled. "I'm sure you'll find something in no time." Jerry had such palpable drive, ambition, and charisma, he was obviously capable of tremendous growth, and I had no doubt that he was meant for success. I felt completely comfortable with him. After the meal, outside the Tavern, Jerry took my hand and we walked back to my apartment. It seemed natural, right.

Inside my studio, seated on a tiny blue foam futon, Jerry asked if he could kiss me. No man had ever been that formal before. His respectful manners charmed me. I said yes. It was easily the best kiss I'd ever had.

Though I'd kissed many men, I'd only slept with two. The first was a sexy, intellectual bad boy from Austin, a tortured infatuation from the start. Then came the older performance artist I met in New York, who served mainly to get over the Texas heartbreaker; he asked me to marry him before running off to clown college.

Hence, Jerry was the most regular guy I had been with, though I sensed that his conforming exterior masked a highly individualistic interior. Like me. It seemed perfectly natural to sleep with him on the first date, a decision that only months earlier would have been totally out of character. But we were already intimately connected, had been from the first moment. I was sure of this person. I trusted him.

Afterwards, we went to a *Daily News* haunt—Jerry had free-lanced for them—and off to Dustin's, Jerry's favorite Eastside restaurant, for dinner, extending our marathon inaugural date well into the evening. Then we returned to Tudor City Park. "I helped save it," he said, gesturing to include the tiny green space as if it were his own. "I fought Harry Helmsley. He was going to put up towers there. The Parks Council gave me its annual award for service to the community." He beamed. So did I. *What an accomplished guy.* I still have the translucent cube displaying a piece of Central Park quartz on my desk. We did not go up to his apartment. Instead, we sat on a bench outside necking. Neither of us wanted the day to end. By the time he put me in a cab to go home, after a mere eight hours together, we were completely besotted.

The next day Jerry sent balloons, a surprise he spoiled by calling before they arrived to ask how I liked them. His eagerness was endearing. I'll never forget the pants he wore on our second date, a day after that: Kelly green Brooks Brothers golf pants circa 1963. When he appeared at my door, he opened his arms in a "ta da" pose to show off the outfit, which included a pink Lacoste shirt. He took me to dinner at a below-street-level Italian restaurant in the Village, followed by cannoli at Café Roma in Little Italy. "It's been on Broome Street, run by the same family, since 1891," Jerry said. As I would continue to discover, he was a font of New York stories. This was the first time that I had met someone who could out-talk me.

On the way home, I asked him, "Do you want children?" I

had never asked such a question of a boyfriend before, but I felt compelled to know.

"Sure," he said, as if it had never occurred to him. "It would be nice to have a boy to play ball with in the backyard." I smiled. The stock response reminded me he was really very young, though only two years younger than me.

Then Jerry revealed that he was a registered Republican. I'd never dated a Republican before. Despite being a registered Democrat, I was essentially apolitical, viewing the world through the lens of the arts, which were my religion, my politics, my everything. "I'm pro-choice and socially progressive," he quickly added. In that same conversation, I told him I was Jewish, a fact he took in stride.

Basic differences out of the way, Jerry wasted no time. "Come to Brooklyn with me tomorrow. I want you to meet my best friend Paul. We met working one summer for the Farm Workers." This had my head spinning. "I used to be a liberal," Jerry said rather sheepishly. "Then I became a neo-conservative." I had no idea what that meant. "To quote the movement's godfather, Irving Kristol," he explained, "a neo-conservative is a liberal who has been mugged by reality."

I paused, not at the political stance, which didn't faze me, but because I felt it was a little soon to meet his friends. Our five-day whirlwind romance had left me winded. I needed a break, but his keenness to include me in his world, to show me off, was irresistible. "How about *next* weekend?" I said.

Soon after, I told *my* closest friend, Kate, that I thought Jerry was in love with me. "What about you?" she asked. "How do *you* feel?" Though this was indeed love at first sight, I was floored by the exhilaration of it all, and I wasn't quite ready to admit, even to myself, how serious I was about him. We fit together effortlessly, in conversation, in each other's arms. In his embrace, my head on his chest, I felt safe and at home. Her question forced me to face what

I knew. "He's the one," I told her.

One month later, I introduced Jerry to my parents—something I had never done with any man, they were so old-fashioned—and it went well enough. "He should have been a lawyer," my mother said. As the wife of one, this was her highest compliment. Such a relief, since my mother could be tough.

That evening, he proposed. Without hesitation I said, "yes," and in almost the same breath, "but let's get to know each other first."

Jerry sublet his studio, moved into mine, and a year later, we rented a top floor Brooklyn Heights one-bedroom on the Promenade, where the final scene of the horror movie *The Sentinel* had been shot. When our living situation became almost as scary as the film—our landlord, pissed that we had questioned her rent increase, kicked our puppy and bit Jerry on the arm, landing him in the hospital on IV antibiotics—we moved to a quiet garden apartment in Park Slope.

In between, I brought Jerry home to Maryland for Thanksgiving, and unlike his first encounter with my parents, this one went awry. We spent the returning plane ride saying how well it had gone, not realizing the damage until my father called to deliver his and Mother's scathing rejection. I was stunned. What happened? Jerry had watched football on TV, revealed that there were farmers in his background, that he was a Protestant advertising writer who had gone to SUNY Oswego and not a lawyer from an Ivy League school. They knew all this when they met him six months earlier. Faced with an alien on their turf, they simply could not accept him. I realized many years later that no one would have been good enough; at the time, I was shattered, but held firm. I trusted my gut. Nothing and no one was going to keep me from marrying this man. In the spring of 1983 we became formally engaged.

After a few false starts regarding wedding locations—the

Carlyle to please my mother, Bargemusic, overlooking lower Manhattan, where I had performed my play about Edna St. Vincent Millay—we decided to get married where we met. We rented a city bus to take our small party from the bus stop ceremony to Rockefeller Center for a wedding dinner at the Rainbow Room. The *New York Times* society page editor, Enid Nemy, refused to run an announcement for a "stunt wedding." We couldn't believe she didn't appreciate how romantic it was. Jerry was disappointed. Social acceptance mattered a great deal to him, since he'd spent his young life climbing out of his small town middle class upbringing.

I wrestled with another disappointment. The night before the wedding, I cried on Jerry's shoulder, as the reality that my parents weren't going to be there sank in. "We're not going to a wedding on the street," my mother had said, but her withdrawal had more to do with a fundamental disapproval than the unconventional venue.

"Are you worried that we won't last?" I'd asked, trying to uncover the source of her problem.

"Oh, no," she'd said. "Once you make a commitment, it will be forever." A backhanded compliment if there ever was one. She wouldn't budge. Mother and Miss Nemy sat side by side in harsh judgment of our eccentric choice. The *Times'* response stung, but my parents' rejection made me feel like someone had died.

September 9, 1983 must have been a slow news Friday, because once the Port Authority's PR department sent out a press release on our bus rental and nuptial plan, it triggered an onslaught of media attention that began with a short item in the *New York Times* Metro section four weeks earlier. The day of our wedding, my distress at my parents' absence faded, and was replaced by a focus on the insatiable news machine, which couldn't seem to get enough of our one-of-a-kind ceremony. The world came to meet us, and to validate our union far more thoroughly than any one-column wedding notice could have. This was in the pre-Twitter, pre-iPhone era, and radio, local television stations, the wire services, all showed up to follow Jerry from the squash club where he was changing into his tux, to my apartment. He called to warn me. "Turn on WABC. I was just interviewed coming out of the locker room shower. Then GO!"

At Kate's place, I put on my cocktail-length white lace Betsey Johnson dress and placed a baby's breath crown in my upswept hair. I wore my grandmother's seed pearls as my "something old." Kate and I watched in disbelief as Jerry, already at the bus stop, was interviewed on the six o'clock news. The reporter tried to create suspense. "Will the bride make it?" Anchor Chuck Scarborough told us to "Tune in at eleven. We'll bring you the results of that wedding."

Along with my maid of honor, Kate—dressed in periwinkle blue to set off her golden hair—and my brother, George—in suit and tie—I traveled up Third Avenue in an ordinary yellow taxi. As we rounded the corner of Eighty-Third Street onto Second Avenue, Kate gasped. The street was blocked by police barricades and a hoard of strangers, who filled the bus lane. I squeezed my bouquet of pink and white flowers, and stepped out of the cab to wild applause. The assembled crowd seemed relieved that I hadn't jilted Jerry. For me, the experience was totally out-of-body.

James Graseck, a violinist we had discovered in the subway, played Vivaldi's "Four Seasons," and "Rainbow Connection" from *The Muppet Movie,* a film in which I'd been an extra. The bus shelter was packed with people, faces pressed up against the Plexiglas, none of whom I recognized except for Jerry's best man, Paul. *Where were our other guests?* There should have been seven other friends. Out of sensitivity to my situation, Jerry had asked his parents to attend the reception we would hold three weeks later instead of coming to the ceremony. Judge Orest V. Maresca, forever known as the pine tar judge to baseball fans, looked flustered, but managed to accept the circus atmosphere. I couldn't hear him, so after a false start, he began the ceremony a second time. The minute he sealed us with, "I now pronounce you husband and wife," cameras and booms moved in.

"How does it feel?" asked multiple reporters.

I'd just kissed my new husband, and now I was practically kissing the reporters' microphones. I don't recall what I said, but I do remember the dismay I felt. One would think that an aspiring actress would have relished the attention. This was my fifteen minutes of fame. But the invasion demonstrated that, for all my ambition, I didn't really want what came with celebrity. This media frenzy wasn't what I had envisioned when Jerry and I decided to get married where we met. I remember wondering, *Was the ceremony even legal?* I had thought it was going to be small and personal, accompanied by the sound of everyday traffic. I'd say "I do," and we'd be off to begin our life together. Instead, I felt hounded and oddly diminished, as if I were there to fill a public need, not the real one—to become Jerry's life partner.

As we stepped out of the shelter, apartment dwellers leaned out windows, waved and cheered. Passersby threw brown rice. A neighboring restaurant provided champagne flutes and bubbly. The bus marquee looped "Just Married," and "Congratulations, Jerry and Roselee." Jerry grabbed my hand and began leading me the few feet to our city bus. "Isn't this something?" he said. Unlike me, my new husband was elated by the attention.

I couldn't wait to get inside, to get away from the crowd and from the "story" that our personal event had turned into, one that no longer seemed to be ours. But as soon as we ascended the bus steps, another reporter whom I recognized, Jane Velez-Mitchell, ambushed me. I couldn't hide my annoyance. "What did you expect?" she said, as she was ushered out of the vehicle. Our guests, whom we hadn't seen until then, were seated on the hard bus seats, waiting for us, and off we went to the Rainbow Room, where mercifully, cameras weren't allowed. It took the entire wedding dinner for me to calm down.

In the airport the next morning, people pointed at us and whispered. On the plane, the captain sent us champagne. When we arrived in Puerto Rico on the way to Virgin Gorda, our honeymoon destination in the British Virgin Islands, we saw our startled faces on the cover of the *San Juan Star*. The whole experience was mind-boggling.

With time, the loss of control and privacy I felt that evening was replaced by pride. We pulled the wedding off our way, with irreverence and significance, with our dear friends, a loyal brother, the MTA, hundreds of strangers, TV cameras, and each other. We couldn't have imagined when we cooked up this wedding that the world would embrace the truth behind the event—that it wasn't a "stunt," that it was a meaningful personal gesture, Jerry's and mine. The story resonated because people recognized the vision: marry where you met and seal yourselves where you fell in love, where you so instantly bonded. We had been true to ourselves.

I collected over 400 newspaper clippings from all over the world, as well as tapes from all three major New York news broadcasts. Over the years, the joy of retelling the story of our one-of-a-kind public wedding far outweighed the private blow that preceded it. I realized it was my parents' loss more than mine. How we met and married—the swift, magically right, meant-to-be beginning of our life together—forged our union, buoyed us up, and set us on a path uniquely our own. I had no regrets about any of it.

10

Day Six continued

Vicky, Ollie, and I sat in the lobby restaurant of the Hilton, where my sister was staying. The hotel was only a three-minute walk from Jerry's apartment. I had offered for her to stay with us—there was plenty of room—but she had declined. Thank goodness. Our sudden reconnection jarred me. Vicky needed her space, and so did I.

I looked over at Ollie, slumped in his seat, undone. Now he knew for sure: his father was going to die, and there was nothing anyone could do about it. Nothing I could do but love him.

Vicky began chattering. "Do you like my hair? I thought I'd try letting it go natural? What do you think? Did you see *Michael Clayton*? You've got to see it. Clooney is amazing!" Movies—her usual fallback topic, along with popular television shows, and office gossip.

Ollie and I took the cue, complimenting her hair-do, naming favorite movie stars: Nicholson, Freeman. All three of us dove into trivia in an attempt to avoid talking about, or even feeling, the calamity at hand, a calamity so huge it surrounded us like a biosphere.

"Then you have to see *The Bucket List,* even though it's not very good.*"

Ollie bristled. I bit my lip. *Really, Vicky? Already with the foot-in-mouth?*

"Oh, sorry," she said. After an awkward pause, she began again. "What about *Charlie Wilson's War?*"

Yes. Jerry and Ollie and I had seen it on Christmas Day. Traditionally, after opening presents in the morning, we went to the movies in the afternoon. Ollie studied his hands. Vicky couldn't have known that this film too, was a trigger. It was the last one our family would see together. The bleak context gave the small talk a new and perverse twist, our mouths disconnected from our feelings, our feelings buried beneath thickening layers of shock. I felt as if all my nerves had been slashed. Every so often Ollie glanced at me, as if to say, *What are we doing? What* will *we do?* I shook my head. No answers. None at all.

A waiter appeared, and we ordered lunch from the bar menu. "My treat," Vicky said. I forced myself to try Dubai's idea of English and American fare—mini-bagels with salmon, and finger sandwiches. "When Mother died, I couldn't eat for a month, and then again on the first anniversary," Vicky went on. *Did she mean that we shouldn't be eating?*

"Everyone's different," I said. I had to eat. I had to keep going. Our mother's death from cancer at sixty-six was nothing like this. It was deeply sad, but not unexpected. This sudden tragedy had blindsided us like a tornado on a clear day. It had ripped us from our foundations.

"And Daddy went so quickly."

Ollie's eyes darted over to me. His eighty-four-year-old grandfather had suffered a brief illness, then died in his sleep. This was what my sister knew of death. She was trying to connect with our experience. *She was trying.* I had to give her that.

In Vicky's hotel room, Oliver went out on the balcony while she lay down on the bed, and I called American Express to find out how we could get Jerry's body out of Dubai. He wasn't dead yet, but I needed to do this. To prepare. Their international emergency concierge spoke evenly and assigned a caseworker to oversee our needs. I found her distant voice calming. She had handled crises such as this many, many times before. This faceless person would help me.

For a moment I pictured how different our crisis would have been if it had happened in the States. We would have been surrounded by family and friends. We would have slept in our own beds. We would have stayed many more hours in the hospital at Jerry's side. Then I snapped back to the present. We were in a foreign land, and we, *I* had to deal with that reality as best I could.

I sent Ollie back to the apartment to rest.

After he left, Vicky stared blankly at me, her hand over her forehead. Then she closed her eyes. "I need a nap. You can stay if you want." I nodded and watched her sleep, envious. Since all this began I hadn't been able to sleep for more than a few hours each night. I attributed her going to bed as much to her usual semi-depressed state as to jet lag. Vicky had always slept more than the rest of us, ten or twelve hours being her norm. When her ex-fiancé a decade earlier had greeted me at the door of her house—they were living together at the time—he immediately pointed upstairs, where at 7 p.m. she was already sleeping, and asked if she was always like this. "Pretty much," I said.

When I returned to the apartment, I called Jerry's parents. We hadn't spoken since Jerry was stricken. His brother Scott had given them the first news. But I owed it to them to make this call myself. His father, Jim, answered the phone. I told him that his son was brain-dead. I waited while he took my words in. Jim didn't speak, but I could picture this quiet man shriveling. I heard Jerry's mother shrieking in the background.

I called Scott. He and their youngest brother, Ross, would fly to Dubai from Seattle and Salt Lake City, respectively. They would leave tomorrow, and not arrive until Sunday. We didn't see Scott a lot due to the distance between us, but his loyal, loving nature had never failed to give Jerry a boost. Right after Jerry's depression was diagnosed, Scott flew to New Jersey to spend time with him. I was certain that my husband would have wanted both of his brothers with us now. I know I did.

"Is there any hope?" Scott asked.

I swallowed. "No," I said softly, "there isn't." I put down the phone—gutted—and looked through the living room window at the glittering Arabian Gulf.

11

Day Seven, Distance

We went back to the hospital in the morning, with Vicky dutifully trailing behind. The ICU doctor told us that they were keeping Jerry stable. This shook me. *Stable for what?* For the moment when we would order them to turn down the machines? Not for transplants—they didn't perform them—something about Sharia law. Jerry had explained that it was Islamic law, based on the teachings of the Koran, and that it governed both personal and public conduct. Like most countries in the Middle East, the United Arab Emirates was governed by Sharia. The thought of it made *me* unstable.

I could barely look at my husband. His already palpable absence created more distance between us than the thousands of miles that had separated us in the last three-and-a-half years. Whatever I imagined Jerry could sense or feel when we first arrived, I could not imagine now. But unlike the day before, I had no impulse to run away. I wanted to be there with his quiet body resting beneath the thin sheet, with his face and its exquisite lashes, with what remained, hooked up to machines that breathed for him, and IV bags that filled him with fluids. I had to be there.

Vicky hung back, wearing her fear like a cloak. Ollie held his father's hand. For him, this was still Dad. Then I contradicted myself. We were on the brink of losing the most important man in our lives, but he wasn't gone yet, not really, not completely. I leaned over and whispered, "Hold on. Your brothers will be here tomorrow."

"You can't go in there." The ICU guard placed his arm in front of Ollie, barring the entrance to the waiting room just outside the ward. *What did he mean?* The tiny space had one small window near the ceiling. Mismatched chairs and loveseats stretched the length of the walls on either side of the door. A rectangular Formica coffee table took up the middle, leaving little room to move. Vicky and I were already inside. Across from us sat a large, dark woman dressed in a turban-like head-wrap and bright rust and saffron robes—Ethiopian, perhaps—and a smaller, much younger woman who did not make eye contact. A middle-aged Indian lady in a deep blue sari sat on the other side of the young woman.

"Why not?" I asked the guard.

"No men allowed," he pointed at the women.

The large woman waved her hand dismissively. "That's absurd," she said in a resonant British accent. "Let him in. I don't care."

Ollie shifted from one foot to the other. The guard shook his head and gestured to the women sitting with her, neither of whom looked up. "It's okay," Ollie said. "I'll wait in the hallway." I considered going with him, but there were no seats in the hall, and I was too exhausted to move. I told myself that I would check on him in a few minutes. Before he left, he mouthed, "It's all right."

When Ollie and the guard were gone, the British woman said

loudly, "I hate this country. Such hypocrisy. I'm from London. My father had a stroke. He's been here for months." My God. How had she coped? *And me fleeing the ward.* "This—" indicating the small woman beside her, "is my father's youngest wife."

"Oh," Vicky and I said in unison, trying to take the revelation in stride.

The woman laughed. "I could be *her* mother," she said, making us smile.

The woman in the sari placed a bag of snacks on the table between us. She gestured for Vicky and me to take something. I felt weak, and accepted a nut bar, a packet of dried apricots, and a juice box, containing an exotic guava. The thick and smooth liquid coated my throat. I thanked her, drinking in her kindness along with the juice. Vicky took nothing. The British woman asked about Jerry, and absorbed my recital of the facts—only the facts— without visible reaction. Then she asked where we were from.

"The United States," Vicky boomed in her public voice, more loudspeaker than human.

"How terrible for you," the woman said with genuine empathy. I knew instantly what she meant—not terrible that we were Americans, but that the sheer distance from home and the unfamiliar environment compounded an already wrenching experience.

Yes, I nodded. Terrible indeed.

12

Day Eight, Sunday, January 27, 2008

Ollie and I sat in the ICU next to Jerry. Before he was declared brain-dead, I had touched his hand to reach the part of him that still might have been aware. *Could it have been only two days earlier?* On this day, it had the same softness and elegant length, though it felt perverse to stroke fingers that were no longer connected to a sentient mind. But stroke them I did. In spite of what I knew, I sent Jerry a message through my fingers to hang on, just a little longer. Scott and Ross would arrive that night.

Vicky had stayed at her hotel, which was fine with me. I'd learned from experience not to press her. In any case, I knew the men would be more present, and would relieve some of the constant pressure Ollie and I were under.

I was worried about my son. His face was ashen, his eyes blank. When he put his head on my shoulder, as he had when we were alone in the apartment the previous night, the tension in his body radiated through me. *What could I do for him?* Stay close, hold him, kiss his cheek, smooth his hair. Not enough. He needed his uncles.

Later that afternoon, at Vicky's hotel, we sat by the pool for lunch with Raine. I surveyed her perfectly manicured nails, plunging neckline, and shiny hair. I felt frumpy and old by comparison. My gray roots were overdue for a touch-up. Then again, Vicky had bravely allowed hers to go natural. And what did I care about how I looked? No amount of hair color would camouflage the sheer nakedness of my fear and the ache of impending loss. They were physical, as physical as my husband's state of suspended animation, which I shared. My mind knew he was by then irretrievably lost to me, but I could not fully take in what that meant. All I could do was give the doctors permission to dial down his life, tomorrow morning, with Jerry's brothers, my sister, and Ollie at my side, and wait together for his heartbeat to stop. *Tomorrow, an eternity.* For now, he was neither dead nor alive, neither here nor completely gone, and I was in limbo.

Raine ordered mezze, Arabic for appetizers—hummus, olives, baba ganoush—for us to share. I gazed at the empty swimming pool. I longed to escape into the water, which I had always found restorative, but it was winter here, with temperatures in the 70's, too cool for a dip. And even if it had been warmer, I couldn't imagine putting on a suit and parading my middle-aged body in front of Raine, the woman who had been the object of my anger and jealousy for months. We nibbled as she offered to assist in any way that she could, perhaps by returning Jerry's rental car. I remembered he had been about to turn it in himself, probably afraid of driving under the influence. Without hesitation, surprising myself, I accepted Raine's offer. I needed all the assistance I could get. Even from the woman I told Jerry to have nothing to do with, the woman he had lied to me about.

Raine called the agency and in peremptory tones told them they *had* to pick up the car without Jerry's say so, that's just the way it was. "This is how you must handle locals," she said. "Demand.

Believe me, I have to do it everyday." Was this how she had demanded my husband's attention?

She and my sister chatted about single life. Raine recounted her broken engagement to a South African businessman, and how comforting Jerry had been. "He wanted to kill the guy." Then she looked me in the eye. "He was the big brother I never had." This struck me on two levels: she had used the past tense, though Jerry wasn't gone yet, and had given the not-so-subtle message, meant to reassure me, that her relationship to my husband was completely innocent. She may not have known what I was aware of—that it wasn't. Not completely.

Two years earlier, spring 2006. Jerry sat on the front steps of our home in New Jersey, smoking. I stood below him on the walk. "What would you say to our giving each other permission to…" He paused. "…see other people?"

"What?" I was aghast. Never would I have expected such a suggestion out of husband's mouth. "You mean *have sex* with other people?"

"Just while I'm away," he mumbled, not looking at me.

"Are you kidding? You know me. I would never."

He took another drag on the cigarette. "But you could. I would understand."

My mouth dropped open. I didn't want him to *understand*. I wanted him to be too jealous to contemplate such a thing, the way he was when we were newlyweds. I'd introduced him to my Texas ex-boyfriend at a party—the attraction between us still palpable—and that evening, my threatened husband insisted, "Let's make a baby." He wanted to stake his permanent claim on me. Where was *that* Jerry? Then the unstated hit me, and my stomach dropped.

"What are you *already* doing?"

"Nothing," he said, a faraway look in his eye.

I gripped the railing. "Tell me. Tell me now."

He stared at his feet. "It was just flirtation. Raine and I…" I remembered the assistant, the beautiful, highly educated young woman he had described to me. "We kissed. That's all. We knew right away we couldn't, wouldn't do anything more." Instantly, I thought, *You might as well have*, considering how shattered I was hearing about it.

I swallowed hard. "So now you want permission to see prostitutes instead?" He didn't answer. "You're out of your mind," I said, and went back inside, slamming the door behind me.

The following month we sat next to each other on a couch opposite a couples' therapist, a small, serious woman in her sixties. I leaned forward and began. "The first year of Jerry's travels started for me as a kind of lark, a vacation of sorts. I could go where I wanted when I wanted, but then the false freedom palled. I miss having my husband with me. I miss him all the time. The daily phone calls aren't nearly enough." Jerry hung his head. "I feel neglected and worn out. When I said I could do this only until Ollie's graduation from college, I meant it. But now that Jerry has taken an apartment in Dubai, it's sent me into a tailspin. I can't stand the idea that his life there is becoming more permanent, without me."

The therapist turned her attention to Jerry. "I love my work," he said. "I know that this situation is difficult for Roselee, but it won't last forever. It'll be worth it in the end." I knew he meant financially.

Then I said, "I'm not sure if we can make it through this."

The therapist asked why not.

I took a deep breath, looked at Jerry, whose eyes were boring a hole in the floor, and I told her about the kiss, about his request for an open marriage. "It was as if he didn't know *me*, that I was absolutely not that person. There's no such thing as just sex, as far as I'm concerned. It's always emotional. Infidelity is something I had never in our twenty-three years together worried about—financial problems, yes, drinking, sometimes, infidelity, never. But this thing with Raine... So we're here."

"What do you want from each other that you're not getting?" the therapist asked.

"An assurance that he will come back to me at the time we agreed upon, and that he will be faithful."

She looked at Jerry. "And you?"

He glanced at me. "Nothing. There's nothing she isn't already doing." This should have reassured me, but it didn't. If there was nothing I could do, I had no control.

Then she asked him another question. "Is this a kind of ego trip for you, this job?"

Jerry blushed and shrugged a maybe, meaning yes.

She looked at both of us and said, focusing on me, "I think you've been very honest and clear about how you feel and what you want." To Jerry she said, "I don't know if this marriage is going to last, but I do know that you will need to be more connected to your own and your wife's feelings for it to survive this strain." Then she suggested I focus more on my own life in Montclair, come and go without paying attention to Jerry's comings and goings, tell myself that this was temporary. I knew what she meant, but I didn't think I had it in me to ignore the pain of my husband's absence nor the pull of his return.

In the parking lot afterwards, Jerry smiled, clearly relieved. "That went well," he said.

I, on the other hand, was stunned by what had just been aired. "What are you talking about? Didn't you hear her? She's not sure if our marriage will survive!"

We drove home in silence. When we got to the house, I went into my study, locked the door, pulled out the sofa bed, and lay down on the thin uncovered mattress. The springs dug into my back.

Jerry knocked. "I have to go to a meeting. I'll be back in a couple of hours. Roselee? Roselee!"

I didn't answer. I couldn't. I had shut down.

After he left, I lay there, staring at the ceiling, contemplating the possible end of my marriage. The thought solidified inside me like a cement block. I was paralyzed with anger and fear.

Forty-five minutes later, Jerry returned early. He pounded on the door. "Roselee, let me in. We have to talk. Come on! I can pick this lock with a nail file if I want to."

I forced myself to get up and open the door.

He glanced at the sofa bed. "You're going to sleep here?"

I didn't answer. I didn't know what I was going to do.

We sat uncomfortably on the edge of the bed and looked at each other for a long time without speaking. He seemed afraid to say the wrong thing, afraid to say anything at all.

Finally, I broke the silence. "I can't do all the emotional work," I said. "You have to participate. I have to be your priority, just as you are mine. I don't care how much money you are making if we aren't operating as a couple. I know I seem strong and independent, but I have needs just like anyone else. I have vulnerabilities. I can't have you thinking it's okay to use that strength and independence against me by ignoring my limits. You have to honor them. I don't want to lose you, but I'm not going to sacrifice myself to keep you either."

Jerry still didn't speak, but the guilt and sorrow on his face were unmistakable. "And there's one more thing," I said. "Promise me you won't have anything more to do with Raine."

Jerry nodded. "I promise."

Then I blurted, "But if you *do* do something, use condoms and don't tell me about it." *Was I bluffing?* Maybe. Maybe not. I thought I was protecting myself.

Jerry tipped his head a millimeter. Not exactly an answer, but I knew he had heard me. Then he took my hand. "Have you eaten anything?"

I shook my head. I was beat and could hardly move. Jerry led me into the kitchen. I sat. Edgar sniffed at my thigh.

"How about I make you an omelet?"

Three days later, Jerry had to return to Dubai. "I don't want to go," he said. "I feel so close to you." And I to him. We had returned only once more to the therapist, confident about our breakthrough, sure we could handle our problems on our own.

"It'll be okay," I said. And for a while, it was.

That June, Jerry took me to Rome for a second honeymoon. We both understood how much we needed to spend undivided time with each other. From the moment we landed and our taxi drove us past the Coliseum, the city's intoxicating mix of ancient and modern history, art and architecture, its sweeping passion, provided the perfect antidote to all we had been through. In the next few days, while we explored the magnificent ruins and the museums, wandered the piazzas and ate and ate and ate, my husband and I fell more deeply in love than ever before. One evening after dinner at an outdoor bistro near the Spanish Steps, we walked and talked, mulling a future long after Dubai, vowing to be together always, a conversation that extended far into the night, as we lay contentedly in each other's arms. When we returned to New Jersey, I knew the glow would have to last a long, long time.

When Raine told me on the phone of Jerry's condition, I was shocked, first by the news itself, and then that this woman was still in his life, a fact that filled me with fury. But in her presence, hearing her talk about her sisterly relationship with my husband, I chose to believe her, that what stopped them from going further was the essentially platonic nature of their bond, the strength of our marriage, and my husband's moral compass. *But even if it wasn't true, what did it matter?* Jerry was dying. He was almost dead. The enormity of that truth trumped everything else. I had no energy

for jealousy. Whatever he did or didn't do, I knew how my husband felt about me. I knew it in my heart. I knew it *by* heart, just as
I did the words of his last email.

I want you to know that my love for you has not wavered in the past twen-
ty-five years.

Raine and I sat uncomfortably in the front seat of Jerry's car,
her perfume filling the space. We had to move the vehicle from the
apartment garage to the hotel lot across the street for the rental
company to pick up. "Here." She opened her purse, and handed
me two little blue pills.

"What are they?" I asked.

"Valium. They might take the edge off."

I inhaled slowly. I'd never been someone who took pills—not
even aspirin, unless I had a fever—but I was actually considering
it. What I *usually* did no longer seemed relevant, now that my life
had been so abruptly altered. I closed my palm and thanked her.
I remembered what Vicky had said about Raine after our lunch.
"That woman is right out of a Danielle Steel novel." She certainly was. I, on the other hand, belonged in *Jane Eyre*, part mad
wife ready to set fire to anything within reach, part blind, crippled
Rochester broken by guilt and loss, and part proud, forbearing
Jane, determined to soldier on through heartbreak. Too melodra-
matic? Perhaps. Once an actress, always an actress. But I thought
Brontë would agree. Life could be extreme.

Back in the apartment, I put the pills in the heart-shaped brass
pillbox that I carried in my purse, along with ancient Aleve tablets.
Just in case.

Scott and Ross arrived in the early evening. They had each
traveled for almost twenty hours. Scott, a ruddy bear of a man
with traces of distant Native American heritage in his wide-set
cheekbones, looked haggard. Ross, the baby of the family and the

tallest, had filled out since I saw him last—no longer a beanpole, but with the same reliable sweetness. I hugged them and said little, simply glad that they were finally there. Scott put his arm around Ollie's neck in a playful lock, then pulled at his long hair, a wordless tease. All at once, Ollie's shoulders dropped, and he relaxed. He no longer had to hold himself together, be the man. Now that his uncles were here, he could give in to the terrified child he had become. And now I could let go a bit, too.

We went across the street to a hotel restaurant—not Vicky's. She wouldn't be joining us; too tired, she said. This hotel was as tacky as the Hilton was elegant. Its décor and the tone of claustrophobic festivity were weirdly ill-conceived—fake palm trees, bamboo torches and glossy wood paneling everywhere, an Arabian version of a '50s Caribbean resort.

I had no appetite, but ordered a pineapple chicken dish anyway. We ate and talked about anything except the reality of what tomorrow would bring: the decision to turn the machines down, the wait until Jerry took his last breath. I was grateful Scott and Ross were there, but deeply sad that their first sight of their brother would be under such wretched circumstances. All through the meal, I was consciously suppressing other feelings too, lest they slip out and swamp me. Just below the surface lurked my terror of my blighted future, my hurt, and my outrage that this was actually happening.

We ordered dessert. I checked my watch. It was 10 p.m. The phone in my pocket—the local one I'd been carrying since Kamilla made such a stink—rang. It was Raine. "Come to the hospital, quickly." I shot up from the table, hardly able to hear her over the restaurant's clatter, although she was shouting. "His heart stopped, they are doing CPR, keeping him alive until you get there. Hurry!"

I shrieked, "Oh my God." Heads turned. The restaurant swirled around me. Scott, Ross, and Ollie stood. "We've got to go,"

I said, blurting out the news, bumping into the table behind me. I began to hyperventilate. We stumbled through the doors.

Scott threw some money at a man behind the bar. "Hurry. It's an emergency," he said as the man tried to count it. "Keep the change," he bellowed, and we ran out the front door and into a waiting taxi.

For a second I wondered why Raine was contacted. I had put my local number on the ward's call sheet. They should have called me, not her. Then I remembered Vicky, and instantly decided that there was no time to get her. At best, it would be a twenty-five minute drive to the hospital. She would have to understand.

Scott and Ollie sat on either side of me in the back seat. Ross was up front with the driver. "Rashid General Hospital, hurry," I said, gripping Ollie's hand with my left, and Scott's with my right. I panted, mouth open in shallow labor-like breathing, but this time anticipating not birth, but death. *We had to be with Jerry, we had to get there in time.* The taxi whizzed past high-rise after high-rise, some lit, some ominously black.

When we arrived at the hospital, we jumped out of the cab, ran inside and up the stairs two at a time. No one stopped us. At the ward, the night guard seemed to know, and quickly handed us gowns. We rushed in to find a nurse doing chest compressions on Jerry's lifeless body. Another nurse counted aloud.

"Daddy, no, no," Ollie cried. Ross grabbed and held him. Scott put his head in his hands.

Then someone let out an animal howl. It was me. I did not recognize the sound of my own voice. A third nurse told me to sit down. No. I couldn't move. She placed me in a chair at the foot of the bed, held my hand, and looked down at me with sorrowful eyes. I keened. Raine ran into the ward, no hospital gown to cover her chinchilla jacket. She looked at each of us, then at Jerry, and clasped her hand to her mouth.

The nurse doing compressions glanced at the clock above the

bed. A doctor nodded. The nurse lifted her hands. I doubled over, all cry, all moan. Scott, Ross, and Ollie huddled as one.

The doctor approached me. "So sorry," he said. "Come, come Missus, into my office." Even in my stricken state, I was aware he found my emotional display unseemly. The doctor was trying to hide me, to get me out of the way. Inside his cramped office, sitting across the table from him, I was sure of it. Oliver and his uncles leaned against the wall to my right. Raine had followed us, but stayed in the doorway. The doctor handed me a tissue, and a paper cup of water. He instructed me to put my head between my legs, afraid I would pass out. I knew I wouldn't, fueled as I was by both sudden loss and disgust at the superficiality of this man's response. The nurses had been sensitive, this doctor, not. "Calm yourself," he said. "It couldn't be helped. These things happen."

Ollie pursed his lips and turned away. I could tell that the doctor's words disturbed him. Ross wiped his eyes. Scott called his wife, his parents.

Raine answered a call on her cell. I stood. She hugged me. "He loved you so much," she said. I answered with a tiny nod, silent thanks for saying what I needed to hear.

Then she handed me the phone. It was Kamilla and her husband, whom I had met only once. The man said something perfunctory. Kamilla told me Jerry was happy that last day, she had had coffee with him, and he was happy. I couldn't respond. I didn't want to hear it. I didn't want to hear from someone who barely knew him how happy my husband had been without me.

I shivered. The shocks of the past week—the call, the flight, the ICU, the diagnosis, the foreign land—were nothing compared to this final blow. My husband was dead. Gone. Forever. A fact so huge, so permanent, so absolute, I couldn't comprehend it.

I spoke to Wali and Sabeen. Then the head of the television station called and told me that Jerry had been his best friend. "He loved you, too," I said, and thanked him for his kind words, though words, any words, sounded empty and distant, as if I were trapped in an echo chamber too tightly closed for anyone to reach. I asked the doctor what would happen next.

"They will take him to the morgue."

I moved to the door. "I want to see him first. I want to see my husband." I left the office and went back to Jerry's bed. He was covered up to his shoulders by a white sheet, his skin yellow and waxy, his face slack and smooth. The tube had been removed from his mouth, the IVs as well, and the bed-railings were down. For the first time since I had arrived, I could reach for my husband and touch him without anything between us. I bent over and kissed his lips. They were already cold. I ran my fingers up and down the length of his arm. This was his body, not him. Jerry Michael Mosier, the man I adored, the man whose sudden and complete presence in my life gave me all I valued, was gone, as swiftly and as fully as he'd come.

I turned away.

When I returned to the office, Raine said that she would call me tomorrow, and left. I asked the doctor where Jerry's wedding ring and personal effects were—his watch, his wallet, the contents of his pockets. Suddenly, I wanted, needed, all of it, especially his ring. Ross and Ollie went downstairs to retrieve them, while Scott and I waited for the staff to prepare to take Jerry out of the ward. As soon as Ross and Ollie returned, I put the watch and wallet in my purse, and put on my husband's wedding band. It was so large I took mine off, along with my engagement ring, and placed it on my finger first, with my own rings guarding his. I held my left hand up to gaze at the three together. This proved what I couldn't absorb: the unthinkable was real.

Then a sharp cry sounded from the other end of the ward. The Ethiopian woman ran out, hand over mouth, followed by a man and the young wife.

"We are ready," the doctor said. An attendant wheeled a

gurney carrying Jerry in a black body bag out through the double doors. Ross would stay with Ollie in the waiting area downstairs.

I took Scott's hand, and we followed the gurney into an elevator and down a long basement hallway. We stayed three paces behind, a slow processional. The world had shrunk to the dimensions of the gray, dimly lit passage. I felt tiny, childlike, a shadow of myself. When we reached the morgue, the attendant on call asked which of us would identify the body. It occurred to me we would not have had to do this if Jerry had died in an American hospital. I looked at Scott, silently asking, *Would you?* Because I knew I couldn't. I had just said goodbye. I couldn't watch the bag being unzipped, zipped again, and shoved into cold storage, a metal covered drawer in a wall. Scott patted my shoulder and went in. I waited by the desk.

Scott returned. "It was him," he said, knowing we needed to hear it to convince ourselves that this was actually happening. Then he signed a paper saying as much, and the attendant handed us a medical death certificate.

It was almost midnight. We went back upstairs to rejoin Ollie and Ross. I had to settle the bill before we could leave. Because Jerry was a legal resident, the hospital charged nothing for a week in the ICU, repeated MRIs and CAT scans, medication and round-the-clock treatments, but the hospital accounting office made us wait before releasing his records. Given our bare bones private insurance—the only kind we could afford, since Jerry had been essentially self-employed—this would have cost many thousands in the United States.

The main waiting area was packed with men. I was the only woman. I sat between Oliver and Scott, and felt the men staring at me out of the corners of their eyes. "Fuck 'em," Scott whispered.

Yes. I raised my chin, defiant. Let them stare.

13

Day Nine, 1 a.m.

The man in accounting told us—no, he told Scott, because he couldn't or wouldn't address me—to go back down to the basement, to the police station, to file the certificate and fill out more forms. Every government building in Dubai had its own police station. I wanted to come with my brother-in-law. I had to, though not one of these bureaucrats considered my wifely status to be of any importance.

The station consisted of a windowless room with a desk, some file cabinets and a few chairs. Two red-capped Egyptian officers with matching black mustaches presided; most of Dubai's police force was Egyptian. The men glared at me and then addressed Scott exclusively.

Their English was terrible, and they repeated questions over and over: *What was Jerry's home address? How old was he? Who was I? Did I have proof of our marriage, since my name was different from his?* I wanted to tell them how utterly married we were, that my commitment to my husband was total, my name notwithstanding, but understanding they wanted answers from Scott, not me, I said nothing.

Thank goodness I had brought the necessary documentation with me. How strange that this was the first time anyone in the hospital had requested identification. I removed the marriage certificate, my passport, and a copy of Jerry's passport from my bag. The officers examined them closely. Not trusting that they could comprehend the papers, Scott put his finger on the address lines on both passports. This seemed to satisfy them. Again, a signature was needed, and one of the men pointedly pushed a form away from me and in Scott's direction.

By the time we were finished, it was after 2 a.m. Ollie and Ross had moved to the waiting area nearest the hospital front door. When they saw us, they rose, as eager as we were to leave and never come back.

A few feet away the Ethiopian woman was seated on a bench surrounded by at least a dozen other women—her family, I supposed—all dressed in richly colored robes and scarves, a vigil of support. I caught her eye, put my hand on my heart, and blew her a kiss. In return she mirrored me, and nodded rhythmically, in silent, shared lamentation.

It was 3 a.m., but none of us wanted to go back to the apartment yet, not even Scott and Ross, who must have been reeling from jet lag and trauma. Instead we went to the Hilton to tell Vicky. I picked up the lobby phone to call her room. A groggy voice answered. "Come downstairs. We're in the lobby," I said. "Jerry just died."

The lobby was deserted and dark, with half its ceiling lights off. We sat in shadow on the cushy orange swivel chairs the hotel had arranged in conversation-encouraging semi-circles. None of us spoke. I faced the men and Ollie, my back to the elevator bank. Scott looked up. Suddenly, Vicky appeared to my right.

"Why didn't you come get me?" she asked, her voice shrill.

Ross and Scott straightened and pulled back. I realized they'd never met my sister before. She'd been in and out of my life so much, and they lived across the country. A family get-together with everyone from both sides had never materialized. Ollie leaned his head on one hand, and with the other shielded his eyes as if from on-coming headlights.

"Vicky!" I wanted to restrain her before she completely lost control, a possibility that was all too familiar. "There wasn't time," I said, telling her an abbreviated version of what had just happened.

"I should have been there," Vicky said and stormed off. Ross and Scott watched my sister, mouths agape. I did not turn around. I knew she would be back.

"What the...?" Scott said. Ollie shook his head and rubbed his eyes.

A minute later, Vicky returned. "Sorry," she said, focusing on the brothers. "Sometimes, I can be a real bitch." Then she held out her hand to each of the flabbergasted men.

"Scott, Ross, my sister, Vicky." They couldn't possibly have known that what they had just observed was the better introduction. The men smiled weakly.

Vicky circled behind them and bent to kiss Ollie. Finally, she sat. "I loved Jerry too."

I had no idea what she meant. She had sided with our parents before the wedding—"You're breaking up the family," she had said—and had hardly been around to get to know him. This night, our reunion under such miserable circumstances after nearly four years without contact, made no sense to my stalled brain.

Then she glanced over at me, cocked her head, and said, "Pete?"

I was dumbfounded. She couldn't have been serious. *Here?* "No, Vicky. Not now." Ollie smirked. He couldn't believe it either.

Scott and Ross looked bewildered. They had no idea what was going on.

"Oh come on," she said. Then turning to the men, "Have you met Pete?"

"Who's Pete?" Scott asked.

Vicky grinned, proud of her insider status. "Roselee's alter-ego."

I was too exhausted to be embarrassed, or to correct her, but Oliver squirmed. This wasn't news to him; he and his father had loved Pete, appreciating the character as evidence of my wild, creative imagination. My son understood that Vicky was outing a private family game under extreme duress, once again proving that she didn't know how to behave. But Vicky needed what she needed. And at that moment, she needed me to be Pete, just as she had on the Christmas morning in 1965, when I opened a box containing an over-sized stuffed owl named "Peter Hoot" that my mother meant for me, and not for my younger siblings. I gave him a high eunuch voice, and a profane personality. I didn't know when I dreamed of being an actress that my longest running role would be a family-only performance.

Two weeks into dating Jerry, I introduced him to Pete. Of course, Jerry had seen him—the apartment was too small to miss a large stuffed owl. But he hadn't *heard* him. I realized that for this special guy to really know me, he had to know Pete. Jerry and I sat on the floor of my studio, leaning against my captain's bed. "There's someone here I want you to meet," I said, looking up and pointing to Pete. Then in his pinched girly voice, "What the hell do you think you are doing here?"

Jerry didn't miss a beat. "None of your business, asshole."

I knew I had found my man.

Pete became our sidekick on weekend trips to the Hudson Valley, shouting, "Road trip!" and babbling a running commentary. I have a photo of Pete in front of the Vanderbilt Mansion, which my then boyfriend took by lying flat on his stomach on the sweeping lawn so the perspective rendered the bird gigantic enough to block out the building's second floor windows. I had to love a guy with whom I could have so much silly fun. I had found my playmate.

On Ollie's college tour in the summer of 2003, we decided that Pete would leave a mark on every campus we visited. While Ollie was being interviewed at Kenyon, Carleton, and the University of Chicago, his father and I found empty classrooms with blackboards. Jerry stood sentry, while I scrawled a chalk drawing of Pete, with a cartoon bubble above his head: *Peter Hoot was here.*

The owl became an inextricable part of my husband's psyche. Once, during an interminable work meeting, Jerry forgot himself, turned to the colleague next to him and blurted, "Pete?" Never in my decades of *being* Pete had I slipped into him in public. Jerry totally believed in the character, maybe more than I did.

Over the years, the very invocation of his name served to comment on political news, a stupid commercial, or as a safety valve during a disagreement. Jerry would cock his head—"Pete?" The owl would say something brilliantly stupid. Jerry would say, "Idiot!" Pete responded, "Savant!" Argument over. The physical stuffed animal had long since retired inside the cedar chest at the foot of our bed, but Pete's voice continued to be a singular element in our constant marital communication, an essential, private language.

My sister once called Pete the glue that held my marriage together, an insight more applicable to our frayed sibling bond. Vicky never really *got* Pete's transgressive nature. For her he was *too* real, as if she were still a seven year-old child who believed totally in the world her big sister had created. For decades, Pete provided the only safe exchange between us. Many times during our adulthood, Vicky would call to talk exclusively to Pete. I usually played along. A cycle formed. Our problems, gone underground, would fester. Pete would buffer, then I would tire of performing and refuse to *be* Pete, at which point she would refuse to talk to me at all. So much for her years of therapy.

Scott looked at me with mischief in his eyes. "Okay. Speak." Vicky, smiled ear to ear, loving this.

I didn't have the will to resist. In Pete's thin, nasal voice, I said, "Hi, guys."

Vicky and the men laughed. Even Ollie grinned. But I could see that he, Scott, and Ross were almost as uncomfortable as I was. I wasn't about to continue. Thank goodness Vicky seemed satisfied. I exhaled, glad to have gotten through this little charade. I glanced at my watch and realized that it was the twenty-eighth.

"My God," I said, looking at Vicky, "it's your birthday." She was forty-nine.

She waved dismissively. "I don't care. I may never celebrate my birthday again."

"No," I said, "we should have some cake." A waiter, who had been watching us the entire time, approached. We ordered drinks, and a small dessert to share; there was no cake to be had at 3 a.m. When he returned, we raised our glasses in a toast—first to Jerry, then to Vicky.

"Don't sing," she said. As if we could. We ate quietly, each in our solitary pain.

An hour later, I called George from the apartment. His wife, Jeanne, got on the phone. We all cried. Once again, George expressed how much he wished he could have been with us. I told him it was okay, and besides, I would need him for something just as important: to be in our house when Ollie and I came back. The return tickets I had purchased were for the following Sunday, and I vowed, there and then, to somehow make that flight. It felt like we had already been in Dubai for an eternity, and another week was all I could stand. Whatever had to be resolved would have to get done in the next seven days.

Then I called Shari to ask her to find a New Jersey funeral home. We couldn't send Jerry's body back without having an official institution on the receiving end. Violating as it felt, the business of death had begun.

Ollie lay down on the living room couch. "That doctor should have let you cry, Mom," referring to the head of the ICU. "You'd just lost your husband." My sensitive boy, his own grief new, yet he was thinking of me. I kissed him and pulled a chenille throw over his shoulders.

"Try to sleep," I said, and then walked down the hall to say goodnight to Scott and Ross.

When I finally collapsed onto my husband's bed, though totally spent, I didn't know how I would fall asleep. As if in answer, a death mask appeared before my closed eyes—face only, no head, no neck, framed in inky velvet, unmistakably Jerry's, with prominent nose and full lips—and hurtled towards my face out of an infinite nothingness, its plaster caste texture and chalky whiteness inescapable proof that he was indeed dead. Then it slammed into me, merged with my face, and my world went black.

14

Day Nine continued, Police Stations

The smell of coffee and the sounds of dishes being set woke me. I pushed myself out of bed, my body a dull ache, and splashed water on my face, not recognizing the slack jaw and haunted eyes in the bathroom mirror as mine. I walked down the hallway to find Ross making scrambled eggs and toast—a real American breakfast, except for the turkey bacon. The four of us sat without talking at Jerry's round glass dining table. Everyone looked ragged. Scott had huge bags under his eyes. Ross's shoulders sagged, and Ollie looked depleted. I encouraged him to eat, which he did mechanically. I took my own advice, without tasting.

An hour later, less than twelve hours after Jerry's death, Scott and I, bleary and bereft, made our way downstairs and next door, to my husband's bank branch, while Ross and Ollie stayed in the apartment. We introduced ourselves to the Assistant Manager, a trim man of about forty with kind eyes, and sat across from his desk. Without saying why, I asked for the balance on Jerry's account. I was already petrified that whatever might be there would be lost, everything Jerry worked so hard for. I opened my purse and produced copies of Jerry's power of attorney naming me.

The manager obligingly told us the amount. I was startled by the huge sum, and quickly wrote down the number. Then he asked, "Is Mr. Jerry away?"

I couldn't answer, and looked to Scott.

"Tell him," he said.

I did, and the poor man burst into tears. "We loved Mr. Jerry, always so friendly, telling funny stories."

After he gathered himself, I showed him the power of attorney once again, as well as a copy of Jerry's will designating me as sole beneficiary, with a specific clause about the Dubai account—something we had put in place for just such a circumstance. I asked that the money be released to me. He said I could have it in a cashier's check, by electronic transfer, or in gold bars. *Gold bars?* Was he serious? I pictured myself lugging bags of booty on to an airplane. Then he excused himself to copy my documents and to speak to the branch manager.

Scott and I exchanged glances. Maybe this would be easy.

The man returned to his desk, and on his superior's orders, froze the account. In an instant the screen went blank. Oh, no. He explained that, according to their legal department, the bank would need a court order—a Sharia court order—saying I could inherit my husband's money. It seemed an American will was not enough. Under Sharia law there were no wills, and all the men in the family—my father-in-law, my brothers-in-law, my son—would have to formally agree to my status as sole heir. Otherwise, the assets would be divided equally among all the relatives.

My stomach tightened. His explanation left me aghast. If only I had had the presence of mind to transfer the money before I left New Jersey. Jerry had shown me how to access his account, but I hadn't—it was all I could do to pack and arrive here in one piece. Now I would have to go through a court proceeding. This was beyond my imagination. I asked if the money was secure.

"Yes, rest assured," the manager said. "Nothing can move in or out of the account until we receive court authorization." Scott exhaled audibly. The man bowed. "So sorry for your loss. He was a good man."

In the lobby, alone, Scott asked if the money would earn interest at least.

"No," I said, "Arabs don't believe in interest." Something Jerry had taught me. "Money can't earn money."

Scott shook his head. "Crazy."

Vicky met us outside, so we could go together to the American Consulate. Ross would spend the day with Ollie. I didn't want to expose him to more trauma. I told my sister what happened at the bank branch. She listened without comment. We got into a taxi. Unforgiving sunlight poured through its dirty windows, which were open—no air conditioning—and once we were on the highway, it was much too noisy to talk. Just as well. I had no energy for chatter.

The consulate was part of the Dubai World Trade Center, a massive complex oddly similar in aura to New York's lost one. We needed an official consulate death certificate, in order to take Jerry's body back to the States. To enter the consulate offices, many floors above, we had to submit to a search of everything we carried. Vicky decided to wait for us in the lobby.

An American woman directly in front of me was escorted by a female guard into a side room, away from the scanning machines, presumably to be patted down. I prayed no one pulled me aside. I didn't think I could bear to be touched by a stranger. I already felt defiled.

Inside the offices sat row upon row of supplicants facing a paneled wall with bulletproof glass partitions on top—part bank, part post office. The bottom of the glass had narrow gaps through which to pass paperwork. We took a number and waited.

Forty-five minutes later, at the window, a woman with a distinctly British accent perused the medical death certificate and Jerry's passport and handed me an instruction sheet. "You will need these forms with these signatures before I can issue the consulate certificates. Come back when you have the necessary papers."

I skimmed the list. Scott read over my shoulder: *Dubai Police Report, Arabic Death Certificate from the UAE Ministry of Health, and attested translation, Government of Dubai Medical Certificate of Death, and attested translation, Mortuary Certificate.* Each step involved a different office, a different location—a gauntlet. I was overwhelmed, yet knew I couldn't afford to be. This had to be done.

We collected Vicky and took a taxi to the nearest police station. It was much hotter than the day before, and we perspired profusely just walking from car to building. All eyes turned to us as we entered the lobby. Rich marble floors swirled beneath our feet, and floor to ceiling columns rose before us—Greek, Roman, I should have known which from my college art history courses, but in my addled state I couldn't remember the distinctions. Scott approached a group of guards, in crisp green uniforms and red berets like the hospital policemen. They told him we were in the wrong place, and directed us to another station not far from there. I sighed, already daunted.

Inside the second station, we were ushered into a cramped waiting room containing nothing but a large fan and a vending machine. I was hungry, but didn't want to deal with finding the correct change in dirhams—Dubai's currency—to operate the machine.

When we were finally brought into the office area to the desk of yet another policeman, he directed all his questions to Scott. This time I was relieved, rather than offended. I didn't have the energy to do more than sit there beside him.

Vicky sat next to me on the other side. She attempted to physically insert herself between Scott and the desk officer, offering suggestions about how to move this process along. The officer glared at her. She wasn't picking up the cue that women were supposed to be seen and not heard. Unless she just didn't care. She'd been a television producer for the past twenty years, the arena in which she functioned best. Vicky was organized, intelligent, quick, and extremely task-oriented. She knew how to make things happen under duress, her strong suit; sensitivity to the unstated, to atmosphere, was not. When the officer ignored her, she began yammering about movies, dating, her last shopping spree. I was too tired to respond beyond a grunt.

Scott grew increasingly aggravated with both the situation and with my sister. He held up his hand. "Vicky. Stop."

The officer whispered in Scott's ear. Scott turned to Vicky. "Leave," he said.

She mumbled, "Sorry" and giggled, then looked at me for reassurance. I patted her hand and motioned towards the lobby, going with her. This was what our brother George had hoped to avoid when he had said he didn't think she would be a burden.

A few minutes later Scott came out. The officer told him we must go to yet another station, this one on the other end of Dubai, in Jebel Ali.

"Are you okay?" Scott asked quietly, indicating Vicky.

"Sure," I said. My relationship or non-relationship with my sister was so complicated, and her behavior so familiar, that nothing about her aimless chatter, or even her bone-headed attempt to take over from Scott, surprised me. Dealing with her strange, out-of-sync actions had been a life-long challenge, one to which I was almost accustomed. Almost, because I had never been able to fully accept how tone-deaf she was, and how she became the center of any situation, even this one. But accept her or not, this was the Vicky I knew.

I quietly asked Scott what the officer had said to him.

Scott rolled his eyes. "Control your women."

It was well past noon and scorching. Again, the taxi's air-conditioning didn't work. I could barely breathe. We traveled down Sheik Zayed Road, past the city's soon-to-be-tallest building in the world, the Burj Dubai, whose underwater restaurant was already open for business. After a while, we were so far from the heart of the city that there were almost no buildings along the highway, and no street signs.

I felt lost, abandoned, and resentful. How could Jerry have died? And how could he have died in such a place, forcing us to cope with its impenetrable bureaucracy by ourselves? It was my husband, my dead husband—the man who could navigate any situation, anywhere, anytime—who I needed to guide me through the morass.

I remembered Jerry's frustration with Dubai's public services. Every time he returned to his apartment from a trip home, the place would be a furnace, because the electricity had been shut off. The utilities' online payment system never credited his account properly. It took days, and multiple trips to the utility office, to rectify the situation. Similar glitches occurred regularly with the cable, Internet, and phone companies. As far as my husband had been concerned, Dubai's new state-of-the-art infrastructure was a total failure.

The long cab ride began to frighten me. *How did we know that this driver would take us where we needed to go? Did he understand the directions?* Just when I was certain we were completely lost, the driver pulled into a deserted parking lot alongside a low-slung concrete building. "Here," he said as he opened the back door of the taxi. A goat walked past. Vicky jumped.

"Where the hell are we?" Scott asked.

"Jebel Ali police station."

Scott told Vicky and me to wait there while he went in. "No sense wasting any more time in waiting rooms if this isn't the right one." Five minutes later he returned. "I knew it. There are *two* Jebel Ali police stations. This is a sub-station, not the main one."

Purgatory.

Station number four: a much larger building with a full parking lot. This time Vicky and I were sent to the Muslim women's waiting room, while Scott was taken to the offices situated behind an imposing wall of doors. Paranoia began to overtake me. *What if Scott didn't come back? What if they arrested him?* I tried to focus on the two women in black burkas sitting directly across from us. Because of their niqabs—the cloth mask covering their noses and mouths—only their eyes were visible. They nodded at us. We nodded back. We must have been as much a curiosity to them as they to us, maybe more. They must have wondered what two western women were doing in a Dubai police station.

Vicky whispered to me, "Don't you think they're hot in their robes?"

"Yes," I said, and told her they could very well be wearing designer dresses underneath, recounting what Jerry and I had seen in the mall.

Then Vicky launched into her dating life courtesy of Match.com, and why she was still single. She mentioned a Canadian guy she'd been on a dozen dates with. Unlike Scott two stations ago, I found her love life, or lack thereof, a welcome distraction. I did what I used to do—told her not to worry, there would be someone—though I didn't truly believe it. Vicky isolated herself. After she broke off her engagement, she never invited anyone, neither friends nor family—George lived a mere fifteen minutes away—to her house, which had been our childhood home. I didn't see how she would be able to really let a man into her world. But I didn't give voice to that thought, of course. I was simply glad to talk about something having nothing to do with my plight.

I checked my watch. Scott had been gone for more than an hour. "Come on," I said. Why should I have to wait in a restricted room? I wasn't a Muslim woman. We moved to the main waiting area where we could see the doors. Just as I was watched in the hospital, the men in this section stared at us with undisguised disapproval.

The doors swung open. "Let's go." Scott marched toward the exit.

"What happened?" I asked.

"One guess."

Vicky and I sat in the back of the cab in station number five's parking lot, while Scott, once again, went inside. It was almost 4 p.m., and the traffic on the road in front of us had slowed to a crawl. Dubai's rush hour started early by Western standards. Our driver, who would go off-duty soon and wouldn't be able to take us back to the apartment, shouted to another driver, who was stuck in the stalled traffic, then attempted to flag down a passing cab to take over. I began to hyperventilate. We couldn't be stranded in a police station parking lot. We just couldn't. All I wanted was to go back to the apartment and lie down.

My anxiety must have been obvious. The driver said, "Don't worry, I'll find someone to take you home." Then he took out his cell phone and made a call. I wondered why he hadn't done that in the first place. He put the phone back in his pocket. "Good, someone will come." The traffic wasn't moving at all now. "I won't leave until my replacement arrives," the driver said. Then he asked me what happened that we must travel from station to station all day. This man, like the nurses and the bank manager, showed genuine sensitivity. Much as I disliked Dubai, I was thankful for the good people I encountered. They made this hell bearable.

"So sorry," he said. "My mother died last month."

I murmured sympathy. Mother, husband, loss was loss.

Finally Scott returned, paper in hand. "I had to strong arm them to get this or they would have sent us to another godforsaken station. This place is…" He stopped himself, suddenly aware of the driver.

A taxi pulled up alongside us, and we switched cars. Scott slipped the first driver a generous tip. The longest day was almost over.

Vicky and I sipped piña coladas served in carved out pineapples complete with pink umbrellas and long bendable straws. We had rejoined Ross and Ollie at the crowded beach bar of Vicky's hotel.

"Boy, do I need a beerham," Scott said, ordering German beer on tap for the men. We laughed at the play on dirham.

Ollie, Ross, and Scott toasted. "To beerhams."

I started to laugh louder, and once I started, I couldn't stop. I laughed so hard my sides hurt, my eyes watered, and my nose ran. I rocked back and forth in my seat. My laugh transformed into silent spasms. No sound came out of my open mouth.

"Mom!"

I flashed on my mother's wild gales after a glass or two of champagne, how her already-red face would turn beet and tears would pour down her face.

"Roselee!" Vicky admonished, as if to say *pull yourself together*, though she was laughing too.

"Wow, doesn't take much to get her going, does it?" Scott said.

His comment triggered a new gut-wrenching wave. I was beyond exhaustion, and out of control. My body, riddled with pent-up emotion, had released me into tragicomic hysteria. My ribs ached. I spewed my drink all over the table.

Scott motioned to the waiter and pointed to Vicky swabbing the table with paper napkins. "We'll need some more."

Afterwards, in the apartment, my chest was sore, but I was calm. Or maybe I was merely spent. I spoke to Shari, who had found a funeral director in a town close to Montclair. When I called him, he volunteered a horror story about a family who didn't get enough Indian death certificates to process all their needs stateside. "Get fifteen. You'll never be able to do this again."

No kidding.

That night we had a formal birthday dinner for Vicky at the hotel. We slouched in our chairs and said little, the weight of the day heavy upon us.

A call came in from the *Montclair Times*, our town's paper, which was planning a cover story on Jerry. I left the table to talk. "He was doing what he was meant to do, and that's what we're trying to hold on to," I told the reporter, giving her a useable quote that left out the rest of the truth—that we weren't succeeding, that Jerry's career fulfillment meant little compared to its cost.

Then friends called. No one could believe it. Kate, my maid of honor, a woman of enormous empathy, who had witnessed my relationship with Jerry from the beginning, wept. "Oh, Roselee, oh, Roselee."

I paced back and forth, up and down the hotel lobby steps. Hotel guests passed me, avoiding eye contact. I didn't care how I appeared or who heard me. "How could this be? How could he be gone?"

When I returned to the table, the cake had arrived—a real one this time, with candles, unlike the wee hours' dessert. We sang, "Happy birthday to you," voices quavering. Vicky seemed about to crack. Ollie took our picture, sisters together after so long. He checked the shot, and a knowing expression passed over his face.

"I don't want to see. I hate pictures of myself," Vicky said.

Ollie handed the camera to me. The photo was raw: my frozen smile, my sister's agonized expression, her mouth twisted, eyes brimming, her face reflecting my insides. The interminable day had ended where it began, in a stubborn celebration determined to mark Vicky's milestone. No matter what.

15

Day Ten, Watched

At the consulate once again, Scott and I, with Vicky in the lobby, stood at the same window talking to the same oblivious British woman. We recounted the previous day's ridiculous chase and how unreasonable it was to expect foreigners to handle the byzantine Dubai bureaucracy on their own. How were we supposed to follow what we now knew to be inaccurate directions?

She listened and passed me fifteen copies of the consulate death certificate, one of which we would need to release Jerry's body from the mortuary and have it transported to the airport cargo bay. "I was trying to save you money," she said, and sent us on our way. According to the instruction sheet, we were far from done. At that point, I would gladly have paid any price to expedite the process.

Outside in the noon sun, we raised our arms to hail a cab, but there were none. The local cell phone rang. It was one of Jerry's friends, Gadin, an Indian businessman. He asked how I was, how he could help. I told him of our frustration, the system's opaqueness. What were we to do?

"I happen to have someone in my office right now who can help you—a professional facilitator. He's done this many times before. I will send him to the apartment this afternoon. And my personal driver will be at your service for as long as you need. He is on his way."

I accepted this offer in the same manner I had the entire ordeal: I surrendered and thanked him. It was a relief to have someone, even someone unseen, looking out for us, though I couldn't help being struck by the timing. *He just happened to have a facilitator in his office? How did he know we were in trouble? Had we been watched this whole time?* Jerry would have said, *Of course you were.*

Scanning around me, I saw businessmen in western suits and Emiraties in dishdashas lined up along the curb, waiting for rides. I didn't know what I was looking for. TV clichés popped into my head: *a man talking into his sleeve*—or was he wiping his nose; *a man in dark glasses leaning on a post behind us*—everyone wore dark glasses; *Maxwell Smart talking into a shoe.* I told myself to stop. Depleted, I couldn't afford more paranoia.

Gadin's driver pulled up. I sank into the car's cushy backseat next to my sister. Scott took the front. My fear and tension receded. I closed my eyes. For a moment, I could let go, and I was grateful.

In the lobby of Jerry's apartment building, Robert, a strapping blond South African with a bowl haircut and flushed, possibly alcohol-reddened complexion, met all of us except Vicky, who had gone back to her hotel to rest. He had a jolly, confident demeanor, and seemed to me to be a bit of an outlaw. Ordinarily, this would have put me off, but nothing about our circumstances was ordinary. I trusted him immediately, convinced that we were in able hands.

We went upstairs to the apartment together. When I put my key in the lock, the tumbler wouldn't turn. Odd. A neighbor from the next apartment, a blonde German woman, opened her door. She shook my hand, said how sorry she was, and called the building manager for us. Two security workers appeared with a master key. It didn't turn either. They couldn't figure out what was jamming the lock, and decided to replace it completely.

Since we weren't going to be able to get inside anytime soon, Robert, the men, and I went back downstairs to talk. He told us that he could handle all the necessary steps for transporting Jerry's body out of Dubai in one day. For six thousand dollars. I called my American Express contact, who wanted to speak directly with Robert. Because Jerry was a platinum business member, they agreed to pay the entire fee, and the cost of flying the body home. Insurance for overseas medical emergencies, including death, came with the card membership. I was extremely thankful for one less expense. Robert would return Thursday morning to take care of everything.

An hour later we were back in the apartment. Scott thought the lock episode very strange—creepy, even. Robert had told us he didn't. "Every American living here is suspect," he said.

Jerry had said the same thing when he first started working in Dubai. "We're all assumed to be spies." The thought of my rubber-faced, motor-mouthed husband as a spy made me smile. He couldn't have kept a secret to save his life.

Images of our family trip three years earlier flooded me: the Mina A'Salam, the stunning luxury hotel where we had stayed when Jerry had worked with the Dubai International Film Festival; Ollie would cover the Festival for his college paper, scoring his first press credentials. The resort had been designed as an ancient palace, complete with minarets, a mote, canals, and gondolas on which we could travel to restaurants, a spa, the beach, multiple pools, and a fully stocked in-house market of shops and cafés called a souk. At the concierge counter, as we checked in, we were asked to turn over our passports, which made me nervous. Jerry took it in stride, just as he had the many security guards posted throughout the lobby. I, however, did not feel comfortable knowing

I was being watched. "Are there cameras in the rooms?" I asked.

"No," Jerry said, "at least I don't think so." Then he paused. "But it could be bugged." Suddenly the trip felt less like a vacation and more like a siege.

"What are you worried about, Mom?" Ollie asked. "We have nothing to hide."

The staggeringly beautiful surroundings demanded appreciation on their own strictly surface terms. To enjoy them, I had to ignore the constant surveillance underneath.

"Now that they, whoever *they* are, know he is dead, they saw an opportunity to go in, find out what he was doing here," Scott said. Ross agreed.

Ollie and I checked the rooms. Jerry's computer was still exactly where we had left it, his paper files appeared to be untouched. It seemed that nothing had been moved, at least not inside the drawers or closets, but we didn't know the contents of the apartment well enough to be certain. Nevertheless, Scott was convinced that someone had been there while we were out. I began to perspire. The suspicions I had squelched earlier on came roaring back. I believed my brother-in-law. We *were* being watched. I didn't think I could take one more minute of fear.

With impeccable timing Scott announced, "Time for beerhams," and we headed to Vicky's hotel.

At dinner, I ate a full meal for the first time since arriving in Dubai. My hunger and sense of taste had returned with a vengeance. I relished the mezze's salty olives, creamy hummus, and spicy peppers. I stuffed rolls, slathered in butter, into my mouth. I ordered course after course, as if I had been starving. But the bottomless pit wasn't my stomach, it was my heart. I couldn't fill its devastated shell, so I substituted the simple pleasure of food. And for the duration of the meal, I was satisfied.

16

Day Eleven, Lawyers

In the morning, Wali and Ross accompanied me to the Ministry of Justice, Dubai's central court, to get an order releasing Jerry's money from the bank account. Scott would stay with Ollie. As Ross and I followed Wali into the government building, its size and the swirl of activity engulfed me. The Ministry's entry hall was vast, with impossibly high ceilings, which gave me vertigo whenever I looked up. Wali spoke in Arabic to a woman at the reception desk, who directed us to a line on the other side of the hall. The line led to a man on a raised platform behind a lectern. His artificial height and this barricaded podium added to my already intense discomfort. The man talked to Wali, who then ushered us outside to tell us we couldn't get a court hearing unless we had two witnesses with us—men—to vouch for my status as sole heir to Jerry's estate. This was a Sharia court, and the American will I clutched to my chest might, depending on the judge, mean nothing here. One of my lawyer father's favorite sayings—*the United States is a government of laws, not men*—echoed within me. In Dubai, I was certainly at the mercy of men, and I felt weakened and disheartened by that certainty.

Next door in a tiny café, we drank bottled tea and strategized. Wali worked hard to stay upbeat. "We will get the money out. I have friends, men ready to appear before the court today as witnesses to vouch for you. And we will need Oliver here, too."

At the mention of my son's name, I froze. I realized that in this world, his status as only son was greater than mine as wife, but I couldn't bear the thought of subjecting him to another ordeal. "No," I said. "I can't put him through anymore this week. Isn't there another way? Can't I get a lawyer to expedite this?" I knew it would be foolish to rush into court to force a binding judgment without legal representation.

Always willing to accommodate, Wali made some calls and found a lawyer who could handle the matter. I spoke to the man on the way to his office. His accent, Indian or Pakistani, was difficult to understand, but I gleaned this much: the Dubai court was supposed to honor an expatriate's will from the country of origin, though just as Wali had said, whether it did or didn't depended on a particular judge's inclination. Get the wrong judge, and I would indeed have to go through a Sharia court proceeding. No way. That mustn't happen.

I asked the lawyer if he could handle an international court action. He hesitated, all the answer I needed. I thanked him and told Wali I was not going any further without an experienced international attorney who could bypass Sharia entirely.

Wali told me that this was why he had put everything he owned in his wife's name. Then he made another call, and we drove to the office of a second lawyer. We entered a modern three-story building and were met, not by the attorney, but by a timid paralegal. His apologetic manner only deepened my mistrust. I was in no mood to be pawned off on an underling. In the conference room, I asked where the lawyer was. The paralegal bowed his head and said quietly that he had been called away. At that point, I could barely sit still. As if in response to my agitation, the paralegal rattled off the necessary filings. I thanked him and left, appalled. In the elevator on the way down, I told Wali that I could not leave my financial fate in the hands of an attorney who didn't bother to show up for our first meeting.

Ross had said little throughout all of this. I relied on his quiet, steady support. I was sure that if he thought I was making mistakes, he would have spoken up. Distraught as I was, I must have been coping.

Wali made another call, and we headed for a mall where we would meet a third lawyer, this one an Emirati, the rare actual UAE citizen. He was dressed in full dishdasha. His English turned out to be limited, but Wali assured me that this attorney had worked for other ex-pats in my situation. The man looked me in the eye, and I was more disposed to consider his services. But the physical toll of the past few days had caught up with me. I swayed with cumulative fatigue, stress, and dehydration. For most of the translated conversation I willed myself to stay conscious, though by now—having felt woozy on a daily basis—I knew I would not pass out. The lawyer bowed and left.

Ross looked at me with concern. "We need to get some lunch." Over sandwiches in an empty mall café, we discussed the legal meeting. Neither Ross nor I was comfortable trusting someone with whom I couldn't talk directly, sans translator, and who had only a one-man shop. I was not about to give such a person a retainer.

That afternoon, just as I lay down on the bed for a much-needed nap, a call from Jerry's US business associate, Bill, interrupted my rest. He asked how I was, if I was "set" with money, and then answered his own question: "Jerry was always good at that." If he meant that my husband was good at making money, then yes, but I was the one who had managed it throughout our marriage. Jerry could be impulsive, and though he always landed on his feet, we had had many financial ups and downs over the years. I had made sure we paid bills on time, paid off credit cards, stayed within our limits.

I said, "I'll be okay," though I wasn't at all sure that I would. He told me the story of his father dropping dead on a golf course at fifty—his demonstration of empathy—before launching into the real reason for his call.

"Did you know about the pending deal? How big it is?"

I sighed. I knew all about it—the one with Ashar, the man who had left Ollie and me on the hospital curb. The deal was simple. Jerry and Bill had introduced Ashar to an American company that could manufacture heat-resistant digital billboards, perfect for the Middle East. If the deal came to fruition, Jerry and his partner would get a finder's fee, a small percentage of the millions involved. Jerry had been so excited—the November email—his last—had said *I made a very big deal tonight that might guarantee us future financial stability.* I also remembered that Jerry wanted Bill to be a silent partner. The man's desperation had scotched plenty of previous plans, and Dubai was no place to be pushy. Jerry told me that in the Arab world, handshake deals, even involving astronomical sums, were honored, and patience and indirection were required to see them through. The bigger the transaction, the more reserve necessary.

Bill continued, "I took the liberty of asking Raine to meet with Jasim to scope out what they are willing to do." Jasim was Ashar's associate. Jerry told me he had introduced Bill, a multiple divorcee, to Raine. Her combination of brains and beauty had, naturally, cast its spell on him. Jerry said Bill had asked if Raine was "his." I wasn't the only one who thought that might be so, but Jerry had scoffed, and Bill proceeded to date her. It must not have gone far. Raine needed someone with more money and less baggage. Bill rambled on about the intricacies of the deal, and all the possible ways it could still happen.

I was much more fixed on my husband's frozen bank account than on a deal that was speculative at best. The account money existed. I had seen the number before the screen went blank, and for Ollie and I that sum would make all the difference. Without it, we wouldn't be able to stay in our home. The deal, on the other hand, didn't feel real. I preferred Bill not take any action, but I didn't have the will to resist. Whatever fight I might have had I had spent dealing with police stations and lawyers. "Fine," I said. "Do what you have to do. But you need to understand, I can't focus on this now. You'd better put it in an email. After the funeral, we'll talk."

That night I said goodbye to Vicky in the lobby of her hotel. She had an early flight to the US in the morning. All through the past few days, I had been acutely aware of the bizarreness of our reunion amidst such extreme circumstances, but there hadn't been a right time, or, in fact, enough strength, to address the elephant in the room. Then, in the middle of another parting, I couldn't help myself. I hugged her and stood back, pinning her with my eyes. "Don't ever leave me again."

She blanched, gaze hardening. "It takes two," she said and turned away. She gave Ross, Scott, and Oliver cursory pecks on the cheek and quickly got into the waiting taxi.

I shrugged. What more could I do? Vicky had a tough time taking responsibility for her actions, and when cornered, she lashed out, but I did not regret confronting her. I had the distinct feeling I might never hold back again.

Ollie put his arm around my shoulders—he had witnessed his aunt's intransigence many times—and the four of us left the hotel. As we walked the single block back to the apartment, the deserted, dusty street spooked me. Its dark, empty high-rises towered over us, their blank windowless facades forming a haunted cityscape.

Though built on giddy speculation that the future of this water-front neighborhood would be brilliant, with money flowing from all over the world to fill its penthouses and high-end shops, the effect was desolate. I realized that Dubai's brash gamble had nothing to offer me in my neediest hour. I wouldn't be leaving Dubai with either my beloved spouse, or—as the banker had suggested—with bags of gold.

17

Day Twelve, Discovery

The next day Scott had to accompany Robert to facilitate the shipping of Jerry's remains, since he was the one who had signed the Arabic death certificate. The body would be released only to him. I was very relieved that I didn't have to go. I didn't think I could have summoned the inner resources necessary to chase through Dubai's dysfunctional underbelly one more time.

Instead, Ross, Ollie, and I went to the second opinion doctor's office across town to pay him. The cab ride was numbing. Even wearing sunglasses and inside the vehicle, I squinted at the glare reflected on the dull expanse of low-rise buildings as the highway stretched away from the city's center. *Hadn't we just done this?* It all looked the same to me, bleached and uniform, occasionally punctuated by a construction crater. I imagined plunging through the earthen pit and emerging on the other side of the world. I longed for green hills, tall trees, deep blue skies.

When we reached the medical office, it was almost noon, the heat searing. The receptionist was kind, and offered us water. She inquired about how Jerry was doing. I swallowed hard and told her. She said nothing, and bowed her head. I charged the bill to my Visa card. The $800 fee for two hospital consultations was the only bill I had to pay for Jerry's care, a small mercy.

We were hungry. The receptionist directed us to the mall across the street. This arcade—more ornate than either the Mall of the Emirates, where Jerry and I had shopped for rugs, or the non-descript shopping center where I had met lawyer number three—sported sumptuously patterned walls and inlaid floors, a garish attempt to marry ancient Middle Eastern art with the mall's purpose: modern consumption.

We stopped at the first eating area we could find. Over a lunch of salads and pita, we began to plan the funeral. I didn't want to, but it had to be done. With Scott and Robert taking care of everything, we were sure that we could finally depart, and therefore set a date. We settled on February ninth, the Saturday after we planned to leave Dubai. This would allow Scott and Ross a bit of recovery time before they had to travel east again. And a weekend would make it easier for other family members to attend.

Ollie volunteered to handle the music. He and his father shared similar tastes, with Neil Young at the top of the list.

When I mentioned that I wanted to speak, Ross asked, "Are you sure? You don't have to, you know."

"Yes," I said, "I know." I knew most widows didn't address the assembled at a memorial. Most sat silently, buoyed by words of comfort addressed to them. I wanted that too, but only after I had said what I needed to say. I needed to tell our story, Jerry's story, because I knew him better than anyone, and because speaking would give me a purpose, a means of control, after having none. It was something I could do.

Ollie wanted to speak as well, I imagined for much the same reason. Ross, Scott, and their sister, Kathy, the oldest, would also eulogize their brother. We listed close friends who could deliver remembrances, and provide live music.

I didn't want to hold the service in Jerry's old church. He'd had a falling out with the minister a year earlier, over her pro-Palestinian sermons. They tried to hash out their disagreement over coffee, but when their discussion reached an impasse and they were about to part, she asked, "If something happens to you over there, do you want me to do the service?" When Jerry told me, I was appalled. *Was she wishing him dead?*

The absurdity of my husband's actual death from natural causes, and not from dangers I had feared and that she had ghoulishly invoked, wasn't lost on me. No, the church was out of the question, unless we could get Reverend Charles Henderson, Jerry's first minister in New York City, who had moved to Montclair shortly after we did. The thought of Reverend Chuck, a brilliant, dry-witted, impeccably sensitive man, gave my non-believer self some momentary peace.

Later that afternoon, Jasim called to give his condolences and to promise me that he and Ashar would honor Jerry's part of the unfinished business deal—the one Bill was so eager to pursue—if it came to fruition. I thanked him and said that one of us, Bill or I, would be in touch. I shuddered, disturbed that this would be yet another thread tying me to Dubai for who knew how long.

Ollie and Ross urged me to take a nap, but the "to do" list had grown, now that we were certain that we could leave on Sunday. I began to sort and pack. I had to. I vowed never to return to this soulless city, no matter what, and I didn't want anyone else touching my husband's intimate belongings.

I opened Jerry's closets and put his designer shoes in garbage bags, which I placed in the public refuse closet down the hall. Jerry's feet were smaller than Ollie's and his brothers'; there was no reason to lug his many pairs back to the States. And besides, I needed to be practical. I had only his one carry-on for whatever I could bring home.

I folded his shirts—beautiful striped Façonnables, Turnbull & Assers, and linen Zegnas—he'd become quite the dresser in the past few years, and I imagined that Ollie would want to wear them some day. I lay the Brioni bespoke suit made in Lebanon, the one he was so proud of, on the bed. Jerry had looked incredibly dapper in it the previous October at the Amal Festival in Santiago de Campostela, Spain, where *The War of Peace*, his film about the various Lebanese religious confessions—as they called factions—was the featured documentary. He stood beside the translator after the showing and answered questions, beaming the entire time. I remembered thinking, *He's at the top of his game; finally he's being recognized for his talents.* As proud as I was, I was also afraid of this success, which was taking him further and further away from me. I had accompanied him on the trip in order to feel closer to him, and to his work, but the temporary fix wasn't enough. By then, on-going conflict over our long-distance life had produced serious strain. I was rapidly reaching my breaking point. We returned to the States, tired and torn.

I carefully put the suit inside the carry-on and dragged his laundry bag onto the bedroom floor. I stuffed the dirty socks and underwear into a trash bag. Then I reached in and retrieved his undershirt. As fastidious as he was about his outerwear, Jerry couldn't have cared less about his undergarments. He had worn the same three undershirts, purchased at the now defunct B. Altman's, for thirty years, longer than I had known him. In the morning, standing beside him, while brushing our teeth, I'd smirk at the sight of his darling barrel chest wrapped in tattered white cotton.

"When are you going to get rid of that thing?" I'd ask.

"Never," he'd smirk back, and then in blatantly Neanderthal justification, he'd add, "it's a wife-beater." I'd laugh. That thin, sleeveless, threadbare garment couldn't do anyone harm. Least of all me. After countless washings, two of the shirts fell apart in my hands, though Jerry accused me of doing them in. He was down to one pitiful remnant; thin was an understatement. It was positively lacey, almost transparent, its ribbing a mere shadow of texture, like an x-ray of an undershirt, not the real thing. Its delicate, near deceased condition was a source of much friction between us over the years. Every so often when I found it lurking among the whites, I'd threaten to get rid of it.

"You wouldn't dare," he'd say, and he was right. I hated the shirt, but I couldn't do away with something to which he was so attached.

"I'll buy you a new one, lots of them."

"Don't," he said. "I love that shirt."

I was glad I hadn't made good my threat. I clutched the undershirt to my chest, inhaling the sweet, sour scent of him, still alive in the fibers. I put my hand inside it, stretching the material over my palm. This tired piece of cloth had touched my husband's chest, had covered his heart, the heart that had stopped beating four nights earlier. I brought the shirt to my nose. There he was. My Jerry. This was as near as I could get, would ever again get to the physical him, to the body I knew so well. The realization twisted within me. I put the shirt back into the bag, and stuffed the whole thing inside my own suitcase to take this last piece of him home.

Then I went into the bathroom, opened the drawer to the left of the sink and tossed out Q-tips, emery boards, aspirin, prescription bottles of Wellbutrin for depression, and his Advair inhaler for asthma. I packed his signature colognes without opening them. After breathing in the undershirt, I couldn't risk inhaling anything more. If I did, I might not be able to continue.

From the back of the drawer, I grabbed a packet with Cialis written on it. For a moment I couldn't remember what it was. *Antibiotic?* Then I realized. *Oh my God.*

At home he used Viagra to counteract the unwanted sexual

side effects of the anti-depressant. I didn't like him taking it too often, because he got violent headaches afterwards. I remembered Jerry saying many common prescription drugs were available over-the-counter in Dubai.

My mind froze. I couldn't absorb what this find might mean. I reached further into the drawer and pulled out packets of condoms and a slip of paper. One side had a picture of a girl, perhaps Filipino, dressed in skimpy black lingerie. The other had a local six digit phone number. I instantly remembered an incident a few months earlier, when Jerry was angry with a British friend who had stayed in the apartment while he was home in New Jersey. The guy, a wild man, had trashed the place, leaving liquor bottles and condoms everywhere. Apparently, he had thrown a hooker party.

I dumped the pills, paper, and condoms into the bathroom wastebasket, and took it immediately to the refuse closet. These remnants of bad behavior seemed radioactive. I needed to put physical distance between them and me. I wanted to believe they weren't Jerry's, only the leftovers from that jerk's orgy. But I wasn't an idiot. I sat on the edge of the bed and let the discovery sink in. I could hardly breathe.

At 6 p.m. Scott returned. "It's done. He's on his way home," he said. My macabre fear that I would have to physically accompany my husband's remains—me above with the oblivious passengers, his inert body below—evaporated. I cried in Scott's arms. Then he and Ross and Ollie embraced. He said we could never have done what Robert did. "The man knew everyone, and had greased every palm many times. The bureaucracy would have been impenetrable to us."

Scott poured out the story. "We went on a tour of every back door in Dubai—the Maktoum Mortuary, where I had to identify him again, the main morgue hospital, where hundreds of poor immigrant workers lined up outside for who knows what purpose.

We had to wait while they prepared his body, then we went to the Ministry of Health to get an official death certificate, then back to the Consulate for a letter of release. It turned out the British woman knew Robert well. My God, why couldn't she have clued us in? Then we went to the airport police station. Counting the hospital station the night he died, that made seven. They interrogated me: Who are you? Why are you here? Robert told me to say nothing more than that I had signed the Arabic death certificate. Finally, we stood outside in the cargo bay and identified the box by number and signed off on the shipment. At least there, five or six people who were shipping packages approached me to offer their heartfelt condolences."

Poor Scott. What an unspeakable ordeal. He looked wrecked.

I sighed. I was in my own version of hell. I needed to talk to him alone. We went back to the master bedroom and sat on the edge of the bed. Then I told Scott what I had found.

He took my hand. "He loved you. He wanted to come back to you. He told me as much last summer when we were in Alaska." They had gone on a men-only family trip. "He said he was done. This—what you found—doesn't mean anything. If he did anything, it was just for a physical release. He was under such enormous pressure."

I nodded. That was what I wanted to believe, but I was also raw with shock and deeply hurt. And I held myself partly responsible. I never thought when I had said, "Whatever you do, use condoms and don't tell me," that he would actually take me at my word. The statement was more bravura than an expression of what I actually wanted. I was acting tough, testing him, and, just in case he failed, trying to protect myself. But I should have known that there was no protection from betrayal. Secrets always revealed themselves, and secrets had the power to wound. *How could he? Did he really think I had given him permission?* I thought he knew me, that I would never stand for infidelity of any kind, that I was bluffing. All these thoughts entwined with my cascading grief. I was aghast and bereaved all at once.

"Are you going to hate him now?" Scott asked.

I exhaled. I couldn't confront Jerry, would never be able to have it out with him, see his face when he told me the truth, whatever that was. *Raine? Hookers? Someone else?* I would never know. And then there was the possibility that he did nothing, that he never actually used the contents of the drawer. This, too, I could never know. I was heartbroken that the conversation, the argument, whatever we would need to do to move on—because no matter what, we always moved on, got through the mess—could never happen. Resolving what we did *together*, as a married couple, was now permanently out of reach. Resolution would be my job to do alone. I was pained, furious, and gutted by the evidence, circumstantial though it was. Nevertheless, I could not hate my husband. I missed him too much.

I looked into Scott's sad eyes, and shook my head.

He went on, "After today, I get it. What he was going through. This place is nuts. I can't imagine living here. Promise me, if you have to come back, for any reason, you won't come alone. That you'll tell me, and let me come with you."

"I'm never coming back," I said. There. I had spoken my vow out loud. I realized this resolve had been building in me from the moment Ollie and I had landed.

"But if you have to, to wrap up the business, whatever. Promise."

I knew that no amount of money would be worth setting foot in this country again, but I gave Scott the answer he needed to hear. "I promise."

18

Day Thirteen, Big as the Universe

Wali and Sabeen had invited all of us to lunch, but Ollie didn't want to go. I understood. He didn't feel up to socializing with people he hardly knew. I, on the other hand, needed to get away from the relentless sorting and packing of Jerry's belongings. Besides his clothes—the ones that Ollie might be able to use someday—I'd managed to cram my husband's office files, his many pairs of glasses, and a few small framed family pictures into his carry-on. Ross sat on the bag to close it. Ollie, Scott, and Ross laid the rugs, largest to smallest on top of each other in three stacks, and then rolled them into bundles. These, along with his books and large framed photos, were all I wanted, all that was important to me. I would ask Raine to ship everything later.

"Don't drink too many beerhams," I said as I waved goodbye to Ollie and the men, who were on their way to Charlie Parrots, the bar in the hotel across the street where we had had dinner the night Jerry died.

"We might have to," Scott said. "It's a jungle in there." And though their destination was tainted for me—it was where we had gotten the call—I was happy to see Ollie smile.

Wali and Sabeen lived with their sweet baby boy in a suburb of Dubai. Their house, white indoors and out, turned out to be the perfect backdrop for my gift: a framed photo that Jerry had taken of a gray-white Moroccan building with curved roof and one dark door against a pale blue sky wispy with clouds. It was my favorite of Jerry's travel photographs. I had another copy in our hallway at home. Sabeen thanked me and hung it in their living room. She wondered how I knew it would be just the right touch.

Then she showed me around the house. Everything was spare, airy, and light. I was the only heavy element, but I was so glad to be far from the oppressive apartment that as I walked through the rooms, I began to forget the weight I carried within me.

Sabeen introduced me to her live-in nanny and housekeeper, a very young woman who said nothing. Jerry had told me that everyone in Dubai had help, mostly live-in, because it came so cheap—hence, the tiny windowless room and bath in his apartment, a room not counted in the three-bedroom, three-bath description. Sabeen snapped in Arabic at the girl. Her tone made me uncomfortable, but the young woman took it in stride.

We sat down to a sumptuous lunch Wali had prepared—another man who cooked. I tried to remember the last time Jerry had cooked for me, and couldn't. When we were dating, his cooking had drawn me in. Ever the autodidact, Jerry had taught himself to cook. His first dish for me, later dubbed "Mosier Chicken," was a marvel of breaded cutlets dipped in egg and lemon, and became, along with many other recipes, a staple over the years. Taking in Wali's cuisine, a mix of Jordanian and Arabic influences—a spicy meat dish with eggplant and dried tomatoes, stuffed grape leaves, falafel and freshly baked flat breads—I thought with disbelief, *My husband will never cook for me again.*

Sabeen, ever the curious interviewer, wanted to know about me—who I was, my history, how Jerry and I met. I began with our bus stop story. Sabeen's bright eyes widened. Wali whooped. Their reaction was why I never tired of telling our love-at-first-sight tale. I went on to recount my previous life as an actress, teacher, and non-profit director, and my current one as a writer. We laughed as I told them how Jerry lugged my props from car to theater in New York City, and how he would run from backstage to the box office, doing anything I needed, when I performed my satire of Queen Elizabeth II, *The Queen's in the Kitchen*, at the Edinburgh Festival; I'd been her professional look-alike.

"I see the resemblance," Sabeen said.

"Jerry and I were a team. He'd design posters for my productions, spearhead the PR campaigns, secure interviews, reviews, and producers." I finished with the present: fiction-writer, my reinvention after ending my long affair with the theater.

In her crisp TV presenter diction, Sabeen said, "Very impressive. I had no idea. You are a *real* woman." A respectful compliment. No one in the States would have responded this way. More likely they would have wondered why I had spent so much of my life at pursuits that didn't pay, and judged me for it.

Then Wali asked how I was emotionally, and the conversation shifted. I stuttered something incoherent. I was still much too stunned to analyze my state of being.

He spoke of his father's death. "The death of a loved one is something so huge, at first as big as the universe, surrounding and swallowing us completely. Gradually it becomes smaller, only as big as the world, then an ocean, then a tree, and then as big as a large person who stands next to us all of the time. Finally, it merges with us, and we carry it inside ourselves, wherever we go." He held an imaginary ball at his side. "It becomes portable, manageable, a part of who we are and will always be."

As I listened, for the first time in almost two weeks, I felt comforted. "That's beautiful," I said. "Thank you." He spoke truth. He had mourned; he knew the terrain of this land I had just entered, and had given me a map of what was to come, for which I was grateful.

Over dessert, I held the baby. His soft skin gave me a moment of elemental joy, even as fatigue cloaked my back and shoulders. The afternoon was winding down. It had been a much-needed time-out. I slumped, and Wali offered to drive me back to the marina. Before we left, I kissed the baby, who had Wali's gentle eyes and Sabeen's spark. An image of Jerry carrying baby Ollie in a backpack flickered before me. It wasn't so long ago that Jerry and I had been in our first home, doting on our own little boy. Gone. All gone.

"Do you think you will ever return to Dubai?" Sabeen asked.

I had not changed my mind, but looking at their kind, expectant faces, I wished I could say I had. "No, I don't think so. But we could meet some time in London, or you could visit New York City." They nodded. Neither of them seemed surprised by my answer. And though we all liked each other so very much—these were the only people I had met in Dubai with whom I could have imagined being friends—we knew we would probably never see each other again.

19

Day Fourteen, Safety

Scott and Ross would leave just after midnight. They did not want us to stay alone in the apartment, not after the lock incident. And Scott was still shaken by the back-alley tour with Robert. He wanted Ollie and me to check into the Hilton for the night. Seeing these strong men so afraid for us alarmed me more than the prospect of actually spending one more night there. I understood their concern. I was nervous too, but neither my son nor I had the capacity to deal with a hotel, even one down the street.

Scott shrugged. "Then barricade the door."

"Don't worry. We'll be careful," I said, and kissed them both goodbye, rattled, but resolving to manage. Our collective fear reminded me of an incident a year earlier.

"Do you want to come with me or stay here?" Jerry asked. It was January 2007, during my visit to Dubai. He had to meet with a production team in Beirut to plan his next documentary on Lebanon. I had come to be *with* him, not to be alone in his apartment. So there was no choice. I went. Even though the 2005 Beirut bombing haunted me, and Beirut, as well as much of Lebanon, was still a war zone, the potential danger didn't concern me as much as being stranded in Dubai without him.

When we landed in Beirut, the airport was almost deserted. Once again, just as I had when our family first set foot in the UAE, I felt my ethnicity acutely, as if I had a Star of David tattooed on my forehead. "I hope you haven't told anyone here about my background," I said.

"Of course not," he said, unconvincingly. Jerry could be quite a blabbermouth. I wouldn't have been surprised if he had confided in one of his Lebanese colleagues.

We stayed at The Albergo, a unique Parisian-Oriental hotel in the heart of Beirut's Achrafieh District. It lived up to Jerry's vivid descriptions. The manager greeted him as an old friend, and they gave us a lovely garden room with its own private patio. The room was layered with ornate patterns on sofas and chairs, tiled tables, and linens. Artwork was everywhere. From the tiny glass elevator, which took us to the hotel's rooftop restaurant, we saw amusing murals in Lautrec style decorating the walls on every floor. The restaurant had a spectacular view of the entire city, all the way to the Mediterranean Sea.

After lunch, we walked down to the tent encampment at the center of town. On each corner stood an armed soldier, with some intersections flanked by huge tanks. I tried to take it all in stride, but I was tense. As we neared the campsite, a guard approached us, and told Jerry to put away the camera. He had already taken many shots of street signs, a photographic theme he and Ollie pursued wherever they traveled.

Jerry complied, and we wandered over to a European-style square for lunch. It was eerily deserted, and the proprietor of the bistro we settled on was overjoyed to serve us, which was tremendously sad. I could see why Beirut had been dubbed the Paris of the Middle East, and why Jerry preferred it to Dubai. There was no contest—one an arid, pretentious space station, the other, an old world city whose history was obvious in its art, food, and architecture. If only its walls hadn't been riddled with bullet holes.

We continued to walk and take pictures, this time avoiding the tents. As we climbed the hill back to the hotel, a soldier stopped us and asked to see Jerry's passport.

"Wait here," he said.

He's got your identification," I said in a half whisper, holding back my growing fear. Jerry was dressed in a black coat and Armani skullcap. I wondered if his attire signaled something suspicious to the police, or if the soldiers near the tent city had alerted them to our presence.

"It's okay. It's routine." Jerry had been through this many times before.

After about fifteen minutes, the soldier returned, handed back the passport and told us to move on.

"No more walking," I said, as we hurried to the hotel.

The next night we met his colleagues for dinner. They were warm, intelligent, passionate people, but I saw clearly then that there were no truly safe places in Jerry's new world, and knew intuitively that there was no one to trust without reserve.

In the morning when Ollie and I woke up, we were alone again, as we were when we had arrived two weeks earlier. We were no longer panicked. Instead, a heartsick numbness permeated us, and we were both very, very tired.

After Scott's warnings, we made a point of not staying inside the apartment any more than necessary. We were packed and ready to go. If only we could have left when the men did, but there was still business to complete. In the afternoon, I would meet with Raine—one more time—to go over the shipping, contact information, and apartment instructions.

Until she arrived, we decided to go to the beach across the street. As Ollie and I walked up and down the shoreline, calm descended upon us. We focused to our left at the water and skyline, and away from the hotel terraces on the right. The smooth cool sand on our feet, the swish of the water around our ankles, the rhythm of the waves brushing the shore connected us to nature, and to the rest of the world we had left behind when we came. Dubai was such an artificial environment that the mere imprint of my bare feet on the sand felt like a balm.

Ollie picked up one of the very few shells in our path, and wrote *JMO FOREVER* in the sand, knowing, as I did, that it would be washed away by the tide. We spoke of our many vacations on Martha's Vineyard, the kindness of Ollie's friends back home, the funeral. The father of one of Ollie's college friends had emailed him a message saying he should resist trying to magically change the past. "You are clever and smart, but not that clever or smart as to make it better."

When we returned, I decided to get a manicure in the nail salon next to Jerry's building rather than go back up to the apartment. I needed to kill time, to distract myself. I never used to get manicures. I came from a long line of women who liked nice clothes, but didn't go in for other forms of pampering. No fancy hair salons, no manicures, no massages. Jerry, metrosexual that he'd become, had begun to get his nails done at this very salon, and back in New Jersey, talked me into the habit. We might have been the only couple to come into Upper Montclair's Pinky Nails for dual treatments.

Inside the Dubai salon, I realized that I had made a mistake. I was not up to anything this mundane, this normal, this frivolous. I was hardly able to sit still, or to make small talk. I was afraid that the young woman doing my nails would ask me questions about my "visit," and, of course, she did. I answered in words of one syllable and forced a weak smile. Usually I welcomed physical contact, but when the manicurist took my hand, the sensation rocked me. I willed myself not to keel over.

Somehow, I got out of there and back to the apartment where Ollie was online, writing to his friends. He missed them so much. I picked up a *New Yorker* I had brought with me. I loved reading, but hadn't been able to read anything since this all began. I flipped to the "Talk of the Town" section, and read the same paragraph over and over and over again, retaining nothing.

I decided to clean out the refrigerator, tossing everything—the wilted iceberg lettuce, the moldy cheeses, the half-empty jars of jam, all but some juice for the morning. Then I did another load of wash. The familiar housewifely duties gave me a small measure of sanity. I could get lost, temporarily, in mindless routine.

In the late afternoon, Ollie and I walked back to the beach. This time, two men with a camel stood in the sand near the parking lot where we accessed the shore. We watched the ground as we made our way past, to avoid stepping in the droppings. The beach was quieter than it had been earlier. We decided to go in the opposite direction, away from the occupied hotels and towards the unfinished ones. Ollie drew another message in the sand: our initials united inside a heart.

At 5 p.m., Raine arrived at the apartment. She was dressed casually, for her: tight jeans, a fluffy sweater, spike-heeled leather boots, dangling silver earrings, hair in a high ponytail, perfume strong and citrusy. She asked about Ollie. I told her he was resting in his room—not the truth—that he didn't want to have to make conversation or worse, accept sympathy from someone he didn't know and would never see again.

I showed her the pile of rugs, books, and pictures that we wanted shipped.

"What about the furniture?" she asked.

"I don't want any of it." I was not sure of much, but I was sure of that.

"I could try to sell it for you. My boyfriend might want the bedroom set." Of course, a woman like this would have a boy-friend—Jerry had told me about him—but I still wondered if the man was real. *Was this a lie to spare my feelings?*

"Take it. Give the couch to Kamilla; she told Jerry she admired it. You both have been wonderful to us." I meant it, despite my doubts and the phone incident. Along with Wali, these two women had been our mainstays.

I sat at the glass dining table, and glanced over a yellow legal pad on which I had written "To do," and contact lists for her to use. All at once, I felt totally drained by what had happened, by what was before me, by what could not be addressed. This was my chance to ask Raine about Jerry's behavior—probably my last chance. Even if she wasn't involved with him, she may have/must have known something. I thought back to the first call. *Had she phoned Ollie instead of me because she felt self-conscious about her relationship with Jerry?*

But I didn't say a word. I couldn't handle a confrontation, and what it might reveal. I didn't want to know more, not now, maybe not ever. And I couldn't risk putting her on the defensive. Once Ollie and I left Dubai, I would have to rely on Raine to carry out a myriad of tasks above and beyond shipping Jerry's belongings. I needed her to handle everything concerning the apartment before the lease ended in March. I recognized why Jerry depended on her. There was competence beneath her flashy exterior. Without Raine, I would have to break my resolve and return, something I was determined never to do. I needed more than anything, more than knowledge of my husband's activities, to be practical.

She asked me about the bank account. I told her it was frozen.

"I know a lawyer, an American, with an international firm and a New York office," she said, looking directly into my eyes. "He's been here thirty years, and just dealt with a British ex-pat situation like yours. It may take some time, but he's the best. I'll give him a call and will send you the information." Relief washed over me.

I thanked her for all she had done and would do. We embraced, her statuesque body towering over my short, rounder one. Resistant as I was to Raine's style, her intimidating beauty, her closeness to Jerry, I needed her, just as he had. Her help had been, and would continue to be, indispensable.

Ollie and I went to dinner at a hipper-than-thou Asian place above the nail salon. As the sun set, our anxiety level rose. We picked at our noodle and seaweed concoctions, sipped limeade, and barely spoke, dreading the evening alone in the stripped-down, echoing apartment. I looked obsessively at my watch, ticking off the time until we could escape. Before going to bed, I lined up our suitcases in the front hallway, and double-checked that the door was locked. I hesitated for a moment.

Then I propped a chair in front of it.

20

Day Fifteen, Flight

Ollie and I got up at four o'clock. I didn't remember sleeping, but I was glad our time here was almost over. The early morning darkness seemed appropriate. We were both extremely anxious to get away, to be sprung from the prison of the past two weeks. I walked through the apartment one more time, opening and closing closets and drawers, checking for some small item I might stuff into my purse or my pocket, but there was nothing more to take.

We descended the glass-enclosed elevator one last time, looking out at the stark cityscape. The full force of this strange vista bore down upon me, the hollowness of it. I saw Jerry's face as he basked in the same view. This disturbing city built on sand had seduced him, like the California Gold Rush had seduced the forty-niners. I understood. Its audacity matched his own.

Downstairs, the night doorman carried our bags to the waiting Emirates Airline car. He tried to catch my eye. He and his cohorts had alternately avoided us, and attempted to engage us throughout our entire stay. I understood they felt guilty, but I was having none of it. The night Jerry was stricken, they found him wandering the halls, and had put him back to bed. They probably thought he was drunk. Understandable. I shouldn't blame them, and yet I did.

"So sorry, Ma'am, so sorry," he said as he lifted the last suitcase.

Ollie looked down. I glanced at the man out of the corner of my eye. His face contorted in pain and embarrassment. I held up my hand to stop him from saying more. What was the use? My husband, Ollie's father, was gone forever. Apologies wouldn't bring him back. His guilt and mine did neither of us any good. He misread Jerry's distress signals, but even if he had read them correctly, Jerry would probably still have died. My own guilt was deeper: the Jewish wife, who wouldn't leave her son alone in the United States to live with her husband in the Middle East. I, too, might not have been able to save him, but knowing that didn't relieve my sense of responsibility. I put my hand down. We got into the car, leaving the man standing on the curb. He and I were alike in that moment, two people powerless to change what was.

In the airport, Ollie and I submitted to two screenings, one before we reached the gates, and one at the gate before boarding—standard security precautions for all flights to the US since 9/11. In the waiting area, worn as we were, neither of us could stay seated. We stood in line, shifting from foot to foot, running in place toward our still faraway home.

On board, I settled into my seat across the aisle from Ollie. The two weeks since the first flight seemed an eternity. We were almost free of this place. Though I knew it was irrational, as much as I blamed myself for not having been with Jerry, I blamed Dubai more. I believed that if he hadn't been working there, so far from our life together, he would have lived. *Crazy?* Maybe. But I had learned, too late, through this visceral life and death experience, the peril my husband had been in. My gut fears had been borne out. For all his accomplishments—the awards, the international recognition, the money—he had spun out in a high-flying life and, on some physical-spiritual plane, this lonely, rudderless trajectory had killed him. Jerry died in Dubai, and with him, so did a part of Ollie and of me. Dubai had changed us. We would be different people now.

Ollie buckled his seatbelt, leaned over the armrest and asked, "Mom, is it okay, when we land, if I go over to Keith's to watch the game?" He was starved for contact with his peers.

"Sure," I said. It was Super Bowl Sunday, the first yearly festivity without his father.

We looked at each other for a long time. The flight attendants bustled up and down the aisles, then took their seats. The captain announced we were next in line. The engines revved. I held my breath until the plane lifted off the ground.

PART TWO

Living After

21

The smoky Chet Baker version of "My One and Only Love" was our song. Jerry played it for me many times throughout the years. We'd cuddle on the couch in the living room, letting the lyrics wash over us.

We owned the record, the tape, and then the CD. I heard the song the first time before we were married. I remember Jerry standing across from me in our Brooklyn Heights apartment, watching my face as I took in the words.

I was speechless, a rarity. Baker's world-weary voice leavened the song's gushing sentiment. I had never heard anything so romantic.

Jerry often said that if anything happened to me, he wouldn't marry again. I would scoff, knowing how needy a man could be. "You would."

"No." He was adamant. "This is the marriage." I felt flattered, but thought maybe he needed my permission, which I gave, more than once.

"No," he would repeat. "I'd have friends, but not another wife. You are my one and only."

"And you are mine," I would say. "I won't get married again either." I hadn't really thought about the subject until he first broached it, but I wasn't merely following my husband's lead. I knew, as I said the words, that they were true. I'd never marry again. I wouldn't want to. Imperfect as we were, this was a real, true marriage. I didn't need another. I didn't want to be anyone else's wife. I could imagine loving again, having friends, lovers, a long-time, live-in companion, but not another husband. Only Jerry, complicated, perplexing Jerry.

My one and only love.

22

Home

When Ollie and I landed at JFK, my relief at finally being back in the United States transformed instantly into gnawing anxiety. I sat in the back seat of the car service sedan filled with a dull ache as I watched New York City landmarks come into view—the Citicorp Building, the Fifty-Ninth Street Bridge—that Jerry, with his architectural/historic preservation passion, had never failed to comment on, no matter how many time we passed them. Dubai had been alienating, and now New York seemed nearly as unfamiliar without my guide. Without Jerry's personal tour, the city where we met and married became, overnight, another foreign land. The skyline he adored had been transformed by sudden loss into an imposing reminder that nothing would ever be the same. The commercial billboards positioned along the highway echoed ones Jerry had proudly helped create years earlier. Manhattan gave me my husband, and I could hardly stand to look at its skyscrapers, grit, and pedestrian hordes. I hadn't realized until then—since we had been living in New Jersey for almost nineteen years—how much I associated the city with Jerry, with us.

When we met, I had been in New York for only two years, and had spent most of my time focused on the theater. Jerry introduced me to a broader urban landscape, giving neighborhood histories, from the Upper West Side and Central Park to the '20s, with his beloved Flatiron Building, to Chinatown and Wall Street. His zest for all things New York rubbed off on me. He introduced me to the Bronx Zoo, where years later we would thrill to our ten-month-old son's first steps. We ate at Luchow's and Sammy's Roumanian. Together, we walked across the Brooklyn Bridge, which so many men had lost their lives to build. Jerry showed me around Fort Greene, where he lived at the outset of gentrification, the Brooklyn Museum, the Botanical Gardens, and Prospect Park, and talked me into moving to his favorite borough. My husband had lived in every one—even the Bronx—during his Farm Workers stint.

In the early '90s, Jerry took me up to what is now the High Line, but was then just weeds and rusty track. "What a view," he said, spreading his arms to the sky, water, and high-rises. "One day this will be a park." I realized, looking out at the city, that he was a quintessential New Yorker, and that, for me, the city without him would be forever diminished.

Ollie and I rode in silence through the Lincoln Tunnel into New Jersey, down Route 3, past car dealerships, strip malls, and diners, and into Montclair, where the territory that Jerry defined expanded before us. He was, many townspeople would have agreed, "Mr. Montclair." He loved local politics, putting his stamp on the town's historic preservation projects and his name on commemorative plaques at firehouses and banks, an organic extension of his early parks work. As we drove down Valley Road, Montclair's main street, I thought, *Plaques, paperweights—no substitute for the man himself.*

The car turned into our dead-end cul-de-sac, and pulled up the long driveway past our expansive front yard. Even in winter, it was beautiful, peaceful. This was our dream home, a mid-century modern ranch set on a private park-like acre. From the moment of Jerry's death in Dubai, I knew I would not be able to stay here indefinitely. Where should I go? I was lost. What dream now?

When my father first saw the house, shortly after we moved in 1998, he called later that day to speak to Jerry; this was something that never happened. My father congratulated him. He wanted my husband to know, man to man, that he approved, meaning he was no longer worried about us, about me. The house had silenced his early concerns. My father respected Jerry's accomplishment.

The garage door opened, and there was my brother in the inner doorway, tilting his head, with its tight, gray curls, towards us. I had called George when we landed, and he must have been watching for us. He squinted, though there was no sun. I got out of the car, and for the first time felt the temperature shift from Arabian dry heat to February chill. George embraced me, his one muscular arm firmly holding me. Then he gave Ollie an extra long hug. George had lost his right arm to cancer only a few months after Jerry and I got married, a crisis that forced my parents to acknowledge my husband's decency and indispensability. George had lived a block from us in Park Slope, and we had seen him through radiation and chemotherapy. Now he would see Ollie and me through whatever was to come.

I looked around. The garage and its contents taunted me. They were all Jerry: his two motorcycles—in the hierarchy of pride and joy, Jerry's vehicles were second only to his son and a bare smidgeon behind me—his helmets, his kayaks, his tools, the car he was so proud of, a black BMW Z4. I had dubbed it his "midlife crisis car," but I too, loved its sleek lines, cute compact body, and the fun we had tooling down the road together for a Saturday dinner out, or a Sunday drive. We had always been at our best in vehicular motion.

Jerry was a contradictory mix of extreme risk-taker and cautious preparedness freak. After 9/11, he created a basement stash of canned food, water, plastic sheeting, duct tape, battery radio, and bedding, so if Armageddon hit, we could hole up in our windowless basement dark room. My husband loved to drive fast, but also took advanced motorcycle safety courses, doing so well he was asked to teach.

I trusted him enough to hop on the back of his bike for a trip into the western New Jersey countryside, via highway as well as country road. Beforehand, he would carefully fit me with my own helmet, gloves, and jacket. Mostly, though, we took short trips to Starbucks, where we'd hold hands over coffee, or to the town diner. On the way home, bombing down the sloping road leading to our street, with my arms wrapped securely around his waist, I'd shriek in sheer exhilaration. I understood why he loved to ride—the heightened sense of aliveness that speed and direct contact with wind, sky, and ground gave him. When Jerry rode alone with his friends, I'd listen for his engine coming down that same road, and smile. He always returned in a good mood.

I looked at the motionless bikes, stung, certain that I would not ride again.

I asked Shari to come over. We sat in the kitchen with George. Ollie couldn't wait to get out of the house to go to Keith's. When he left, I told my brother and my friend what I had found in the apartment bathroom.

After an awkward pause, George said, "He loved you."

I sighed. "What am I supposed to do with this information?" Neither of them had an answer, their faces reflecting confusion and concern.

The muscles in my chest and back seized. "I'm afraid I'm going to have a heart attack," I said. I had read somewhere that the recently bereaved were far more vulnerable to coronary incidents than most people—something called broken-heart syndrome.

George rubbed my back in slow circles. "No, you won't," he said, and for a moment I believed him.

Beyond exhaustion, I said goodnight, and went to our bedroom—it was still *ours*—bringing my purse with me, though I usually left it on a kitchen chair. At the last minute, I had taken the undershirt out of the suitcase and had decided to carry it on, hidden in the bottom of the bag, as if it were a precious piece of jewelry. Jet-lagged, undone, I placed the unwashed shirt, wadded into a ball, under my pillow, and fell into a deep, dreamless sleep.

The next day, since I was in no shape to get behind the wheel, George drove me to my appointments. We went first to my attorney. In his wood-paneled conference room, we listened while he outlined the steps needed to make my status as executor official. I said that I needed to update my own will immediately, making my brother executor. Then I told the attorney that I had a lead on an international firm to handle the business in Dubai. My lawyer recognized the firm's name, and said he would check on its credentials. This startled me. The simple act of connecting our longtime lawyer to the unresolved issues in the Middle East made the past two weeks real in a way they hadn't been. I didn't want to have anything more to do with Dubai, but the pending financial business meant I had no choice.

Afterwards, in the parking lot, I asked George if I had been coherent. I really wasn't sure.

"Totally," he said, as we got in the car to go to the funeral home.

The funeral director informed us we couldn't have an open casket—not that I wanted one—because the body "wasn't prepared to US standards." I didn't understand what that meant, but I pictured Jerry's decaying remains wrapped in a thin sheet, then tried to erase the image from my mind. My husband hadn't liked the idea of cremation, but joked that I should travel to Martha's Vineyard, put him in one of his kayaks, set him out to sea from Edgartown Harbor and *then* light him on fire, a Viking funeral. I picked the plainest casket available, and handed the director my credit card. I was terrified about my future financial state, but I told myself to spend whatever I had to, and think about it later.

At Mt. Hebron Cemetery in Montclair, I picked out a plot. In the office, I discussed my options with the eccentric gentleman in the plaid vest and golf beret, who handled such matters. Then he took us outside, and we walked from plot to plot in the cold, assessing the real estate. I rejected the less than prime locations: too close to the street, too "crowded," until we found a spot under a massive oak, near the carillon, with a winter view of New York City—Montclair and New York united.

Back in the car, George's eyes grew moist. "You just bought your own plot," he said.

"Yes. I know." I had decided in the instant to buy a double-stacked plot. I would be buried on top of my husband. "It's surreal, knowing where my remains will be, but necessary. For Ollie. It will be one less thing for him to deal with someday." I had faced the reality of my own death. How strange, when I hadn't yet accepted Jerry's.

George nodded in solidarity, and turned the key in the ignition. We had to make one last stop: the insurance agency. I had only met our agent, a tall man with soft eyes and a firm handshake, once before. He gave his condolences. I filled out the forms. He told me it would take about ten days to get the money to me. Thank goodness.

As we talked, I remembered I had to call the other agent, the one with whom Jerry had filed, but not finalized, a second policy. After my husband quit smoking the previous spring, following a COPD scare, he had decided he could pass a life insurance exam to greatly expand our coverage. As soon as we returned home, I called.

"Oh, Mrs. Mosier, I have your husband's policy here on my desk, ready to sign." All through December I had been bugging Jerry to find out what was taking so long, why the paperwork wasn't ready, when he'd passed the exam with no problem. It seemed that large policies took time.

I stopped the man from saying more, and told him what had happened. He mumbled how sorry he was. All I could think of was the timing, and if only the insurance company's comprehensive testing had found the aneurysm. Petrified as I was about money, I told myself that whatever I had been left with would be enough. It would have to be.

The service was to be held at the funeral home, since the church, in light of the tensions with its minister, was out of the question. But later that day Keith's dad said, "No way. There are going to be hundreds of people. Everyone loved Jerry." With the help of another friend, we were given the use of the Montclair Art Museum's main hall. This felt right. I had served on the Montclair Arts Council with the museum's director, had participated in museum committees, and had performed in the hall for an art and literary collaboration. Jerry, Ollie, and I loved museums, this one, mere blocks from our house, in particular. Intimate, classic, it was the town jewel, and Jerry had only recently shared with the director his experiences of art in the Middle East.

By Thursday night the house had filled with family who had flown or driven in from Nebraska, Utah, Seattle, Maryland, and Virginia. Every available towel, sheet, bed, and couch had been taken. Strung out, not fully in my body, not fully in my head, I went through the motions of playing the "hostess," directing sleep assignments: Jerry's older sister Kathy's family downstairs; Scott's son, Eric, on the living room couch; George and Jeanne camped out on air mattresses on my bedroom floor; their son, Leo, who was the image of my father, with Ollie; Ross and his wife, Robyn, in the family room on yet another air mattress; Scott and his little girl Sydney on the pull-out couch in my study. Leo's twin sister, Isabel, a quiet girl with her parents' insight and beauty, would sleep next to me in the king-sized bed that Jerry and I had shared. She would take his place, delaying for a night or two my having to sleep alone. A blessing.

Bringing the two families, the Bloostons and the Mosiers, together—something that had never happened on such a scale before—meant that I had to translate references to "Mike" whenever Leo and Isabel were in the room. To them, my husband had always been Uncle Jerry. Jerry's family of origin, however, called him Mike. I found this out early on in our relationship. Everyone who had met Jerry from college onward knew him by his first name. Everyone who knew him before that called him by his middle name.

The oddity of this split didn't really sink in until I traveled with Jerry to his parents' house in Salt Lake City for our first Christmas together in 1981. Jerry and I had already experienced the disastrous Thanksgiving with my insular family. My parents' disapproval hung over us. After tearing into my choice once again, they begged me not to go to Utah with him. "They're the kind of people," my mother said, "who will assume you are marrying their son." I didn't see anything wrong with that—Jerry and I were already committed to each other—so I went. I have often wondered what my parents would have thought if they had known that Jerry proposed to me the very June evening when they were introduced.

Jerry had been born in a small town in western Pennsylvania, and grew up in another tiny community in upstate New York. By the time his father had been transferred west, Jerry was out of the house and on his own, so Utah was disorienting for both of us, though for me it was all about his dual identity.

Mike, get the turkey platter…Mike, how about a game of touch football?

"We never thought Mike would get serious about anyone," his sister said. Then she told me that she was the reason they all called him Mike. "I couldn't pronounce Jerry when we were little."

Her explanation made sense, but I felt shut out. I immediately stopped referring to my boyfriend as Jerry. I began calling him, "your son, brother, uncle," or just "he" or "him." This continued for decades, whenever I was on the phone with any member of his family, or in person, and it was odd none of them had any problem talking to me about "Mike," though they knew full well he didn't use the name in his adult life. It felt as though I was married to someone other than the man they had raised or grown up with, that we weren't talking about or to the same person.

But with my husband gone, I resolved to reclaim his first name—another gut decision that I wouldn't have anticipated, like buying double-plots, but that seemed perfectly appropriate. The Mosiers, young and old, were in our home, and I could no longer pretend Jerry was someone else. I knew him best and longest, day in, day out, for nearly twenty-seven years.

Leo cocked his head, confused, as little Sydney rattled on about how much she missed "Uncle Mike."

I hugged my nephew. "She means Uncle Jerry." Then I whispered in his ear, "I'll explain later."

Vicky called. Since returning from Dubai, she had phoned daily—"Just checking in," she'd say—and changed her mind as often about whether or not she would come to the service. This time she told me she couldn't. "I have a washer-dryer being delivered tomorrow."

I was in the kitchen. At her weird declaration, I held the phone away from my ear. Kathy, a small woman with a round smooth face unlike her brothers', was sitting at the kitchen table, and looked at me quizzically. "Gotta go," I said, and hung up. I repeated Vicky's words to my sister-in-law. I tried to absorb their absurdity, and failed. This was Kathy's first introduction to my sister's strangeness. She shook her head. There was nothing to say.

In the evening, while the family ate pizza in the kitchen, my writing teacher, Alice, came to visit. She and the entire workshop group had kept in close touch via email throughout my time in Dubai. There weren't many people whom I wanted to see, but I welcomed her support. I introduced her to the family, and then we went to my bedroom to talk. We sat on the embroidered couch opposite the bed—our first major purchase for our first house, a tiny Dutch colonial in Upper Montclair. I curled my legs under a wool throw and launched into the story of the past two weeks. I hadn't had the energy to write the details in my emails.

After listening silently, Alice said, "You're so present." She must have expected me to be catatonic.

Then I said, "I know I will have to write about this to survive it." I thought about how, from the very beginning, Jerry whole-heartedly supported my creative pursuits, accompanying me to comedy clubs and theaters, laughing at every joke, no matter how many times he had heard it. Though I made next to nothing, my husband never treated my work as less valuable than his own. He understood ambition, even the non-earning variety. And he was sensitive to the toll the effort had taken, especially the multiple events I had produced for my non-profit writers' group. "Why don't you take the energy you're giving to everyone else and apply it to your own goals?" he said. I listened, valuing his opinion more than any other. When he died, I had been polishing a novel, about an inheritance battle and an estrangement between sisters. Jerry's generosity made my artistic life possible, and my family life too. My husband made everything possible.

Alice nodded. "Of course you will write about this."

But first, I had to write a eulogy

23

Memorial

At dawn on Saturday morning, the day of the memorial, with Isabel sleeping beside me in Jerry's place, George got up from the air mattress at the end of my bed, where his wife was still asleep, and crawled in on the other side. Neither one of us had gotten any rest. "It's best that Vicky is not here," he whispered, reading my mind. "It'll be easier for me to give my eulogy without her. I have things to say she won't want to hear." *What did he mean?* Then I told him what Ollie had said in Dubai, about needing his father to show him how to be a man. He listened without comment.

We arrived at the museum early to set up. The service would be at 9 a.m. to accommodate the gallery schedule and the requirements of the cemetery, which couldn't schedule burials after noon on a Saturday. I put my coat on the back of a chair in the first row, directly in front of the podium. The day before, at the funeral home, a long line of people had paid their respects. We had agreed on an extra day of public mourning without realizing what it would require. The cumulative pressure of each person's pity and the casket in all its solidity bore down upon me, compounding a grief I had barely begun to grasp. After embracing the last person, shaking the last hand, I sat and then collapsed in Kathy's arms, my head in her lap. "Yes," she said, stroking my hair, "it's so terrible. Let it out. Let it all out."

I felt better the next day, anticipating a sense of control and celebration the visitation had lacked. But the experience in Dubai and the whirlwind of the week following had caught up with me. I could barely move. I calculated I could walk the few steps from the chair to the podium and back. Because I had to.

Then something clicked within me, and I switched into familiar directorial mode. I spoke to the museum technician. We tested the microphones, and I insisted that each of us—George, Scott, Ross, Kathy—stand at the podium and speak. A dress rehearsal. I had done this before, many, many times, and most recently in this very space, preparing a multi-media reading in response to a contemporary portrait show. But I would not be performing a monologue based on one of Cindy Sherman's personae. I would be myself. *And who was that now?*

Ollie arrived. Since I didn't have room for his friends from Chicago, he had stayed overnight with them at Keith's. Ollie looked shaky, but handsome in the gray suit Jerry and I had bought for his twenty-first birthday five months earlier. It would be the first time he had worn it. He kissed me on the forehead, put his coat on the chair next to mine, went to the podium and tested the microphone.

A designer friend of Jerry's entered carrying huge wrapped poster boards, enlarged photos of Jerry for the easels on the hall's small stage. "Are you ready to see them?" he asked. The family looked anxiously at me. I nodded. Though I had selected the shots myself, I wasn't prepared to see my husband, almost life-sized, in front of his motorcycle in one, and in the other, a broadly grinning, rosy-cheeked man in his office, the nighttime neon of

Times Square flashing behind him. This was my favorite picture of Jerry—jolly, mischievous, winning. I got a charge whenever I looked at the smaller version on my desk at home. Here, huge, it was too much for me. I had to look away.

The screen above the stage lit up: "In Celebration of Jerry Michael Mosier, 1955-2008." Everyone helped by placing a program on each seat. I had taken the cover photo during our weekend in Beirut—Jerry, in skullcap and sunglasses, against a clear blue sky, in his element, surveying the ruins of a bombing.

People began to trickle in. I recognized the mayor, our councilman, members of the arts council, the Historic Preservation Commission, parents from Ollie's elementary, middle, and high schools. Most glanced at me, looked down, and quickly took a seat. My college friend Robyn rushed forward and knelt in front of me, taking my hand. "This isn't supposed to be happening," she said. "You'll come visit me on the Cape this summer."

Shari and her family entered. I had asked them to sit in the front row across the aisle. I spotted Kate and her husband, other old friends, followed by Alice and the writers. All of them drifted to the back. Keith's father had been right. The hall filled. Hundreds of people had turned out for Jerry and for us.

For the first time, I noticed the music, which had been playing since the doors opened. Ollie had chosen Neil Young, Springsteen, jazz, and, just for me, an instrumental version of "My One and Only Love." He knew the words would have been too hard to hear.

At 9:10, it was time to start. Worried about being late to the cemetery, I signaled the house manager. The crowd grew quiet. I licked my lips, but my mouth remained dry. Reverend Henderson ascended the stage, and welcomed everyone. His open, intelligent face and calm manner set the tone.

Then it was my turn. I had planned to speak first, knowing I couldn't have gotten through the other eulogies if I had to wait. I looked out at the upturned faces—our whole history in front of

Roselee Blooston

me, some who loved us and whom we loved, as well as those who hadn't known Jerry well, but had admired and respected him. I inhaled deeply, adjusted my glasses and began.

> *My husband was many men, all of them marvels of energy, passion, talent, and generosity. I want to thank all of you for being here to celebrate a life well-lived, though it seems impossible to celebrate without the man who was the party.*

I told the bus stop story, from meeting to quick proposal—the audience laughed when I said that we ought to get to know each other first—to wedding day, our fifteen minutes of fame. Faces smiled up at me. I had never enjoyed telling this story more than at that moment, bittersweet as it was, because while I spoke, I had him with me. My voice surprised me—loud, clear, resolute—though it shouldn't have. Years of acting training meant that I could rise to any occasion, even this one. The helplessness of the past weeks evaporated, and I could share my man.

> *Although he was an unemployed copywriter driving a Checker cab, I had no doubt that this guy was going places, and no doubt that he was the real deal: loyal, funny, sweet, and incredibly interesting. Just walking down a New York street with him was a lesson in history, not to mention a rant about litter. I've never met anyone who had broader and deeper knowledge. He was brilliant—I dare say, a genius in his field—wildly creative, engaged, voraciously curious, and though I would often throw up my hands in exasperation, I was never, ever bored.*

I told of Ollie's birth the night before our third anniversary, and of Jerry's fatherly devotion. Ollie sat right in front of me, but I couldn't look at him. I was afraid if I did, I wouldn't be able to go on. I described our political debates:

At first we were Carville and Matlin, with me as the bald guy, but over time I pulled him left and he pulled me center. How he had looked forward to the 2008 elections.

The audience chuckled at Jerry's sartorial evolution from Brooks Brothers ad man to a Brioni clad jet-setter who carried a man-purse, "or 'murse,' as he liked to call it," and his trendsetter status, "taking up kayaking before kayaking was chic." I cited his many interests, his volunteer and career achievements, and then I spoke of recent times.

...because Jerry was so alive, so willing to leap without looking, because he was so unafraid—he truly had the courage of his convictions—I was often afraid for him. When the job of a lifetime called for him to travel to dangerous places and use his vast creative and communication skills on the world stage, I knew it was his destiny, and there was no choice but to support him in his quest. After all, he had supported me through my many artistic risks. You see, ours was both a traditional marriage of stay-at-home mom and bread-winner, as well as an unconventional one, both of us pushing our respective envelops while watching each other's back. It was a partnership that expanded and redefined itself whenever our needs changed.

Though we both felt the pain of loneliness and the sacrifice of the other during these last three-and-a-half years, we knew that Jerry was at the height of his powers, a genuine fulfillment of his potential. The night we met, he was working on short films with his college buddies; at the end of his life, he produced serious documentaries about countries in crisis. His work was important to him, and to the world. He lived large and loved it. Fifty-three years young. Taken too soon. But what a life.

I paused, then addressed him, my voice suddenly quavering.

My darling, I will miss our long walks with the dogs, laughter after a good row, our telepathic connection, and holding hands, especially holding hands. It seems impossible that a light so bright has gone out. That our lives must go on without you. But you have given Oliver and me so much. And it will have to do.

Oliver, I love you with all my heart, just as your Daddy did. I'm aware as I speak about my beloved husband, to our son, to our incredible extended family, to this sterling community, that no stories, no lore, no words can assuage such a tremendous loss. But I hope you will cling, as I will, to these three: Love never dies. Love. Never. Dies.

Carefully, I gathered my papers, and watched the steps as I went down; I hated walking in heels. Scott met me at the bottom, and helped me to my seat. I kissed Ollie's cheek. He put his arm around me. Then I leaned into George. I wanted to crumple, but I could not. I owed everyone here my full attention, though my whole body was vibrating with the magnitude of what I had just done.

Jerry's brothers and sister went to the podium together. Kathy explained "Mike," and described their grandmother's dream of their brother, all in white from helmet to boots, riding a white motorcycle to heaven. A friend played Duke Ellington's "Solitude" on the guitar. Then Paul recounted their days as United Farm Workers organizers, and how my husband "never shrank from defending a neighbor's right to talk openly about his or her opinions and beliefs, even if he didn't agree with that person." When he was done, George stood and patted me on the shoulder before addressing the assembled.

When you love someone, they inhabit you. Think of them and it's as if you are them—you see with their eyes and their expressions become yours. With Jerry there was the knitted brow as he listened. There were the double raised eyebrows of surprise. There was the scowl, the eye roll, the shake of the head in dismay. There was the quick laugh and the buoyant smile and the mischief-maker's grin of delight. There were the explosive rhythms and rumblings of his voice. And under it all was the engine inside him endlessly revving.

When Jerry married Roselee, he became the first new member of the Blooston family in more than twenty years. This was a dubious honor. Joining our family was like a warped version of college admissions. Jerry got in, but he wasn't accepted.

The room erupted in laughter. I laughed too. My God, I couldn't believe what my brother was doing.

I, for one, never expressed reservations about Jerry, but Jerry suspected this was only out of loyalty to my sister. Well, it wasn't only out of loyalty to my sister. Like many families—and the typical banana republic—

The laughter swelled.

—the Bloostons were a repressive regime.

I laughed louder than anyone.

But Jerry was irrepressible. And while my parents were caught up in their own childish fears, Jerry—hard-charging Jerry, all of twenty-six—HELD HIS FIRE. He was the adult, far kinder and more understanding of my parents than I could have been.

So this was what George didn't want our sister to hear. Vicky considered our parents infallible—couldn't tolerate any other vision of them—and here our brother was publicly airing their worst behavior.

In the end, of course, my parents saw their error. And Roselee and I learned that our father, forty years before, had gotten the same rough treatment from our mother's family. So you might say Jerry simply received the traditional welcome.

A smattering of chuckles reverberated through the hall.

But here's the point. We all need examples in life. Roselee and Jerry are mine…From them I learned that love and adversity often go hand in hand. Jerry seemed always to know that being yourself—and letting others be themselves—is worth all kinds of heartache and struggle. And that amid struggle, you can reap all kinds of joy.

Jerry was a walking, talking liberation movement. But he knew that life isn't a manifesto, it's a conversation. It's an exchange. Jerry was so free with himself, he made living look easy even when it wasn't.

We are all shocked by Jerry's death. Jerry wasn't done, he wasn't nearly done. I keep thinking, "It's unbelievable," and in my mind can hear Jerry saying it: unbelievable, a term of disapproval he reserved for an umpire's bad call or some knucklehead driver. But this is unbelievable. I know it is true. We are all here; it must be true. But I can't absorb it.

Here's another phrase of Jerry's: "What it is." This is the rejoinder to "unbelievable," a concession to reality, as in "It is what it is." I don't know if this will help, but I'd like all of us to say these phrases together, just to keep the conversation going. We'll do this twice, because when Jerry liked the sound of something he'd say it again just to savor it. Think like Jerry, shake your head, and this will work. Repeat after me:

UnbeLIEVABLE.
The audience erupts: "Unbelievable."
What – it – is.
"What – it – is."
UnbeLIEVABLE.
"UnbeLIEVABLE."
What – it – is.
"WHAT – IT – IS. "

The room crackled. Relief swept through me. I had carried the weight of my parents' initial rejection for so long, I hadn't realized how much a part of my very being it was, how burdensome, until my brother publicly acknowledged all that Jerry and I had gone through. George gave us a gift. He had lifted a stain on our union and vindicated us as a couple, and Jerry as an individual. After he sat, I kissed him and whispered my thanks. *If only Jerry could have heard it.*

I drifted through the Twenty-Third Psalm, the friends channeling my husband's humor and irreverence, the strains of Beth Chapman's "Say Goodnight," until the moment I had been waiting for arrived, and Ollie rose and took the stage. He would close the service. Before he opened his mouth, George said, "He looks like an angel." Yes, with his flowing hair framing his ivory complexion, and his big blue eyes, hooded in sadness, he did indeed.

There we stood in the bitter cold, waiting in the bowels of some godforsaken Manhattan parking garage. A self-righteous Soccer Mom (please excuse the redundancy) with her three rug rats decided to block the exit with her station wagon in a warped act of narcissistic parking defiance. Some people defended her despite the obvious selfishness. My father wasn't one of those people.

"I sure picked one hell of a day to leave my handgun at home," he said, ostensibly to me, but really for the benefit of all those painfully waiting around us. Within five minutes, the woman swallowed her twisted pride and left. Problem solved. That was Jerry Mosier, my father.

As a child, there seemed to be no subject he lacked in expertise. He could recall the genesis of the Baltimore Chop, explain why milk is essential to Bolognese meat sauce or fill me in on why The North should have won at Antietam. To me, he knew it all. Before I began developing my own strong opinions, I followed his. I supported his crusade against the absurdity of wind-chill, his opposition towards fake coffee (better known as decaf) and was fully behind his war on visors. I mean, it's only half a hat.

...I was privileged enough to learn the "Code of the Beemer," an unspoken truce between BMW drivers. I talked like him. I listened to Miles Davis and Neil Young like him. I even gestured like him. In my youth I would tilt my head down like my father when skeptical of someone, mimicking his own classic response. He would tilt his head and his glasses. It only turns out that I was doing this out of reverence, and Dad was doing it because he desperately needed bifocals to see.

...From an early age, he treated me like a peer. Whether I was chef-helper in the kitchen, or navigator in the car, I was always involved. He also instilled in me the importance of skepticism and independent thinking, something for which I can never truly repay him.

...In only fifty-three years, he packed in several lifetimes.

He started out as Mike. Continued as Jerry. Became JMO, and lest we forget, that brief ill-advised period in the late '90s where he went by The Mose. To me, even as the progenitor of JMO, his son, it was different. The man who taught me how to score a baseball game, tie a bow tie, and drive stick was always the three-letter title he treasured most. Dad. I always called him Dad, never Daddy or father or Pop. I never channeled Jean Shepherd and referred to him as "my old man." My only wish was that he got to become one. This is a farewell, without forgetting. I love you, Dad.

There it was: Jerry's intensity, wit, and depth alive in our son's words, and in our son. Ollie made us laugh and cry. He embodied his father, while being totally himself. I had never been more proud. As Ollie left the podium, George leaned in and whispered, "He is already a man." I smiled. It was true.

I waited for the music, which didn't come. In the silence, I stood, and the crowd slowly followed. For a few minutes, Ollie and I stopped in the small outer hallway to greet our friends, but there wasn't time. I would see them at the house later. No sooner had we settled into the limo that would take us to the cemetery, along with Reverend Henderson, than Ollie spotted Leo weeping. He leapt out of the car to wrap his arms around the shaken boy.

It was drizzling as Ollie and I walked slowly towards the burial site. The flower-decked casket loomed. It seemed twice the size it had been at the funeral home. *But Jerry was so slight.* A few relatives and friends stood by; I spotted Bill among them. They watched us with mournful expressions. I looked at the ground. Reverend Henderson said a few words, while white roses were distributed to the family. Ollie and I placed ours on the casket, and returned to the car. I sank into the seat, a blank satisfaction filling me. It was done. My son and I held hands all the way home.

24

Aftermath

The house was crammed with people, food and drink. I circulated round and round through the rooms, talking to people I hadn't seen in decades—an old friend, who had disappeared from our lives for long periods and vowed to stay in touch; a close colleague, looking gray and disheveled; a renowned photographer, who had worked with Jerry and taken Ollie as an intern. "If you could do that," he said, referring to the service, "you are going to be fine. You are one strong woman."

I was not so sure—I was operating on automatic pilot—but I took his encouragement on faith. "Help Ollie," I said, "anyway you can."

The woman from whom we bought our first house described how Jerry had "jumped for joy, clicking his heels like Donald O'Connor" when the deal was done. At the dining room buffet table, a member of my non-profit group, whom I had not seen in a long time, rushed towards me. "Are you going to get married again?"

I stared at her, holding up my hand like a traffic cop. "I just buried my husband."

She blathered on, "Because *I* want to. I just broke up with my longtime partner, but I like being married." *What was wrong with this person?* I left her in front of the salmon platter.

Friends told me repeatedly to sit down. As soon as I did, Jerry's literary agent and his partner, a Morticia type, ambushed me. I had always found them creepy, and the man's last-minute attempt, earlier in the week, to insert himself into the service had been presumptuous. "Roselee, do you have the draft of Jerry's new novel, the one on the Middle East? I was thinking I could reconstruct it. I know it'll sell if I can get it out there." I didn't know what Jerry had told him, but I knew there was no draft, only an outline and some notes. I said as much. His face fell.

I excused myself, rounded up the writers, who had gathered in the kitchen, and ushered them down the hall to my bedroom. I needed to get away from people who didn't give a damn about me. I needed my friends.

I sat on the bed, and put my legs up. The women formed a semi-circle around me, some on the sofa and some on the edge of the bed. It felt as if I were holding court, except that what power I had, the events of the day and the past two weeks had leeched out of me. I had no words of wisdom and neither did they, but their mere presence in the space that only Jerry and I had shared was balm enough.

That night, after everyone but the family had left, Scott and George sat with me. They had met only a few times before, but the trust between them was palpable. We talked of Dubai, the horror of dealing with its underbelly. Scott reiterated his warning, "Don't go back there alone."

I shook my head vigorously. "I'm never going back."

"But…"

"No buts." I told them about my lead on a good international lawyer.

George said, "My crazy brother-in-law. How the hell did he do it?"

I didn't answer. I couldn't say what I was thinking: he didn't. It killed him, the city of false fronts, the strain of living in two worlds. In my mind, the burst aneurysm was inextricably tied to the disorienting life he led.

Later, when we were alone, George said, eyes watering, "If only we had all known each other better, spent more happy times together as a family. This," he gestured to the sleeping bags and air mattresses, "is how it should have been." He was right. The distance between all of us had been less geographic than emotional, permanent fallout from the earthquake of our parents' insularity. The initial mistrust between the two families had diffused into a passive longstanding habit, more benign than the rift, but resulting nevertheless in irreparable separation, which we all took for granted. It became *the way things were.*

The next morning, before George and his family left to go back to Maryland, he stood in the driveway, put his arm around Ollie and whispered in his ear, "You'll have days when you feel alone. You're not."

Ollie returned to Chicago soon after. Though he had planned to take the quarter off, he needed to be with his peers. Ross and Robyn stayed an extra two days. They didn't want me to have to face a suddenly empty house. They stocked my bathroom cabinets with paper products—towels, toilet paper, and tissues—and my refrigerator with milk, eggs, fruit, and bread. Robyn prepared hearty meals. I was grateful for her cheery take-charge style, and the natural compassion Ross exuded.

While Robyn cooked and Ross puttered around the house, I went to my study, cleaned off an area on my desk, and placed a file holder there. Then I began arranging folders for all the business ahead—banking, Dubai notes, estate issues. I knew I was using organization—one of my strong suits—to bolster the illusion of control, though much like in Dubai, I had none. Just as it was in the UAE, I could not make anything happen, nor could I unmake what already had occurred. For someone used to initiating, taking charge, creating, this was profoundly unsettling. I hardly recognized this woman, this passive person buffeted by circumstance who could only react, only respond to what had befallen her.

Over dinner, Ross, Robyn, and I talked, for the first time ever, about the Mosier family dynamic. "I can't believe my parents weren't at the service," Ross said, shaking his head. "Mom's in bad shape, with that infected knee. Her surgeon really botched the replacement operation. But we all begged Dad to come, offered to drive him up and back, to arrange for someone to stay with her. He just wouldn't leave." Then, after a pause, "It was wrong." Yes, I silently agreed. He should have come. She should have, too. We could have gotten her a wheelchair. They should have been there, for their children grieving their brother, for their grandson grieving his father, for themselves, and most of all, for Jerry. I was glad that he couldn't know.

By the time Ross and Robyn left, I was ready to be alone. Or thought I was. I walked through the living room, lush with plants, orchids, lavish arrangements. I picked up a copy of the *Montclair Times* from the coffee table. There was Jerry, top left. I couldn't read past my own quote, "He was the best guy I had ever met."

I did my laundry, finding solace in the automatic movements of loading and folding. I defrosted the comfort food left by neighbors and ate without tasting. I walked the dogs. I cried. Dreamless sleep alternated with hours lying awake, rigid with fear. I read the condolence cards that came in the daily mail. I realized I was still in shock, one month after the call.

When the petals shriveled, I cleared the house of their sickly sweetness. I put Jerry's framed picture—the one with the twinkling eyes and rosy cheeks, the small version of the memorial poster—in the front hall, a statement to anyone who came to the door. Each day I took care of one piece of business—credit cards to close, bank accounts to reconcile, official notifications of his death. In every phone conversation, I had to tell the stranger on the other end, "My husband died." I didn't fully believe it, but I needed to say it, because it was true.

On Valentine's Day, less than a week after burying Jerry, a friend drove me back to the cemetery. I placed a red rose on the freshly packed mound. We were supposed to be in Mexico—our compromise holiday, since I had refused to plan further ahead to our September anniversary. When I told the reservation manager and the airline representative the circumstances, I got a full refund of the airline tickets and the hotel deposit, a welcome break given my mounting worries about money. The insurance check couldn't arrive fast enough.

A few days later, I scrolled through Jerry's computer files, and found reservations for two at a resort in the Maldives for the same week. My sleep-deprived brain slammed immediately into high alert. The words on the screen jolted me, triggering the underlying hurt I had kept in check since leaving Dubai. *My God, was he going there with another woman? A mistress? How could he?*

I called George. He didn't know what to say.

I hung up, and howled at the walls. Then I remembered. *We* had made those reservations in December, wanting to combine a trip to the islands, which were close to Dubai, with a possible jaunt to Goa in India. Jerry had forgotten to cancel them when we arranged the Mexico trip. *I* was the mistress.

I called my brother back, mortified, but the confusion revealed how deeply wounded I felt, and how uncertain I was of where I stood with my now-dead husband.

I went back to the computer and continued sifting through file after file of messages and documents. I inserted one of Jerry's many pocket flash-drives. The only thing on it was a poem. Jerry had written me a number of poems over the years, a flurry when we were courting, and an especially memorable one sent via email the previous spring.

Nine time zones and
7500 miles separate us.
Me from you
You from me
How long can this go on?

It is dark here
It is light there

People are in bed here
People are at lunch there

This work
This quest

Time is ticking by and
I ask myself

Is it worth it?

Time cannot be recaptured
We have only the present

But my present is not yours
My past is before yours
My future is behind yours

I stood on the beach tonight
Looking out
Seeing lights
Ships

And I think of you

The night is falling
My strength is failing

Can this go on?

His pain then, mirroring mine, had moved and reassured me. We were in this struggle together. But the newly discovered fragment rocked me. I read it once and deleted it. I knew if I looked at the words again, I would commit them to memory, and they would torment me. Once was enough. Something about "the desert sand …your hair…don't think about husbands…" *Had he written to a married woman? Was this for Raine, referring to her canceled engagement?* I would never know. All I knew for sure was that it wasn't written for me.

25

Tizzie & Rita

It was snowing, hard. Our lawn crew, who plowed in the winter, was out front clearing the driveway and the paths to the front door. I wrestled with myself. *Should I go out and tell the young man, who loved Jerry, saw him as a father figure, that my husband had died?* No. It was cold, and dark. I couldn't. I just couldn't. I had told so many people who didn't know him that one more announcement, especially to someone who would have an emotional reaction, was one too many. As it was, each declaration felt like a punch in the gut. I stayed inside, hugging Jerry's gray jacket sweater around me, its Nehru collar warming my neck, its too-long sleeves covering my hands, and listened to the truck engine, watching the bright headlights move up and down the driveway, until the work was done.

The only thing I *had* to do, no matter what, was walk the dogs. Old Eddie, lumbering and soulful—dare I say, wise, the Yoda of dogs—had to be walked apart from Tizzie. He couldn't keep up with her. I'd do one loop of the nearby streets and bring him back home. Our beloved companion had grown ancient overnight.

Then it was Tizzie's turn. She was named for Tisbury, after the town in Martha's Vineyard, just as Edgar had been named after Edgartown. She was Cleopatra beautiful, with dark-rimmed eyes and a honey coat, but I could hardly stand her bouncy energy, so out of sync with my own exhaustion. When we came home from Dubai, I immediately noticed the chewed-off kitchen cabinet corners, evidence of teething and distress. I couldn't even muster a reaction. In contrast, Eddie's very presence soothed. He embodied our family's love, a decade of it.

Tizzie got on my nerves. I resented her undiluted demands, her sheer puppiness, and then felt guilty that I was merely going through the motions. She was our fourth dog—we'd had two Springer Spaniels before Ed. The first, a black and white female we named Deco Bauhaus, entered our lives when we first moved to Brooklyn. Jerry broke down my resistance—I'd never had a dog before—by crying and throwing himself on our bed. When he brought her home, I melted. I was a sucker for puppies. I found their cute faces and ultra-soft fur irresistible, but this time I felt disconnected. I couldn't get out of my head what Jerry had said last fall about Tizzie.

When we brought Tizzie home for the first time, Jerry had assured me that this second dog meant that he'd be coming back for good, sooner rather than later. As if to prove his commitment, he did all of the night walks for the first couple of weeks. He had been home from Dubai for a longer stretch than usual, partly to avoid the extreme summer heat, and partly for a much-needed rest. I loved having him with me, and had visions of walking the two dogs together through our neighborhood in Montclair for years to come.

In August, we took them to the Vineyard for two weeks. We stayed in the same house we had rented for the past dozen years, between Edgartown and Katama, on dead-end Gerts Way. Rental or no, it felt like our home away from home. We loved the secluded woodsy property, the deck with gas grill, the vaulted ceilings and the comfy couches. Ollie brought three friends to stay with us. They had a great time, kayaking, body surfing, eating lobster.

After the boys left, Jerry and I sensed that something had irrevocably changed. We looked around the house and agreed its time in our lives had come to a close. This was where our family had enjoyed peaceful summer idylls, but Ollie was almost grown, and now life was all about us, as a couple. It had been a near-perfect vacation. I'd rarely seen Jerry so relaxed.

On our last night, we went out with both dogs, tiny Tizzie unsure how to walk on a leash, either spinning in circles or sitting immobile, and Edgar leading the way. We looked up at the stars, and vowed that the next time we returned, it would be to a Vineyard house of our own, a place to one day retire to, though it was hard to picture Jerry not working.

In autumn, after another homecoming, Jerry stood in the kitchen, leaned against the sink, and looked down at me, seated on the floor holding the puppy. "I'm glad we got her," he said. "She'll replace me."

I had been petting Tizzie. His words stopped me mid-stroke. "What? Replace? What do you mean *replace?*"

Jerry shook his head. His face flushed. "No, no, I just mean keep you company."

"But you said *replace.*" And the word, the *thought* that he needed replacing, lay there between us.

In my winter grief, irrationally, I held Tizzie responsible for Jerry's ridiculous, disturbing solution to the problem of our separations. I held her responsible for it not working. I wanted to scream at him, *See, no little dog could ever replace you. How could you think such a thing?* Instead, I stood outside in the cold on the snow-covered ground, and shouted at this innocent pup, a baby dog, who only wanted what I wanted: love and safety, warmth and care.

Less than a month after Jerry's death, I was at the bank, sitting with one of the managers—I practically lived there, I had so much to attend to—when I overheard a woman asking Rita, one of the tellers, how she was. Rita's kindness and competence had kept my husband and me coming back, though other banks had better offers. The tone was so solicitous, I knew immediately she was either ill or bereaved. I looked up. She was wearing black.

Then I heard her answer, "It's hard. I can't believe he's gone."

The manager handed me papers for the teller, and I took my place in line. When I reached Rita's window, I passed her the check and deposit slip. She had black and blue circles under her eyes, as if she had been beaten up, but she greeted me with a genuine smile, and said, "Hello, Roselee." Then she read the slip. It was made out to "The Estate of Jerry Mosier." She looked at me through the glass. "Oh Roselee, did you lose Jerry?"

"Yes," I said. No one had asked me in quite that way—lose, as if he had been misplaced. Then she told me that her husband had died a month earlier. We stared into the mirror of each other's eyes. Though the facts differed, we were in this together. She told me about a support group at the local hospital, which required only that the loss be at least six months old, a recognition that fresh grief couldn't be socialized, it simply had to be endured.

Once home, I thought about it, and put the contact information near the kitchen phone. I'd never been much of a joiner, but I'd never been so needy, either. I tried to imagine where and how I would be in five months, but I couldn't. I couldn't imagine the next week.

26

Proof

AIG, our life insurance company, sent me a letter. The ten days that the agent had said it would take for me to get the money had passed. It had been over two weeks, and I was becoming extremely anxious. The letter said, "Please accept our condolences on the loss of your husband, Jerry. Since this death occurred outside the USA, we must verify the circumstances of the death." Oh no. The letter went on to state that the company had assigned a specialist "to investigate the claim." I called their 800 number, got the name, and called the investigator.

She was a cheery, efficient sounding, young—I assumed—woman. Her bright, chirpy manner may have been natural, but it seemed to me a practiced front intended to minimize the panic on the other end of the line—in this case, mine. She informed me that this was standard procedure for a death in the Middle East, nothing out of the ordinary. They needed to be certain that he hadn't faked his death, or disappeared on a desert island in order to later cash in on the policy. I took this personally. In that case, I would have been his accomplice in a fraud. She assured me that once I had returned the requested documents and filled out the accompanying questionnaire, she would promptly process it. As she continued to talk, I visualized Jerry's dead body on the ICU bed, waxy, covered with a sheet.

The questionnaire and the list of documents were daunting, almost as daunting as the trudge through Dubai's police stations. They sent me back psychically to where I never wanted to return, and hit me like an assault:

> *Authorization and consent to disclosure of information, (signed and*
> *witnessed);*
> *Questionnaire (signed and witnessed);*
> *UAE Ministry of Health Death Certificate;*
> *Translation of death certificate;*
> *Government of Dubai Medical Certificate of Death;*
> *US Department of State Report of Death of an American Citizen*
> *Abroad;*
> *Letter from Consulate regarding release of Jerry Michael Mosier's body;*
> *Consular Mortuary Certificate;*
> *Dubai Police Report;*
> *Department of Health and Medical Services Transit Permit;*
> *Copy of airway bill;*
> *Funeral home bill;*
> *Cemetery bill;*
> *Gravestone bill;*
> *Jerry's social security card;*
> *His UAE driver's license (I couldn't find his New Jersey one);*
> *His passport photo page;*
> *His alien registration card;*
> *A recent photo of Jerry;*
> *The front-page article on his death from the Montclair Times;*
> *The obituaries;*

The Emirates Airlines cargo manifest for the return of his body;
His unused return ticket information.

And they wanted things I didn't have: an autopsy report; a passport stamp verifying when Jerry entered the country (he had auto-entry); photos of his body in the funeral home or burial site—the funeral home director was appalled at this. "Of course, we don't take photographs! This whole thing seems illegal to me."

I spent the next three days frantically collecting the paperwork. I had to enlist Raine and Kamilla to obtain the names and phone numbers of the doctors at the hospital, all the while feeling like a suspect. I had to prove that my husband died in Dubai, that it wasn't a hoax. *But what if, against all the evidence, they didn't believe me? How would I survive?* I had no idea when or if I could extricate the frozen bank account. I had been counting on the insurance payout.

My brother attempted to calm me down. "Don't worry. It's just procedure. They *have* to release the money." His assurances took the edge off my alarm, but only the edge. I was more than worried. I was angry and terrified. How could this be happening?

Shari sat with me as I filled out the questionnaire. The night of the phone call came roaring back. Here, once again, was my steadfast friend seated across from me in my study, anchoring me as I followed the instructions: "Describe in detail the events and circumstances *leading up to and immediately following* the death of Jerry Michael Mosier. Please detail the events beginning at onset of illness." The use of italics seemed particularly confrontational. It was too soon to have to relive this trauma, but what choice did I have? I decided to write in the simplest *Dick and Jane* prose. Since I already felt like a criminal from the investigation's implied accusation, I figured any elaboration beyond the bare facts could be misinterpreted by the insurance company and turned somehow suspect. Though of course I hadn't killed him. The brain hemorrhage had.

> *On the morning of Sunday, January 20, 2008, I got a call from my husband, Jerry Michael Mosier, from Dubai, in which he said he had 'the worst headache of his life.' Several hours later I was informed that he had been taken, unconscious, to Rashid Hospital. My son and I flew to Dubai on Monday, January 21ˢᵗ, landing on the 22ⁿᵈ. We went directly to the hospital ICU Ward 9 to see him, and were told that Jerry had suffered a brain aneurysm and was not expected to survive. We visited Jerry in the ICU every day. On Sunday, January 27ᵗʰ Jerry's brothers arrived from the United States. That evening we were called to the hospital because Jerry's heart was failing. When we arrived at the ICU the nurses were doing chest compressions. A few minutes later, he was declared dead. Then my brother-in-law, Scott Mosier, and I accompanied Jerry's body downstairs to the hospital morgue.*

The entire process of assembling the multiple proofs of his death pummeled me. I felt besieged. I called my local lawyer. I wanted his office to send the packet, so that the investigator and the insurance company would understand that I had representation. He requested that the originals of the medical and Arabic death certificates, which AIG had insisted on—the ones with colorful postage stamp-like seals—be returned to me, along with the photo of Jerry.

It was now twenty-one days since Ollie and I had arrived back in the States—the longest Jerry had ever been absent. My body yearned for him, in the hallway, in the bed, at the kitchen table. I focused on the garage door, willing it to open, for my husband to walk through, for all this to have been a bad dream.

The day the investigator received the documents, she called me, amazed at how quickly I had amassed the information. Two days later, she called again. "It's done," she said. She told me that she had contacted the hospital and the doctors, and remarked on how easy I had made the verifications, that sometimes, when dealing with the Middle East, things got murky. As if I didn't know. She went on, "It was very straightforward. I'll write my report, and your claim will go through."

This was at four weeks, a month since the day my husband died, and the reality that he was never coming home slammed into me, full force. My body had been waiting for him, against my mind's evidence. I gasped for air, no longer able to hold my breath.

When the money finally arrived two weeks later, in the form of an entry in a special bank account checkbook—which the insurance company considered safer than a check—I stared at the long number representing my loss and my gain. It was more money than I had ever known, and although I had the distinct feeling that I deserved it, had even in a perverse sense *earned* it, I felt poor, poorer than I had ever thought possible.

27

Dolls

I spoke with Shari and Ollie every day. The daily sound of Jerry's voice had anchored me; now, theirs did. In the second month, I understood why the word "shock" was often followed by "waves." Without my friend and my child, I would have drowned.

There was nothing, and everything, to talk about. One day, early in March, I said to Shari, "I'm not married anymore."

"Yes," she said.

"I'm single."

"Yes."

"'Til death do us part."

My friend fell silent.

Saying the words wasn't enough. I needed to take concrete action to convince myself of my new reality. The next morning, before I opened my eyes, I visualized moving my rings, and his, to my right hand. I had worn Jerry's wedding band between my own and the engagement ring on my left hand from the night he had died. And I had never, ever, taken off my wedding band. I got out of bed, and before I had washed my face, I transferred the rings. I knew full well that the bare ring finger of my left hand made a public statement. It signaled my new, unwelcome status. Now I was a widow—the "w" word that I had a hard time writing, let alone saying. I couldn't entirely accept the label, even though I had checked the box on my gynecologist's forms. I told myself I was just *me*, me without him, not a whole new category. I held my right hand up to the light that streamed through my bedroom window and bounced off my engagement ring and the two gold bands, compared it to my naked left hand, and saw the undeniable truth.

Later that week, Shari came over and brought me goodies. She was a fantastic cook. "Now you will always know what love is," she said. *How could she say that, knowing as she did about my discovery and the hurt that it had caused?* I asked what she meant. "He loved you. He wanted the job and the separation to be over." Was she telling me what she thought I needed to hear? Yes and no. She knew me. She knew my husband. "You were such a good wife." My friend wanted me to focus on the totality of our union, and not on my doubts. But I couldn't, not then, not yet. That union had been fractured, by loss and by doubt.

My pain was more than emotional. The vise that had been put in place six weeks earlier, from the first phone call, continued to clutch my heart, squeezing it into a knot of agonizing tension. Despite my brother's assurance that I would not have a heart attack, I still felt at risk.

The day I sat down with my bank's investment advisor, a lovely sympathetic young woman—and their representative from Wealth Management, a more predatory professional, who clearly saw dollar signs when she looked in my direction—my body revolted in a head-to-toe clamp. After the rep pressed to "take me to lunch," to talk about "my future," all I could manage through my clenched jaw was, "I'll think about it." I couldn't breathe until I got back to my car.

At home, I lay prostrate on the couch, closed my eyes, and shut down. Even alone, the pain between my shoulder blades didn't abate. The tightness in my chest and back were constants from the moment I woke up, until I went to bed at night. Hot baths, massages, and long walks offered only temporary reprieve. Then the clutch returned.

My appetite, however, roared back. I ate ravenously, though no matter how much I consumed—I had dropped any semblance of good dietary habits, downing cake, ice cream, brownies, grilled cheese sandwiches, and muffins—I lost weight. My body, mind, and heart were working so hard to stay upright, alive, and functional, to do what had to be done, and the stress was so consuming, that extra pounds melted. When friends noticed how slender I looked, I'd say, "It's the grief diet. I don't recommend it."

And when the daily store of sorrow threatened to crush me, I cried. Buckets. If I tried to hold back tears, I became nauseous. I couldn't suppress the tsunami of emotion. I wailed and dragged myself down the hallway to my bedroom, averting my eyes from the gallery of black and white photographs that told the story of our happiest times: Vineyard vacations with Ollie on the dunes, running towards us along the beach, proudly holding a shell aloft, and then, holding the conch to his ear, listening.

I slept in our king-sized sleigh bed as I always had, on *my* side, the left side. There was plenty of room for Edgar. He sprawled across the bottom of the bed, horizontally, taking up the space where Jerry's feet would have been. After the first week, Eddie had moved up to the area once occupied by his master's torso.

Whenever my husband returned from a business trip, the first thing he wanted to do was climb into bed with the dog and me. Edgar would crawl between us and put his head on our merged pillows, as if to say, *Here we are again, exactly as we are supposed to be, all's right with the world.*

I was so exhausted after a day of wading through estate demands that I hit the pillow and slept dreamlessly. But waking up alone was much more difficult than going to bed alone. The emptiness of Jerry's place, the smooth sheets beside me, the fluffed un-dented pillow, tormented me. When I opened my eyes each morning, I was forced to face the void where he should have been. This feeling was unlike my loneliness when he traveled. I'd miss him then, but I had something to hold on to—the fact that he would always come back, take his place inside the bedroom and out. This new and horrific missing had no end, because it was an end, a permanent state of goneness.

One morning, I picked up Jerry's pillow, stripped it from its case, and threw it in the trash. Then I moved my pillow to the center of the bed and placed the decorative ones around it, including the pillow embroidered with Martha's Vineyard's landmarks—the beach, the lighthouses, the Black Dog Tavern—that I had given Jerry for his fifty-third birthday, three weeks before his death. The gift had been my reminder to him to keep our goal of an idyllic island retirement in mind. Now the pillow taunted me with its depiction of a future that was not to be. That night, I crawled into bed, my pillow centered on it. In the morning, I woke to find that I had migrated left.

All through a March too dreary to be outside except to walk the dogs, I cleaned closets—his, mine, ours—dumping the contents of his sock drawer, removing his footless shoes, well-pressed pants, and belts that had hugged his slim waist. Every discard wrenched, but I plunged in, regardless. If I could face the things Jerry had left behind, maybe I could face his loss.

One day, when I needed a break, I opened my own closet, reached up and pulled down a box that I hadn't looked at since we moved to the house ten years earlier. Inside it was my foreign doll collection. I hadn't been interested in dolls for decades; the last time I added to it was during my teenage stint with a traveling theater troupe through Europe. I'd been saving the collection for a daughter.

I opened the lid and found the dolls still in their native garb, though the French girl had deteriorated considerably; her foam rubber head had turned a rusty orange, and her nose flaked as if she had leprosy. The Italian troubadour couldn't turn his neck, and the Greek shepherd had lost his head altogether. Otherwise, the dolls looked exactly the same as when I had displayed them in my childhood bedroom, only a bit dustier. I wrapped them up again, careful this time to pack for posterity, with plenty of room to lay each one straight. I had no desire to give them away—perhaps I'd have a granddaughter one day—nor did I want to display them again. That would have been ridiculous.

Or so I thought, until I looked up at the highest shelf in my closet. I climbed a stepladder to reach it. There, I found The Widow. I'd never actually thought of her as one, but in my current situation, it seemed self-evident—dressed all in black, her head covered with a mantilla trimmed in black lace, her soft legs hidden in black stockings. Her face, in contrast, was moon white, her eyes unfathomable. She seemed the quintessential Italian widow, mourning inside her room with the curtains closed. The total effect disturbed me. But that didn't matter. I felt compelled to put her on my bed. She sat in my place. She stood in for me, representing my sorrow. Only I couldn't shut myself away—didn't really want to—though on a bad day, that old-fashioned formal year of isolated mourning made sense. I understood the primal urge to withdraw. But with the doll in position, I didn't have to go that far. The Widow would do it for me.

Then I uncovered Rosie. When Maurice Sendak's book *Really Rosie*, came out, it was accompanied by a doll, complete with display stand. My mother presented her to me without embarrassment. It was 1986. I was thirty-three years old, with a child of my own on the way, but as far as Mother was concerned, there was no statute of limitations on giving a daughter a doll. Rosie—a self-satisfied little girl dressed up in her mother's long red gown, over-sized shoes, and feather hat with matching boa, eyes closed—imagined herself a grown-up. Over the years her resonance grew. In my play *Mad Moms*, the main character, Rosie Ann, played dress-up all day long, becoming different versions of her mother. And my father called me Rosie.

In our first house, I had kept her on my dresser, and The Widow on a child's chair near my side of the bed. Though Jerry never complained, I decided that the new bedroom needed a more adult, less girly style. I put Rosie and her dark counterpart away, and forgot about them. Now the room was mine again. Only mine. I brought Rosie down from her shelf and placed her bedside to watch me, and to balance out the sad, keening vibe of The Widow, keeping her company—together, the bookends of my life so far.

28

Dubai, Dreams

Week after week, I had put off calling Jasim, Ashar's assistant, about the pending business deal. All the more ordinary estate business took precedence; huge chunks of my insurance money was being eaten up by Jerry's business creditors. I told myself that an executor had to do this, pay the deceased's debts. Trying to think reasonably didn't help. Whenever I needed to write a check in the mid-five figures—too often—my hand shook. I had cut out every extra expense I could think of; I fired my cleaning lady, turned down the thermostat, found a budget hairdresser. These tiny savings wouldn't be enough, and I didn't have the energy to look for work. Managing the estate was a full-time job. I couldn't afford to ignore any potential financial resource, even if picking up the phone meant deliberately going back to Dubai, at least mentally—an action I avoided unless, as with the insurance investigation, I was forced to do it.

Due to the time difference, I called Jasim early in the morning so that I would reach him during business hours, which ended there at 4 p.m. Although I was merely following through on the brief conversation we had had while I was still in his city, I was afraid of saying too much or too little, of pushing him, or of not being clear. So I wrote out a script.

"Hello, Jasim. This is Mrs. Mosier, Jerry's widow." When I got married, I kept my name. After all, my Actors' Equity card said Blooston. I only used Mosier for Ollie's school, and his pediatrician. And in these circumstances, I was not above using my new status for whatever sympathy it might engender.

"Oh, Mrs. Mosier, how are you? How is Oliver?" Jasim's voice was higher and lighter than I remembered. Or perhaps he was uncomfortable talking with a woman.

I told him that Ollie was back in school, and would be graduating in a couple of months.

"Oh, I hope he will consider working in Dubai."

I stifled a gasp. *Not in a million years.*

He went on, "We have many opportunities for bright young people. I'm sure Ashar would be glad to help Jerry's son in any way possible."

I found this laughable, considering how Ashar had left us standing outside the hospital without transportation, to fend for ourselves, as he rode away in his limo. But instead I said, "Thank you. That's very kind." Then I paused and asked, "Is there any progress on the deal that you can tell me about?" I had no idea if the US billboard manufacturer, the one with the heat-resistant product Jerry had introduced to Ashar, was even in contact with him. It seemed unlikely that this handshake agreement would ever reap the huge finder's fee that Jerry and Bill had hoped for, but my husband's frozen bank account was still inaccessible, and I had to pursue every possible money source, including this hazy arrangement. My future might depend on it.

"Oh. Not yet. But rest assured that your husband's and your interests will be taken care of when the time comes. Rest assured. Call me next month. I should have news then."

I thanked him again and said goodbye. I slumped. The strain of even such a brief, innocuous exchange drained me. Every moment felt loaded and murky, just as it had in Dubai. I felt lost, and didn't know what I didn't know. I marked next month's call on my calendar, and lay down on the couch.

Raine had emailed me about the apartment. Jerry's lease would run out at the end of the month, so she had been busy closing the Evision cable and Internet account, the Dubai Electrical and Water Authority account, and had, with my permission, sold some of the furniture. Now she was arranging to have what remained shipped back to me in New Jersey. We set a time to talk.

Raine sounded upbeat on the phone, and hurried. Cars honked in the background. She told me that she wanted to deduct the sale proceeds from whatever the shipment cost. Then I could pay her back. Fine with me. I appreciated it. This would have been so much more difficult without her, maybe impossible. Then she said, "I've been wanting to move from my place for a while now and I've decided to rent the apartment." *What?* She went on, "It's such a nice building, and they know me now. And my boyfriend thinks it's great."

I gave an ambiguous grunt, which she took as approval. I was floored. *Jerry's* apartment? Where she found him in the foyer unconscious lying in his own vomit surrounded by shattered glass? Ever since she had described the horrifying scene to me, it had been seared into my visual memory so vividly that I needed to remind myself that I hadn't actually been there. But *she* had. *How could she bear to live there?*

As soon as I formulated the thought, I knew the answer. For her, the trauma of Jerry's death didn't run as deep. However much she may have liked my husband, her feelings were superficial. This perception matched my sense of Dubai itself. Nothing there, not even relationships, had much real depth. Even big gains and big losses seemed less consequential in a city of appearances. For a passionate guy like Jerry, this must have been incredibly disturbing. He had friends, Raine among them, but how far did any connection go? From her cavalier appropriation of his space, evidently not that far. No wonder my husband had been in free fall.

While I was still in Dubai, Shari, after spending a great deal of time on the phone notifying my friends, had said, "A death reveals who people really are." She said that my strong and caring friends responded just as I had said they would, with thoughtfulness and compassion, but that—and she hesitated to tell me this—a self-involved one had been true to form.

"What do you mean?" I asked.

"She wanted to know where she was on the list?"

"The list?"

"My call list. Her first concern was where she stood in the hierarchy of your friends."

I shook my head. "Wow. That's…" For a moment I was speechless. "Are we still in high school?" I sighed. Why was it necessary to rank our relationships? I realized this was exactly what I had been doing in regard to Raine, ranking her feeling for Jerry, judging her. In truth, I didn't really care whether or not she rented Jerry's apartment. It wasn't my business. But knowing she was there provided another stark contrast to my life in the home my husband and I had shared. She wasn't haunted by his loss. I was.

The absence of his presence was everywhere: in every room, every wall, every ceiling, every floor. I pictured him in the kitchen, standing at the stove stirring taco meat, and in the family room, sprawled in front of a Jets game and screaming at the television when the team inevitably blew its lead. I heard him coming through the garage door, and calling *Hello, where are you?*, then sweeping into the living room to tell me about his day. I saw him in his basement office, staring myopically at his large computer screen, waving me away with *I'm working* or *Just one more chapter, I'll be up in a minute.* He barreled down the hall to the bedroom, bursting with some new line he'd written for an ad campaign, wanting my First Reader approval, or with a bit of gossip from the Historic Preservation meeting he had just chaired. I heard him clear his throat, a tick from his ever-present phlegm. I watched him brush his teeth, squint into the mirror, shave, slap on cologne—a smell, the very memory of which, slayed me. I rolled over in bed towards his place, and saw him lying on his side, facing me, hand under head, eyes closed, long lashes against alabaster skin. I rolled away, turned off the light, closed my eyes. I saw him still.

On March twenty-fourth, exactly eight weeks since the night that Jerry died, I finally dreamed of him. In our daily conversations, Ollie had told me about his many dreams of his father; in the most striking one, Jerry filled the night sky. I was glad Ollie had that comfort, and a bit jealous.

And my dear friend Kate told me that she had dreamed of Jerry shortly after his death. She saw the three of us in my living room, Jerry standing behind me, speaking through me to her. He directed Kate to tell me that he was sorry, had never wanted things to turn out this way. I was thankful to hear it. Though I was no believer in angels or ghosts, I was paradoxically starved for some word from the other side. So I appropriated her dream as my own. The silence in my own head worried me. *What was wrong with me that I couldn't dream of my dead husband?*

And then I did.

Jerry's hair was dark, thick, and wavy, as when we first met, his face fuzzed out, like the subject of a TV investigation whose identity had to be hidden. But fuzz or no, the young man was definitely Jerry, frenetic, eager-to-please Jerry. He ran out for White Castle burgers, the square ones we had eaten only once. I said, "Bring French fries." He nodded, and then in unison we said, "Comfort food." Or perhaps we just read each other's minds, which we had done regularly, especially where food was concerned. We sat across a table with the burgers in Styrofoam containers before us. I said, "I don't want to be alone."

I awoke lighter. My husband had finally come to me. He fed me and took care of me, if only in a dream. That was something.

29

Brunch

On the sidewalk corner in front of an Upper Westside restaurant, I waited. The day was unusually hot for March. People walked past me in shorts and sandals. I tried my friend's number again and got nothing but her voicemail message. We were supposed to meet for brunch. I lived for these meals with my girlfriends.

Since the winter, I had made a point of seeing at least two people a week for lunch or coffee or tea. And everyday, I talked on the phone with someone, anyone, friend or relative, to lessen the thick layer of isolation still surrounding me. And the nakedness in public places. Waiting for a table, any ordinary interaction with a waiter, hostess or busboy rendered me an exposed nerve ending, like a burn victim. A layer of my skin was missing, the protective layer. It must have shown—my raw pain—I thought, as I peered into the restaurant one more time to see if she might have been sitting there all along.

Driving into the city, I had been acutely aware that this was the first time since the car ride from the airport that I had been in

Manhattan. The reverse ride through the Lincoln Tunnel rattled me. Visions of trips that Jerry and I had taken to spend the afternoon at a museum, out to dinner, to see a show flooded me. I felt him in the car, in the driver's seat—he almost always drove when it was just the two of us. I gripped the steering wheel, palms slick with sweat as I passed familiar landmarks—Forty-Second Street, the Intrepid docked next to the West Side Highway, the swooping tree-lined exit at the Seventy-Ninth Street boat basin. I held myself together with the idea that I had someone, an old friend to see, to chat with, to take away the sting of his ever-present absence, if only for an hour.

But she wasn't there.

Starting to panic, I reentered the restaurant, walking up and down past the packed tables, scanning the faces of loud, happy New Yorkers sipping mimosas and gobbling eggs benedict. I avoided making eye contact. *I must look like a crazy person.*

Outside again, thirty minutes later, about to leave, the phone rang. *Sorry!* She got confused, made a mistake, she would make it up to me, which she did a month later by taking me to a lovely formal tea, and presenting me with flowers. But at the time, I mumbled that it was okay, though it wasn't. I wasn't. I could hardly walk back to the parking garage. All the way home in the car, I sobbed. When I stumbled into the house, I frightened my dogs, who followed me around the kitchen wagging their tails, asking for attention I was in no shape to give, and then retreated to the family room, when I didn't respond.

I called Kate. She talked me down. "It's the abandonment. The last thing you need."

30

Outings

I needed to go grocery shopping. It was April, and I'd run out of almost everything. The refrigerator held a few dried out lemons, some orange juice, ancient Parmesan, a container of pine nuts, some condiments, and a couple bottles of sparking water. I had eaten all of the frozen food that considerate neighbors had brought, things I normally wouldn't have touched, like beef stroganoff, and macaroni and cheese. I ate these meals mindlessly and thankfully. For the past two months, cooking had been out of the question. Even scrambling an egg was beyond me.

Although my cupboards were bare, I resisted going to the store. I found everyday activities harder than dealing with the ongoing Dubai business, because what was once automatic could no longer be taken for granted. The smallest, most trivial action required Herculean effort, as if I had had a stroke, and needed to learn to walk and talk again. I grew painfully self-conscious, observing myself going to the bank, driving the car, washing clothes, taking out the garbage. I thought, *Look at you, following your daily rounds as if nothing had happened. Amazing.* But that wasn't the truth. I handled regular tasks with the constant awareness of exactly what had happened. I never forgot for a second, even while watching some vacuous show on television, going out with friends, or playing with the dogs. My husband had been the context of my life; now, his death was.

Going to the grocery store became the most challenging mundane activity, because I loved it, both with Jerry, and for him. Though I was the daughter of a bona fide shopoholic, I had never been much of a shopper, except when it came to food. I loved browsing the aisles, comparing varieties of pasta or rice, checking out the produce, loading up with arugula, kiwi, Honey Nut Cherrios, and Ben & Jerry's—both my guys' favorite ice cream brand. I got a rush from filling the cart, adding something that wasn't on my list, a special treat for Jerry. Sometimes it would be small—a new salad dressing, or fancy olives. Sometimes it would be big—maybe key lime pie—my husband's dessert of choice.

I had a regular grocery store, Kings in Upper Montclair, that was small but well stocked, the checkout clerks unfailingly pleasant. When I started shopping at the store, we had just moved from Park Slope. Ollie hadn't turned three yet. He sat in the cart, chubby legs dangling, while I basked in the sensuous pleasure of suburban groceries. Even when we moved to the other end of town, I continued to drive the extra ten minutes to shop there. Now I had to push myself to walk in.

I had liked shopping alone, but it was more fun when Jerry and I shopped together. It felt like a date. Jerry and I dated a lot—I don't mean Saturday nights out to dinner and a movie, though we did those, too; I mean going out for a morning coffee and a scone, Sunday brunch at the local diner, or a trip to the hardware store. Even errands were occasions for "just us" time. On the way out the door to get leaf bags or furnace filters, he'd say, "Come with me," and I'd be excited to join him. This had always been the case, even before his work overseas separated us. But the spontaneous transformation of ordinary tasks into intimate moments became even more important afterwards. It was a way for us to acknowledge how much we needed to *be* with each other.

We'd trade off pushing the cart. We'd part—Jerry would check out the meats, while I continued on to canned goods—then reunite in the detergent aisle. There was nothing like seeing my husband at the end of that aisle, the split-second of recognition. *There you are*, I'd think, and then we'd continue on in tandem. He'd bag, I'd pay, and we'd drive home, satisfied that we'd accomplished something. That night he would cook—Jerry found preparing dinner soothing and creative—and we'd enjoy the meal together.

With this history haunting me, I decided to frequent a new store in a neighboring town. The Whole Foods in West Orange was much larger than Kings, and much closer to home. Jerry had liked it too, but we didn't go often enough for it to have been *our* store. Its vastness kept me from feeling claustrophobic. I couldn't bear to encounter familiar faces. They made me feel lonelier. Their very sameness reminded me of how different *I* was, how apart from myself. It was a chore just walking up and down the endless aisles, keeping myself together. I didn't have extra energy for small talk.

As I loaded bag after bag into my car, I couldn't wait to drive home. I had stocked up, so that I wouldn't have to shop again for at least a few weeks. One day, I hoped that I would be able to shop with pleasure, but perhaps I would have to settle for keeping myself fed, for sustenance. It was my partner who made the everyday fun. We loved taking care of each other at this most basic level. Now I would have to learn how to take care of myself. I could do that, I thought. But I didn't have to like it.

The following week, I treated myself with a ticket to see Patti

Lupone in *Gypsy*, my favorite musical. I should have realized, though, what attending a Wednesday matinee would mean.

My mother had always insisted that I was named after the legendary stripper Gypsy Rose Lee, and not my paternal grand-mother, Rose. Mother had big dreams for me, and as a child I didn't know where hers left off and mine began. It was exhilarat-ing to see the mother-daughter struggle played out against a back-drop of half-naked ladies and a soaring score. I didn't much care for musicals, but I couldn't get enough of this one.

I'd seen four revivals, each marking a different phase in my life. I saw Angela Lansbury in1974, when I was a grad student madly in love with acting. Then in 1989, when I'd been a strug-gling actress Off-Off Broadway for a decade, clinging stubbornly to my aspirations, I sat in the front row watching Tyne Daly rip into "Rose's Turn." The 1993 TV version starring Bette Midler served as a reality check. There weren't any successful actresses getting discovered at forty-one. I skipped Bernadette Peters' 2003 revival. By that time I had left acting altogether.

By 2008, I had made my peace with the stage, and looked for-ward to simply being an enthusiastic member of the audience. I hoped the familiar score would distract me from a much deeper wound than a stillborn career. I hoped attending the show would transport me back to the girl I was before Jerry, to the woman whose passions he'd supported and whose disappointments he'd understood.

But in line outside the theater on Forty-Fourth Street, waiting for the doors to open, I was surrounded by a population I hadn't bargained for when I bought my ticket: retired people, including dozens of elderly couples, the Wednesday matinee set. I wasn't prepared for my visceral reaction to these men and women in their sixties, seventies and beyond, laughing together, holding hands, arms entwined, walking in lock-step. *Oh, I'm never going to have that.* I reminded myself I didn't know what I was looking at. Not all of these couples were long-married. Not all of them were happy. But logic had nothing to do with the emotion that blindsided me. I was riddled with envy.

Inside the theater, I leaned forward in my seat, riveted to the stage from the moment Lupone made her first entrance. But during intermission, I couldn't stop staring at the couple chatting in the row in front of me. The way the woman tilted her head towards the man, the man's hand on his wife's—or so I assumed—shoulder. Their intimacy unnerved me: the woman's fingertips lightly, absently tapping on the man's jacket sleeve in marital Morse Code, the casual chemistry only decades together could have produced.

Even if I managed to move on to another relationship, that future man would never know me whole the way Jerry had. No one else would ever read my mind without a guide, automatically translating my glance into action, transplanting the roots of a bad mood just by intuiting the source; no one else would share our history. There were only two witnesses to that history, and one of them was gone.

I cried all the way home. I cried for what I would never have. The show had delivered as promised—the poignant past, the painful present—but it could not deliver what I most desired: a future with my husband. I missed what would not be, the possibility of sitting next to my longtime love—the one who had seen me through my theatrical journey, and given me a life beyond it—whispering in each other's ear at the 2030 revival of *Gypsy*, starring Adele as Mama Rose.

From the moment I picked Ollie up at Newark airport, I was concerned. I hadn't seen him since February. His uncombed hair was longer, his face unshaven—I had no idea that his beard was so red—and his eyes were tense and haunted. He seemed a beaten version of himself. Ollie complained that he'd been stopped on the way through security. Again. Sure, I thought, he was the image of Ted Kaczynski.

Once home, Ollie retreated to his bathroom to wash up, and must have caught himself in the mirror. He asked me if he should shave. Ollie only asked such a question when he already knew the answer. I said it was up to him. He closed the door and came out smooth, his essential good looks restored. Then he went out for a haircut. Also his idea.

That night, I sat in our family room, waiting for Ollie to bring popcorn from the kitchen. We had planned to watch something mindless on TV. Suddenly, he ran into the room and threw himself on my lap. "He's never coming through the door again. He's never coming back." I held him and we both sobbed, as if we were still in Dubai, clinging to each other. Only now the foreign country was our own home. It didn't feel like ours without the husband and father who had made our family complete.

All the next day we looked forward to the coming night out. We really needed the company. Ollie and I had been invited to dinner at the home of his favorite high school history teachers, the Branigans, who happened to be married to each other.

It was a clear spring evening, a cool breeze gently moving the cherry blossoms visible from our hosts' front porch. This was the first social occasion the two of us had attended together since the funeral. Geoff and Gillian bubbled with charm. Their two little girls darted in and out. No one mentioned Jerry, or anything verging on our situation. It was exactly what we needed. I sipped wine, nibbled nuts, and olives, and told myself how well I was doing.

When it was time for dinner, Geoff excused himself to take charge of the backyard grill. We all followed. As I passed through their kitchen, I spotted the program from Jerry's service with the cover picture of him overlooking Beirut posted on their bulletin board. The couple hadn't been able to come; one of the other teachers in attendance must have given it to them.

The children played in the grass. I nursed my wine, and made small talk. Geoff turned the chicken breasts. Then Gillian brought out plates, and distributed them randomly on the patio table. It was all very casual, to be arranged as place settings later.

I looked down at the blue-edged porcelain and counted: two small plates for the girls, and one, two, three, four large ones for the adults. *Oh,* I thought, *there should be five.* I studied the plates and counted again. One was missing. Definitely. I wondered if I should say something? No. They would realize the mistake when we all sat down. Maybe I should be helpful, go inside, and get one more. I decided to wait. But the missing plate bothered me. I counted yet again: one for Gillian, one for Geoff, one for Ollie, and one for me. Oh. God. Four. There were four of us.

Not five.

I swallowed, broke out in a cold sweat, and told myself to breathe. Thank goodness I hadn't said anything. The evening had been going so well, so *normally,* they'd have thought I had lost my mind. Ollie would have been upset because, for the past ten minutes I *had* lost my mind. For those interminable minutes, staring at the plates, counting and re-counting them, over and over, I had been thinking magically á la Joan Didion. I couldn't leave my husband out of the count.

For the remainder of the meal I felt broken, as if something inside me had cracked. This had been the first time since the January phone call summoning me to Jerry's bedside overseas that I had lost contact with reality. I had faced every aspect of what was required of me head on. I had been strong. I had been present. Until that night. For all my stubborn insistence on coping with what was, I still had not truly accepted the most basic fact—that Jerry was dead, and, as Ollie had said only the night before, that he was never coming back. There had been three of us; now there were two. Two and two made four.

At the end of the evening, as we approached the car, I asked

Ollie to drive. We got in. Then I told him. He nodded, "It was a family dinner. Before this, we would never have gone to Geoff and Gillian's without Dad." Ollie removed his fingers from the ignition, and we sat in silence for a long while, looking straight ahead at the empty street.

31

Family

"Pete?" It was Vicky, who had been calling regularly. I had not unleashed the entertainment—a great frustration for my sister—since the night Jerry died, in the wee hours of her birthday, when she outed Pete to my brothers-in-law.

I sighed. "Yeth," I said in Pete's trademark stress-induced lisp.

Vicky giggled with delight. "How *are* you?"

"Don't asthk," I said, hoping this would end a performance I couldn't sustain.

"You sound down, Pete," she said with genuine concern.

I paused. "I can't, Vicky. I just can't."

"Oh. Sorry. I'll check in later." Click.

George and Isabel came up for the weekend. I hadn't seen them since the memorial and I wanted to, but the moment they arrived, I realized I wasn't up to it. At all. I could hardly speak, and of the three of us, I had always been the talker. Long silences hung in the air, freighted with what we could not directly address.

Having my family in the house made Jerry's death somehow more real. Their presence threw his absence into high relief.

Just before we went out to eat, George and I stood in the front hallway staring at my empty living room. "It's unbearable," I said. "Am I going to survive this?"

George walked to the picture window, and glanced at the sill where I had placed the purple and white orchids that my New York girlfriends had sent me. He pointed to the little clip on one orchid's stem, attaching it to a rod, which held the bloom upright. "Who put this here?" he asked.

"I did. It was flopping over."

"You'll be okay," he said quickly.

"What do you mean?"

"You noticed what the flower needed—a small thing—and you cared enough to respond." He smiled. "You'll be fine." I didn't quite believe him, but I wanted to.

All weekend I kept my wretchedness within. After George and Isabel left, I rushed into the living room and collapsed in racking sobs. Family coming and going, Jerry gone. For good. When the tears stopped, I stood and faced the window. This view of our expansive front yard had captured me when we first looked at the house, and it was my favorite spot in which to practice T'ai Chi Chih.

I didn't know how to go on, but I began to move. I moved through sorrow, disorientation, and anxiety about my future. Unlike my practices on the day of the phone call and in the Dubai apartment, I was able to put my attention on the soles of my feet and to keep it there. Pain ebbed and flowed. I did not resist. I shifted my weight backward and forward, side to side. For the duration of the practice, I was inside my body again, whole.

More visitors. Scott, his attractive, athletic wife, Gina, and both daughters—six-year-old Sydney, who had come to the memorial, and Kira, who was eighteen—came from Seattle to see me. In the days before they arrived, I pushed myself to clean house, set up beds and bathrooms, stock the refrigerator. The effort felt monumental. It was nearly midnight when I drove to the airport to pick them up. Waiting in the near-deserted baggage claim area, I felt stranded, though I was about to see familiar faces.

When they finally appeared, Sydney ran to hug me. I smiled and tousled her blonde hair as she wrapped her small arms around my waist. There were kisses, hugs, and searching looks from Gina and Kira. Their arrival did nothing to temper how isolated I felt, as I worked mightily to put up a brave front. I wasn't comfortable enough to let them know what rough shape I was in, as I had with George. Though I hadn't let go completely with my brother, there was an understanding between us. Scott's family were dear relatives, but not true intimates.

They stayed for four days. On the last, Scott checked out Jerry's sports car, which he planned to buy. This was fine with Ollie. "I'm twenty-one, Mom. I can't be driving a car like that." Scott offered to let Ollie drive it whenever he visited.

"You too," he said to me.

I nodded, but knew that I didn't want to ride in the car again. Scott wore one of Jerry's motorcycle jackets, the only one that fit; his shoulders were so much broader than his brother's. And he would take a winter coat, too. Earlier in the day, watching him try on Jerry's clothes ripped me up, though I had offered, though I truly wanted him to have them.

"I'm glad I came," Scott said, peering under the hood. "It helped me, being here again."

I couldn't say what I was thinking: that this visit was too soon for me. I was too raw. I hadn't realize how raw until they were actually in the house. If I had, I would have postponed. For months.

Then, apropos of nothing, Scott said, "At least you kept your name. That should make it easier."

I shook my head vigorously. "No, no, it doesn't. I may have kept my last name," my voice wobbled, "but I was completely married to your brother. I still feel married to him."

"Oh, I didn't mean..." He moved towards me, arms outstretched.

"I know," I said, resting my head on his chest, on leather that smelled like Jerry.

That evening I leaned against the doorway of Ollie's room while Scott and Gina packed.

"There's something we've been thinking about," Scott said. Gina nodded. "We would like to name you as Sydney's guardian?"

My mouth opened, but no sound came out. I was bewildered. Besides the fact that I lived three thousand miles away and had only seen Sydney a handful of times since she was born, I wondered why they wouldn't name one their four older children. Each had two from their previous marriages; Eric, Scott's oldest, was twenty-one, as was Gina's eldest. He and his siblings were the logical choices. I said as much, and they responded that none of them were grown up enough to handle such a responsibility.

"Guardianship takes a real adult," Gina said.

However undone by circumstance I was, what my brother-in-law and his wife saw when they looked at me was a mature, responsible woman who could handle anything. But it wasn't true. I couldn't. Not then.

Their faces glowed with expectation. "There's no one we think more highly of," Gina said.

I was flattered and disturbed. *Please don't ask any more of me,* I thought, though I said, "It means so much that you trust me. Let me think about it."

As soon as I left the room, I began to panic. This request was so off-base. I had the feeling that my brother and sister-in-law were trying to take care of me by asking me to take care of their daughter. They wanted me to know that I was still part of the family, that there were people who needed me. They seemed to think I needed to be needed. But I didn't. At least not by anyone but Ollie. I wanted to scream, *I* need to be taken care of. They wanted so much to give me purpose, to make things better for me, that neither Scott nor Gina recognized that guardianship would be a huge burden.

The next morning, after I dropped them at the airport, I wrote an email to Scott politely but firmly turning down the proposal. I had stayed awake most of the night imagining what it would be like if I had to take this child in the immediate future. The very thought overloaded me, and filled me with dread. I could barely take care of myself. *How could I take care of her, too?* I told Scott as much, that I didn't know how long it would be before I felt stable, but for the time being, I had to focus exclusively on myself and my son. He answered that he understood. He and Gina hadn't meant to add to the pressure I was under.

It occurred to me that setting limits, saying no, trusting my gut reactions was exactly what taking care of myself meant. I had learned something. It didn't matter who understood me, or who didn't. It only mattered that I understood myself.

Ollie called his grandfather on his birthday. After a brief chat, Jim asked him to hold on, and shouted to his wife. "Janet! Oliver's on the phone." Ollie's grandmother had not spoken to her grandson, or to me, since Jerry died, almost three months earlier. I found this very difficult to understand. *How could a grandparent, no matter how bereaved, not acknowledge her grandchild's loss?* But then I had trouble understanding why neither of them had shown up at the funeral.

About a week later, Janet finally called me. "I was afraid to speak to you. Afraid I would cry," she said, her thin voice shaking only slightly more than usual.

"That would have been okay," I said. "We would have cried together."

This opened her up. "I can't stop thinking that he didn't know how much I loved him."

"He knew," I said. I didn't say that just before he died, he was beginning to face the depth of his anger and disappointment concerning their relationship.

Then she told me, more firmness in her tone, about the memorial she was planning on July nineteenth "for Mike" in the Pennsylvania town where he was born. Kathy had already told me about it. I said there was no way I could come. Ollie too, had expressed revulsion at the idea of a second service. "It's a violation," he said. I told Kathy it was difficult enough to move forward without doing a funeral replay less than six months after the real one. And who would be there? People who knew Jerry when he was six? She understood, and must have told her mother our reaction.

"Perhaps you could write something for someone else to read," Janet said.

"No," I said, suppressing my rising fury. "I already wrote and read. In February."

My mother-in-law didn't get it. We watched Jerry die. We planned and held a memorial. Hundreds of people came. Friends spoke. We buried him. And we were still mourning. *How could she put us all through such a thing again?*

I spoke to Scott. He didn't want to attend another memorial either. No one did. Except Janet. But when he asked his parents to cancel it, his dad said, "Your mother needs this to mourn." She was willing to put her children through more hell, because she couldn't get herself together to be there when it counted. People attend funerals in wheelchairs, on oxygen. One of our friends told me of a dying father on a stretcher, attending his child's funeral.

I knew I was being hard-hearted, but this wasn't the first time Jerry's mother had not shown up for our family. Four years earlier, while Ollie received his high school diploma, she was sacked out in the back of our station wagon. Jerry almost missed the ceremony too, between ushering her out of the church and dealing with the EMS technician, who asked what she'd taken, and wanted to bring her to the hospital. She refused, said she just needed to sleep. I'll never forget my father-in-law's loneliness at the celebration dinner afterwards.

A pattern of absence. Belatedly, I understood why Jerry was so furious with his mother. And I understood, more completely than ever before, how parallel our positions in our respective families were: both of us were the odd ones out. My parents hadn't attended our wedding; his hadn't come to the funeral.

I asked Scott not to tell me anything more about the July event. "When the day arrives, I don't want to hear who was there, who spoke, nothing." I had a vivid imagination, and didn't want pictures in my head of a misguided ceremony to supersede the original memorial, the one that had been for me and for my son the only real tribute.

It had been a long month, with family coming and going, magnifying my sadness. But on a Sunday, late in April, I woke up well, happy. Weekends had been particularly tough. They had been our time, Jerry's and mine. And the onslaught of spring, the forsythia bushes' yellow assault in the beginning of the month announcing that nature would go on, would in fact celebrate itself, seemed a personal affront.

But not that day. On that day, when I walked down the driveway to get the paper, the canopy of apple and cherry blossoms, which turned the front yard into an orchard, delighted me, just as it always had. How lucky I was.

I didn't know why I was able to appreciate nature's beauty on that particular day, and not on the day before. No matter. I put on my sunhat, a wide-brimmed blue straw I had inherited from my mother, and brought the *New York Times* out to the patio. The dogs followed me. Tizzie busied herself with sticks, chewing and chewing, working one after another down to a nub. Edgar sat under the deck, content simply to be. Every so often he got up, changed position, moving to a spot near the fence line under a holly. Then, after a while, he'd move back.

The same sun that had boiled in Dubai warmed me on my home ground. I sat on the Adirondack chair where Jerry used to loll when he wanted to smoke a cigar, or talk privately on his cell. I would watch him from the kitchen window. Today, unlike last week, when I couldn't look at the empty chair, this wasn't sad. Something had shifted inside me. I wasn't simply coping, wasn't soldiering through. I was genuinely enjoying the afternoon, my yard, the silky sky, my dogs, solitude.

All at once, I had the urge to write.

I brought my laptop outside on the deck table and placed it so the sun was behind me, and the umbrella shaded the screen. Tizzie trotted after me, stick in mouth. Then she curled herself under my feet. Edgar stayed below, on the path overlooking our neighbors' yards, surveying his domain. I felt content, ready. I could begin to work in earnest, for no other reason than the sun.

32

Dealing

In the conference room of the blue chip international law firm that Raine had found for me to handle Jerry's estate affairs in Dubai, I waited for the attorney I had never met, and gazed at the dazzling, unobstructed New York skyline. I had been to the top of the Empire State Building—I remembered crowds pushing against each other to get a prime view—and to the top of the World Trade Center, as well. Jerry had accompanied me both times. During the latter trip, my fear of heights took over. I could hardly look out, and definitely not down. Jerry had no fear.

But seated alone in a cushy leather chair at a long polished wood table, swiveling back and forth to catch the breathtaking view—this was the top of 30 Rock after all—I had no vertigo, physical or otherwise. I knew I was in good hands. For a moment, I fantasized that Tina Fey, a.k.a Liz Lemon, would walk in, or better yet, Alec Baldwin as Jack Doneghy. Well, at least the attorney's name was Jack.

I had put my trust in the firm to open and retrieve Jerry's

frozen bank account, though beneath my rational choice lay a constant thrum of concern about my future. Immediately after returning from the Middle East, I didn't have the will or concentration to push for action overseas. And I was afraid, afraid to go back to Dubai, even in my mind, but again and again, I found myself having to do exactly that, first for the insurance investigation, then with Jasim and Raine, and now with a lawyer, without whom my future would remain precarious. The fees would be steep—not a surprise—though based on an hourly rate rather than a percentage. Given the circumstances, the firm kindly waived their usual retainer—a blessing, since the more ordinary estate requirements continued to sap my resources.

The previous month, in my best daughter-of-attorney mode, I had sent the lawyer a list of questions and a summary of facts, not the least of which being that Jerry had amended his will a year earlier, clarifying that I was the beneficiary of his bank account. Jack's answers made the process seem doable, albeit counterintuitive. *Why was the will, an unambiguous directive, not necessary?* Even with the services of a high-powered lawyer, I didn't trust my situation in the UAE. My experience there had left me deeply insecure. In our phone conversation, Jack had assured me that the money wasn't going anywhere. "Not to worry. Once it is frozen, it remains so." And besides, he added, "This will take some time." I could tell from his calm, seasoned manner that he was the right person to handle my problem. But that didn't stop me from worrying.

Jack entered the conference room, an imposing man in his sixties, still handsome. We shook hands, and he described his strategy to extricate the funds. Every paper sent to Dubai, including the Surrogate Certificate—the testamentary letter naming me as Jerry's executor—would have to be notarized and "attested" by the New Jersey Secretary of State, the US Secretary of State, and the UAE Embassy in Washington, DC. The firm would handle everything. Thank God.

I signed a document giving him power of attorney; two, in fact. One was in English, the other in double column format— Arabic on the right, English translation on the left—because I was uncomfortable with the notion of signing an Arabic copy I couldn't read. Then I gave Jack a packet of documents, including copies of Jerry's corporate papers and bank account statements, listing me as beneficiary. I still didn't understand why that and the will weren't sufficient.

We discussed Jerry's documentary film company. "This may complicate things," Jack said. "Dubai's incorporation laws are a bit convoluted. If there is resistance on the part of the bank, you may have to become the company's director." The prospect seemed both intimidating and ridiculous.

Then we talked about the pending business deal. I still didn't know if Ashar's company had a formal agreement with the American billboard manufacturer to whom Jerry and Bill had introduced them. And if so, was there any chance I would ever see the promised facilitator's fee? Against Bill's wishes, I asked Jack to contact Ashar's assistant, Jasim, on my behalf. Our monthly telephone conversations had worn me down. I had the distinct impression I was being "handled," and I didn't like it. I pictured giant liquid crystal display screens shining in the desert sun. *What did this have to do with me?* Bill had also spoken to Jasim, and didn't think involving a lawyer was a good idea when in delicate negoti- ations with Middle Easterners. I disagreed. Once again, I needed to trust my gut. It was all I had. I needed resolution. I needed to know if the arrangement was real, or if, as I continued to suspect, merely the phantom legacy of my husband's outsized ambition.

After the meeting, far below in Rockefeller Plaza, I made my way past throngs of tourists and office workers enjoying the mid- day sun. I felt elated and proud of myself. The world-class set- ting, the demands of the situation hadn't thrown me. I had han- dled what was required and would continue to, despite my rage at the enormous mess Jerry had left behind, the complications that had become a full-time job. But I should have expected as much. My husband was a complicated man with a complicated life. Of course his death and its aftermath were complicated.

Shari and I stood in my garage in the empty space where Jerry's sports car used to be. The day the moving truck came to take it cross-country to Scott's house in Seattle had been bittersweet. The car represented Jerry's sense of fun, his need for speed and flash. Another piece of him gone for good.

We spread out the rugs, books, and framed pictures that had finally arrived from Dubai in a giant cargo crate. Even this had not gone smoothly. Extricating the shipment from the arrival area in New Jersey had involved multiple calls, paperwork, and, of course, more fees.

We layered the rugs one on top of the other, just as the salesmen had done in the mall store where Jerry and I had purchased them little more than a year earlier. There, the intense colors and lush textures, the history woven into elaborate patterns, contrasted sharply with the store's fluorescent lighting. How strange that here, in my dark and dusty garage, their traditional designs seemed somehow more authentic, more at home.

Shari and I brought the rugs inside the house. I put the runners, which had warmed the marble of Jerry's apartment hallway, on the floor of our narrower, shorter one, and a handsome thick Iranian piece on top of the Spanish tile in the foyer. Then I placed the spectacular Afghan we had picked out for our bedroom in front of the bed. "That's stunning," Shari said. The rug's raised midnight blue and camel rectangles perfectly echoed the room's colors and shapes. Jerry's gift to me completed our bedroom. Correction: *my* bedroom.

I put the framed photographs of Middle Eastern scenes Jerry had shot on my dining table. The previous owner of our house must have been a photographer too, because he had built a dark room and display cases in the basement. Our downstairs hallway had a gallery vibe. I used to tiptoe down that hall and listen outside the door to my husband and my son conferring on what to print, when to take the paper from the chemical bath, and which photo had turned out best. I'd wait for the red light to go off to see what they had produced: black and white shots of the Vineyard, old Italian men in undershirts, stone homes in Avebury, England, a garden in Provence, scene after scene of our family travels. Inevitably, once digital photography became the norm, the dark room got less and less use.

The pictures on the table, all in color, were taken in Dubai and Morocco. I had already chosen which ones I wanted to keep for me and Ollie: a tiny truck driving over caramel dunes, sandals outside a mosque, an old man from Casablanca in a feathered hat, large blue and white ceramic bowls, stone arches framing a blue door. The rest I wrapped to send to his family and mine, along with DVDs of the memorial and a book I had compiled of eulogies, obituaries and condolence notes. I especially wanted, needed Jerry's parents to see the DVD, to know how we had honored their son.

33

Mother's Day, Father's Day

My daily conversations with Ollie were usually brief, just checking in to hear the other's voice, to know that the other was still there. But every so often, my son called me in open pain. "I can't stand it," he said. "I miss him sooo much." If we had been in the same room, I'd have listened, stroked his hair, held him. But all I could do on the phone was say, "I know, sweetheart, I know."

Two calls that spring stood out. On a weekend night, a rare one when I was out of the house celebrating a friend's sixtieth birthday, Ollie called to tell me that he had met a girl he liked at a campus party, but couldn't bring himself to tell her about his father. We talked about wanting to be normal, to enjoy ourselves. What we really wanted was to bury our sorrow, if only for an evening, and to move about the world as if nothing were wrong, so that no one who didn't already know our loss could discover it.

And then there was this. " I can't do it, I can't." Ollie had been pushing to finish his senior project, an original film entitled *Goin' Back to Canada* about Neil Young's hometown. "I have eighteen hours of footage. I don't know where to start." He had shot the film the previous summer. Along with three of his closest college friends, Ollie had filled my station wagon top to bottom with rented equipment secured by Jerry, and driven from Montclair to Omemee, Ontario, where he had interviewed townspeople, many of whom had known Young as a boy. This was more than a degree requirement for Ollie. It was a passion project, and in the wake of his father's loss, a nearly unbearable one. Jerry had introduced Young to Ollie, and passed along his admiration of the singer-songwriter's originality, purity, and rebellion.

"Breathe," I told him. "Work on one little piece, take a break, then look at the next piece. It will come together." I put down the phone, a plaintive chorus echoing in my head: *helpless, helpless, helpless*. I longed to see my son.

So when Mother's Day was upon us, I decided to visit him in Chicago, as I had the previous spring. It was the one thing I could do for Ollie, be with him. And I had another motive. Mother's Day was a month before graduation. I knew that being in the city, in the same hotel where we usually stayed, without Jerry, was going to be hard. Getting on a plane for the first time since coming back from Dubai, even harder. I needed to desensitize myself, so when graduation day came, I could focus on celebration.

As I entered the lobby of the InterContinental, its corporate formality felt alienating, and though there were people milling about, I felt completely alone. Once in my room, a carbon copy of the one I had shared with Jerry, I began to cry at its generic sameness. I told myself to pull it together. I was meeting my cousin Tuckie at the Art Institute for lunch, a short walk down Michigan Avenue. I knew the way, but I felt lost.

In the museum's lobby, my cousin, a sprightly woman in her late sixties with elfin features and a platinum bun loosely piled atop her head, embraced me. "You're here," she said, as if I had just crossed the finish line of a marathon. Tuckie knew sorrow.

She and her husband, Arnie, had lost their daughter many years earlier when she died from septicemia, after delivering their first grandchild. I remember how shocked the entire family had been that such a thing could happen. Tuckie understood from experience that merely moving from one point to another was a monumental achievement.

Over lunch in the elegant Institute dining room, she told me she didn't have much use for counselors or support groups—"the grief industry," she called it. She didn't believe in a one-size-fits-all remedy for bereavement. "It never goes away, but it does get better." Her only advice: "Do something ordinary every day—go out, see people, make a call, shop. Keep moving." I took everything she said as gospel.

The next day was Mother's Day. Ollie looked better than he had in April, but still pale and distracted. We had reservations at a restaurant featuring a jazz brunch, the same place we had gone the year before. With Jerry in Dubai, that Mother's Day trip to Chicago had been a lark. At home, the holiday had always revolved around breakfast in bed cooked by my two men, and a trip to the garden center to pick out summer annuals. With Ollie in school and Jerry away, the brunch for two could have begun a new tradition. This time, though, the mellow music and smiling families struck us as funereal. We both whimpered through the meal, only stopping when the waitress came to the table. She looked concerned, but we couldn't possibly have explained what was tearing us up: that this was how it would be from now on, our family permanently ruptured.

After the meal, I went to campus with Ollie, hung out in his room, which was crammed with books, papers, and dirty clothes, and took him and his friends out to dinner. By the time I got to the airport the next day, I was jumping out of my skin to get on the plane. When we landed, I dashed to my car. As torturous as re-experiencing Chicago without Jerry had been, reentering our home

without him, after being away, was far worse, worse than returning from Dubai, because this time, I was no longer in shock, and
didn't have my loving brother awaiting me.

I climbed into bed, and the full force of the weekend's immer-
sion overtook me. I paced, pounded pillows, screamed, *I miss you
so much. I'm scared. I. HATE. THIS.* Edgar looked at me with his
mournful eyes, then burrowed his head under his paw.

The next morning, I awoke with tired satisfaction, as if I had
accomplished a tremendous feat. I had done what I'd set out to
do. I had inoculated myself, and by extension, Ollie, against what
Chicago had meant to Jerry and to me, our hopes and dreams for
our son. I had been afraid I wouldn't be able to face it alone. But I
did. I showed up for Ollie, for myself. And I knew I could return.

A month later, when I came back for the graduation, it wasn't
a flood of memories that concerned me. The Mother's Day practice run had taken care of that. I was anxious for a different reason. This would be the first time Jerry's parents would see me or
Ollie since his death.

When I came down to the hotel's lobby to meet them, I saw a
crumpled, frail woman in a wheelchair and a haggard older man
behind her, and I felt sad. They were clearly crushed. I kissed them
both, and held Janet's hand. "I'm glad you came," I said. And I
was. I had the sense, though, that I might not see them again after
this, until there was a wedding. Or another funeral.

On his way to the hotel to meet everyone, Ollie called to tell
me that Tim Russert had died suddenly. Vicky worked for him.
In the hotel room I would share with George—Vicky had wanted
her own room—I sat her down and broke the news. She turned
white. We switched on the television. *She might bolt*, I thought, but
to her credit, she didn't leave, though the entire weekend was suddenly skewed in her direction. Ollie, George, and I noted that she
reacted more strongly to Tim's death than she had to Jerry's. And

there was the added parallel of his wife and Tim's only son—about Ollie's age—both overseas when it happened.

In spite of the shadow of this additional loss, we had a fine dinner at Café Spiaggia. Janet sat dolefully throughout, saying little. I felt for her. This was her first concrete experience of life without Jerry. After the meal, I wheeled her into the ladies' room. On the way back, she thanked me for the DVD of the memorial. "It was amazing. I don't know how you and Oliver did that."

"We did what we needed to," I mumbled. Perhaps now she understood why she shouldn't have expected me or Ollie to attend a second funeral.

Then she asked, "Where did he come from?"

Jerry had often said he felt like a changeling. His mother and father never really *got* their son, either as a child, or as a world-traveling, big-city-living, self-made man. Like me, he had pushed his parents past their comfort zone. They were astonished by Jerry's unstoppable drive, his boldness, his ability to take on the world. I could understand that his fearlessness inspired fear. It had in me as well.

Where had he come from? "From you," I answered.

Graduation the next day was hot, clear, and as Shari had predicted, joyful. I was so proud of Ollie. In spite of deep grief, he had finished with his class. The ceremony was long, with over a thousand graduates. Jim and Janet left early to go back to the hotel to rest. When we finally heard, "Oliver Blooston Mosier," we whooped and applauded, though we could hardly see him. Scott managed to get a blurry photo. After the ceremony, we gathered the rest of the family and Ollie's friends for more pictures. Ollie looked a bit disheveled from the heat, but dapper in his bowtie, and enormously relieved.

That evening, we shared a celebratory dinner with his friend Rob's family in the downstairs "cellar" of the Firehouse Restaurant. The boys had arranged everything, a huge help. They held court—Ollie grinning ear to ear, and Rob, the steady guy sporting a five o'clock shadow. The room was dank and dark, but nothing could dampen our collective sense of triumph. Though Jim and Janet had trouble managing a smile—oppressed as they were by the new, palpable reality of their son's absence—everyone else beamed: Scott, Ross, Vicky, George, cousin Tuckie, and her wise-cracking husband Arnie. I was grateful for them all.

Rob's father, a pleasant man in his fifties, took me aside. "What you must be going through right now." I assured him I was okay. Truly. I was buoyed by Ollie's achievement, and my own. We'd done it. Made it through a major milestone without our man.

Ollie's younger classmates appeared—the boys who had accompanied him and Rob to Canada, acted as crew and on camera, searching for Neil Young and themselves: intense, hyper Charlie, lanky, laid-back Henry. I was so glad that my son had such friends. Jerry and I had always worried that we had done our son a great disservice by not giving him siblings, but he had found them on his own. These were his brothers.

The next day was Father's Day—a poignant coincidence that Ollie and I had obsessed over in the preceding weeks, but that seemed entirely fitting once it was upon us. After all, there could have been no graduation without Jerry, no son without the father. I left for the airport, satisfied we had made the best of it. Before I boarded the plane, Ollie called me, ecstatic. "The whole weekend was everything I needed it to be. I love you, Mom." For the first time since January, we were both truly content.

34

Nightmare

I dreamed Jerry wasn't really dead, that it was all a bad dream, and more disturbingly, that he didn't remember our commitment to each other. He stared at me when I reminded him that we had gotten married "again." I didn't call it a renewal of vows, something in our real lives we considered unnecessary, and perhaps bad luck. *Weren't our first vows enough to last a lifetime?*

I got out of bed and went to my jewelry box. I picked up the rings, though I hadn't been wearing them every day, instead putting turquoise and silver on the ring fingers of each hand, or the anniversary ring with sapphires and diamonds Jerry had given me for our twenty-fourth anniversary—our last. When I had asked him why he didn't wait until next year—he knew I wanted an eternity band for our quarter century—he shrugged, and said he just felt like it.

For the graduation weekend, I had purposely worn the engagement ring and the two wedding bands on my right hand. I wanted Jerry with us, at least symbolically. Now I held the rings in my palm, closed my fingers over them, and put them back into the box. For good. I knew I would not put them on my finger again.

But I did want to be able to wear them from time to time. I decided I would put the rings inside a locket, kept unseen, private, near my heart. That morning, I went to our local jeweler, a man who'd sold Jerry many gifts. Together, we examined one locket after another—too big, too small, too shallow, too ornate. He would have one designed for me. "Something simple," I said, "and it has to be ready by September ninth, what would have been our twenty-fifth anniversary."

I had a nightmare in which Jerry came back from the dead to tell me he wanted a divorce. I awoke, breathing hard. This was my deepest fear. He was in terrible turmoil living a double life, here and in Dubai. Our marriage had indeed been at risk. And now, it was up to me to live with the unknowable. *What if this dream had come true? What would I have done? What should I believe, considering I could never know what was in his heart or mind?* He had said, "I don't want to lose you," said it a month before he died, told Ollie how much he wanted to come home, how hard the separation was on me.

I surprised myself with my quick response. "Then don't." *Don't lose me.* Years earlier, I would have given him what he wanted— reassurance that of course I would never leave him. After a year of therapy and another year to digest it, I understood that if he was going to tank our marriage and himself in the process, I had to take care of myself. There was nothing I could make him do or not do. This broke my heart.

I began remembering other things Jerry said. Many times, after a discussion of our future had reached a standstill, he would say, "Trust me." I hated that. Trust was a given, part and parcel of the vows we lived every day. We had trusted each other for decades, but the more he said the words, the less I did. His depression, his self-medication with alcohol, his declaration that he wouldn't mind having an "open" marriage for the duration of the job, gave me plenty of reasons to do no such thing. And I told him as much.

Jerry started labeling himself a "mediocre husband." I disagreed. Jerry wasn't mediocre at anything. And he would blurt, apropos of nothing, "men are pigs." I assumed he was talking about *other* men. No matter how distressed I was, or how disappointed, I never thought of my husband as a pig.

Maybe he was afraid *I* wanted to leave *him*. *Was he giving me permission to walk away?* Yes. I believed he was trying to release me, even though he knew as well as I did that I didn't want to be released.

At no point during our long marriage were we afraid to argue. My sister had dubbed us "The Bickersons." We relished sparring, hashing things out, voices raised, doors slammed, profanity shouted, whatever it took to air the issue, secure that no matter what we said or did, we could recover, be *us*. Disagreements existed on the continuum of our marital conversation, unsurprising given how opinionated we both were. But we rarely went to bed angry. Pete saw to that. Jerry would cock his head, address him, and we would let go of the grievance with a laugh, a hug, a *What was that all about?*

But not during his travels. The miles between us had created an unfamiliar formality. I begged him to please tell me what was going on. *Weren't we each other's best friends?* He'd say, "I tell you everything, except what might hurt you. I don't want to do that again," referring, I supposed, to the kiss that sent us to counseling. Then he'd purse his lips, as if squeezing them would lock them shut and prevent hurtful news from leaking out. What did *again* mean? Was he referring to Raine? Someone else? His drinking? Or all of the above.

I had put on a tough show. "Use condoms, don't tell me." If my husband was going to be a fool, I wanted him to protect himself, and me. He didn't realize his withholding hurt me, too, though maybe he sensed I didn't really want to know the truth. I was too terrified that distance and opportunity might have undermined our long history together. I didn't think I could stand it. Now, alone for good, I wanted to know everything, and I couldn't. Ever. A blessing? A curse? I didn't know. But it was certainly a torment.

I took what was left of the clothes in his closet and threw them on the floor of the windowless dressing area, where for years he had quietly gotten ready for work while I slept. I screamed, "You bastard, you fucking bastard," over and over and over again, my voice loud, low, a savage bellow. "I hate you. I love you. Did you love me?"

When my voice was gone, I sat in the heap, and remembered doing this once before, when Jerry was alive, when a regular skirmish turned into a rare all-out fight. He had picked me up, held me. In the echo chamber of my mind I heard him whisper, "Of course, I love you."

I could go mad.

Instead, I wrote everything down: memories, rage, grief, confusion, black letters on white paper, words in order, sentence after sentence, building into pages, releasing me for the limited period while I worked, creating the possibility that this relentless ache was manageable, comprehensible, and ultimately survivable.

The next night, a third dream: Jerry on "borrowed time." It was a Thursday. We both understood he had little time left. I leaned against a counter in front of a woman from whom we needed something, my husband to my right. She said, "Oh, he's here."

I answered, "Yes, but only until Sunday." I had a tremendous urge to kiss him again and again, the awareness too late that there were never enough kisses and now there would be no more. In the morning, I realized it was the twenty-seventh—exactly five months without my husband.

That very day, Ollie wrote me a letter. He had decided to stay in Chicago for the summer. He didn't really have a plan, but I suspect he simply wasn't ready to inhabit the house yet, to face on a daily basis the void within it. He needed time and distance, and though I missed my young man, I understood.

Later in the week, as I sat on our front steps after the postman came, sorting out the junk mail and opening bills, I spotted Ollie's return address. Inside the envelope was a full-page yellow legal sheet in Ollie's rapid half-print, half-cursive scrawl. The date on the top right: *6/27/08.*

Dear Mom,

I know this may come as a surprise, but I do, from time to time, stumble across something worth writing home about and forgoing the ever-popular electronic email. In the process of writing an abundant amount of "thank you" notes, I quickly came to a singular conclusion: I need to thank you, the person who has marched forward with me during this painful year. As you know, these past few months have been extremely difficult, so much so that words only scratch the delicate and horrible surface.

The letter you wrote to me prior to graduation served as comfort, an emotional stilt propelling me across the finish line. As you have said, "You can't choose your family." Despite such an assertion, I know that, given the choice, I cannot imagine a better mother than you. I almost said, "I'd choose you in a heartbeat," but you already know my well-documented disdain for the cliché.

Mom, you are my rock, the person who both comforts me and pushes me to strive towards new heights. With Dad's death, I lost my father and my best friend. I realized then, more than ever, what great parents (keep in mind the plural) I have. I know that whatever travails and hurdles await in the hazy future, you will be there, and I will be there for you.

Love,
Ollie

I gazed out over the front lawn, eyes brimming, and could not imagine a better son.

35

July

I went to the Fourth of July parade, fully aware it was my husband's holiday, his parade, and stood on the usual corner, a half-block from the viewing stand, at the end of the route. I wished Ollie were there, but he was still in Chicago. This was my guys' favorite holiday. They both loved the corny patriotism of flags flying, burgers on the grill and thunderous fireworks, not to mention the lack of religion, formal sit-down dinners, or obligatory gifts. And it didn't hurt that our town put on a terrific parade every year, one Jerry had had the thrill of participating in on multiple occasions.

Friends stood with me and told stories of Jerry revving his motorcycle engines to the dismay of bystanders. We laughed at the memory of my provocateur husband, leading a pack of fellow weekend riders. He had beamed on his Beemer, then posed in front of it dressed in full biker regalia.

The Montclair parade kicked off with a long line of cars, some antique, some not, often with an ancient veteran in the front seat of a white Cadillac circa 1963, and some blatant advertisements for town government—the mayor or a councilperson perched on top of the back seat of a '50s convertible. The first year Jerry participated, he walked as coach with Ollie's Little League team. The eight-year-olds in their Giants uniforms proudly marched the entire three-mile route.

The next time, my husband and two friends drove their Miatas, not antiques—one red (Jerry's), one white, and one blue—with children in the passenger seats. The huge pâpier maché cigar Ollie and Jerry had lovingly designed, complete with *Hoya de Monterey* label wedged against the grill, got plenty of laughs from the crowd. I still have the cigar.

Jerry relished any chance to stick it to Montclair's most politically correct elements. In 2003, he managed a county campaign for a Republican. The candidate and family rode high on the backseat, while Jerry drove the requisite two miles per hour. How my husband basked in the boos and hisses of the townspeople lining the curbs. I was in the crowd, and though I voted Democratic in national elections, I was sick of local machine corruption, and loudly cheered while taking pictures.

Watching the makeshift floats and high school marching bands pass by without my husband either among them or by my side stung, but this was still our town, where we had raised our son and built a life together. Looking up at girls on stilts, banner-carrying political action groups, and a string of fire trucks, ambulances, and vintage roadsters, I conjured my curmudgeon of a husband atop his cycle, waving to the crowds, and giving me a special helmet-headed nod.

One morning, I found myself draped diagonally across my mattress, one hand reaching up to where Jerry's pillow used to be, as if I were attempting to reclaim his body's territory, and all at once I was compelled to change the position of the bed itself. I needed to realign the space by angling the bed from one corner, and *voilà*: the room's energy moved in a dynamic circle, making it smaller, cozier, suitable for one. Jerry was still present, of course, in the many photographs I surrounded myself with, but the process of making the room my own had changed it from a reminder of what I'd lost into a private haven.

The bathroom presented its own challenge. All I had to do was look at Jerry's sink—no toothpaste scum, no sprinkle of beard, goatee or mustache—and I missed him. Just as he shuttled between names, my husband hadn't been able to make up his mind what look he wanted; the closer his return to the Middle East, the more likely his attempt to grow facial hair. The absence of his tiny quarter-inch shavings, months on, still upset me. We used to bicker over his messiness. I'd have given anything for evidence of his living, breathing self, spackling the basin next to mine. Instead, there was an empty bowl, pristine with disuse.

I contemplated renovating the room, something I would have to do if I wanted to sell the house—a real possibility, given my unresolved money problems. Yellow tile and Formica counters didn't measure up to neighborhood standards. But I wasn't ready to relinquish what had been ours, however dated. A designer I consulted suggested a single sink. Every so often I washed my sweaters in his sink, but most of the time—unlike on the bed—I stayed on my side. After all, there was my sink, the right one, and his sink, the left one, the one he left behind. "No," I told her, "this has to remain a bathroom for two."

During the first few weeks after the funeral, I had removed one object from his side every day: first the toothbrush, which I tossed, then the comb, and the soaps. I kept the old-fashioned shaving brush he loved. I had always gotten a kick out of seeing him lather his face with soap from a wooden dish. Years earlier, I had watched our toddler son gaze in awe at his father's manly ritual, then sit on the closed toilet seat of our apartment bathroom, in serious grown-up mode, while Jerry covered his smooth little face with cream and handed him an empty razor. The two of them would proceed to "shave" in slow, rhythmic strokes until all the white foam was gone.

Just as I had with the bed, I tried to take over Jerry's side of the bathroom. I filled his wicker container with nail polish remover, air freshener, and bath powder, and stored toilet paper and tissue boxes in his cabinets. I emptied his vanity drawers, threw out prescriptions and extra razor blades, put the men's colognes on my son's bathroom counter, keeping his *Vera Wang for Men* in the cabinet below my sink. The mere memory of its familiar hearty scent undid me. If I looked at it for more than a moment, the spiciness of my husband's freshly shaved cheek enveloped me. I dared myself to open the bottle. I took off the black cap, put my nose near the nozzle, and inhaled. No need to spray. The perfume was rich, heavy. A chill shot through me. I reeled backwards. *There he was.*

July twelfth: the day I didn't cry. I had cried every day since I had gotten the call, but not that day. I hadn't cried so much since college, when I would lie on the bed in my tiny dorm room every Saturday night and whimper from virginal yearning. What had I expected when I chose a school whose newly coed population numbered ten women for every one man? Now in my virgin widow state, saturated with feeling, I cried with abandon. I cried to clear myself out. I cried, because I couldn't not. Until the day I didn't, like a faucet whose constant drip mysteriously ceased, though no plumber had touched it.

"Have you seen any movies?" It was Vicky. I was still wary. As long as our conversations stuck to pop culture I felt safe.

"I saw *Dark Knight.*" Not my usual fare. In fact, I would have only gone with my husband, who loved Batman. But this was Heath Ledger's last performance, and his sudden death over-lapping Jerry's had merged the two in my mind. I had to see it.

"Well. What did you think?"

"Ledger was great," I said. His face—a white Kabuki mask, the mad eyes, the slashed mouth—tumbled before me. I didn't tell her the film had triggered an onslaught of Dubai flashbacks. *Ollie and I watching CNN: Ledger dead at twenty-eight; Jerry on a gurney in the ICU; walking the hospital's basement hallway hand in hand with Scott on our way to the morgue; police waiting rooms; barricading the apartment door on our last night; monochrome landscapes of sand and unforgiving sun.* The intensity of those two weeks in which I could only react to one horror after another had reverberated throughout my first six months at home. I left the movie theater shaken. The tragedy of a young actor's unfulfilled promise, the scenes of epic destruction seemed inextricably linked to our family's loss.

I told my sister, "It was pretty intense."

"Go see *Sex in the City*," she said. "You'll have more fun."

At the end of the month, I spent a few days at Robyn's Cape Cod home, taking my college classmate up on the generous offer she had made at Jerry's memorial. It was the first "vacation" I had had on my own. Joan, another classmate—like Robyn, sharp and energetic—came as well, and the three of us became girls again just as we were in Vassar's drama department thirty-five years earlier. We had a wonderful time on the beach, and especially at the movies for a Streepfest. Meryl had preceded us at Vassar, and haunted us too—her legendary success setting an impossibly high bar—but we loved seeing her films together. *Mama Mia*, or "Meryl Mia," as we called the latest, was bubbly, silly fun. Because we knew each other before life had irreversibly happened, spending time together renewed me.

Robyn took us to a play at the Monomoy Theatre in Chatham,

where I had done two seasons of summer stock during college. Such a considerate gesture. After the show, we went backstage to the theatre office. The couple running the place, Alan and Jan, had been student actors in the same company as mine. We embraced and smiled at each other's middle-aged faces, eyes crinkling. Then they opened their arms to a ceiling papered with hundreds of headshots—every young thespian who had graced the theater's stage. "There," Alan said, pointing to a round-cheeked innocent with long wavy hair and big eyes. "There you are."

36

Becoming Jerry

After months of no real movement on the Dubai business deal, I knew Bill was becoming anxious. He told me he had discussed the situation with Raine. It seemed he was using her as a sounding board on Middle Eastern business practices. She thought the deal was dead, that he/we had nothing to bring to the table. Bill proceeded to instruct me on exactly what approach to take, directing me to play the bereaved wife to whom they had made promises at Jerry's bedside. I found this condescending, and the description made me cringe. I didn't have to *play* the bereaved wife, I *was* the bereaved wife. He warned me not to push them, or they would end the relationship. He didn't want that to happen. Patronizing and desperate. No wonder my husband wanted to handle the deal himself.

I asked my lawyer to weigh in. I had grown weary, and needed his advice. He responded that it was best to go slowly, that my call would serve as mere fact-finding, and that it was unnecessary to play the unsettled widow, since I was only trying to sort estate matters. Exactly. I appreciated his respect. Unlike Bill, my attorney was not concerned that I would make a fatal misstep.

When I called Jasim, he told me more time was needed for approvals, etcetera, and that our "interests were protected." He asked if Jerry's estate affairs in Dubai were being handled satisfactorily. I mentioned my attorney and his firm. Later, I relayed our exchange, as well as the underlying message of patience, to both Jack and Bill. Maybe Raine was right, maybe not. I only hoped that if the deal was indeed dead, we would find out soon. I wasn't cut out for such prolonged, murky business. The uncertainty tore me up, only adding to my mounting anxiety about the frozen funds. *Would I ever see the money, and if not, what would become of me?*

At the end of August, Jack updated me on the bank situation. As he had warned, the firm had decided that the best strategy for freeing the account was to declare me the director and shareholder of Jerry's UAE company. Not a simple matter. Once again, the certificate stating that I was my husband's executor had to be attested by the State Department, translated into Arabic, and sent, along with my complete curriculum vitae and a reference letter from my local bank manager verifying my identity and character, to Dubai Media City, the governing body. In addition, we would need a Dubai Court order to change the signatory arrangements on the account. Simply to unfreeze it, I had to become my husband in Dubai—something I had already experienced at home in New Jersey.

When I sold Jerry's Ducati to a used motorcycle dealership and had to stand up to a salesman who tried to pressure me into lowering the figure we'd previously agreed upon, I told him I didn't *have* to sell it, which was true. It was paid off. But the guy pushed anyway. I said no, I'd walk away, or he could. He accused me of lying about the condition of the bike, which was mint. He said his driver had found a nick in the mirror, the same guy who told *me* the bike was in amazing shape. I quoted the young man to his boss and held my ground, the way Jerry would have. A widow friend had told me that I would take on my husband's traits, the ones I had relied on for ballast, the ones that had acted as an invisible net to catch me when I fell. She said, "You will become more like him than you ever thought possible." She was right. I got my price.

And so, the newest twist overseas, becoming the company's director, unimaginable mere months before, seemed part of a larger shift, a formal absorption of everything Jerry had been. Though I was uncomfortable with all things Dubai, I was fairly accustomed to legal matters—my father had seen to that. But I was not comfortable with how much this work cost. My nerves were shot from living the paradox of small economies—every nickel spent on gas or groceries started an internal debate—and large expenditures. The monthly legal bills equaled my mortgage and property taxes combined. The slow trek through Dubai's labyrinth meant that the federal and state estate forms couldn't be filed on time. The extension created yet another expense from my accountant. *But what choice did I have?* This was the only way to get the money released to me. And I knew I was going to need it, all of it. My decades-long artistic path had yielded much satisfaction and little cash, and Jerry's multi-faceted career had not included anything as conventional as a pension. I had to trust that the tens of thousands of dollars I was spending on extricating his account would be worth the investment.

I received a letter from the apartment building manager about Jerry's security deposit. They owed me a couple thousand dollars. I glanced down the itemized accounting of their costs from January twentieth—the day Jerry collapsed—until March, when the lease was up. Below the astronomical air conditioning charges it said, "Cooker Glass Cover Replacement Charges." Once again, I saw my stricken husband, out of his mind with pain, flailing around his kitchen, slamming pots and pans against the stove, sending glass flying. And then I pictured Raine, comfortably ensconced in the flat, curled on her couch, cocktail in hand, gazing out at the Iranian mountains in the distance.

The Dubai court judge requested a copy of Ollie's passport, as well as the originals of Jerry's death certificate. *Why?* I thought we were asking the court to honor American estate law. Wasn't this the reason I had hired this big law firm in the first place, to avoid Sharia? I said as much to Jack, and that I was loathe to hand over original documents. He explained that ordinarily we should not have to deal with the court at all, but the bank manager wrongly believed he needed a court order, and each judge operated on whim. Again, I heard my father's mantra: *the US is a government of laws, not men*. In Dubai, the government was men—volatile, arbitrary men making up their tribal laws as they went along. I was stuck there, if not physically, then certainly financially and mentally. So I had no choice but to comply. I longed for Jerry to witness and give me credit for dealing with this mire of his making, for doing a passable job of being his surrogate. And I wanted my husband to tell me it would be okay.

37

Hope

In August, an old friend visited from abroad. She and her ex-husband knew our family in Park Slope, and then later, we all moved to Montclair. Her son was close to Ollie's age. Her visit was a peculiar affair. Before she arrived, she said how good it would be for both of us, but now that she was in my home, I saw that her agenda and mine were not aligned. We spent the afternoon driving around Montclair, to her old street, her old house. The owners invited us in. My friend wept as she walked through the tiny rooms of her once intact family's home.

When we returned to my house, she said, "That was so hard. What this must be like for you!" It seemed she came to put her own ghosts to rest. I lived with mine. Unlike widowhood, divorce was a choice, in this case a bitter one. Her husband had recently married a much younger woman and had a new baby. But though I felt slightly used—I was after all, taking care of *her*—I appreciated her excellent advice, which applied to both our circumstances, and which I would repeat to myself often in the years to come. "Don't let anyone tell you how long this is supposed to take," she said. *This*, meaning my recovery, potentially moving away, and—impossible to picture then—my eventual new life.

At the end of the month, Ollie returned from Chicago to Montclair. When he and a friend pulled up the driveway in a station wagon full of belongings, I was ready for him. Or so I thought. I had come a long way towards accepting Jerry's death, towards coming to terms by myself. But witnessing Ollie's daily struggle with that void set me back. I faced with Ollie the loss of his father in all its concreteness: *there was my boy, watching baseball by himself, no Dad to trade stats with, cooking Bolognese sauce alone, no longer sous chef.* My son's pain merged with mine, and reopened wounds that had barely begun to heal. But I soon realized it could not be otherwise. True healing could happen only with each other. What we had gone through in Dubai together had to be finished together.

With Ollie home to help with the dogs, I decided to visit my brother and his family in Maryland. On the train, an elegant Indian gentleman sat beside me reading the *Economist*. He glanced over at my *New Yorker*, and we began to chat about our destinations. The attraction was palpable. He got off at Philadelphia, hesitating before he left. I had the distinct impression he didn't want to leave me.

Then I remembered an airport encounter in July, on the way to the Cape. In the open eating area of Logan, a trim graying man, all in black, asked if he could sit with me at a small table for two. He told me he had just spent a week at the Omega Institute in Rhinebeck, New York, and was going home to Dallas, to his daughters. I listened, volunteering almost nothing. Only in retrospect did I realize this man had been hitting on me.

And there was the guy at the car repair shop who couldn't take his eyes off me, commenting on how my turquoise outfit and jewelry set off my eyes. It was an encounter that excited me, that reminded me I was still alive, still a woman attractive to men. I was far from ready for a new relationship, but when I was, I would have to keep the theme in mind, planted long ago at a bus stop: transportation flirtation.

Perhaps, when the time was right, a helicopter?

Throughout the summer, I went every week to the park in town to join my T'ai Chi Chih group for an informal practice. Sometimes I led the group, and began to consider becoming an accredited teacher. When eight years earlier I had stopped teaching theater to form the non-profit, I was sure I wouldn't teach again. But unlike acting or writing, the meditative movement practice wasn't about words. Its silence complimented my literary life, and had already given me so much. In my vulnerable state, the slow, soft, deliberate movements anchored me. And outdoors, in the group, I became part of the circle, held up by collective energy. I could feel the earth under me, focus as far in the distance as my eyes could see. And further.

It was during one of these practices that I realized Wali's image of loss as big as the universe had shrunk, just as he said it would that day in Dubai at lunch in his home with his wife and baby. *How big was my loss, seven months on?* In the shimmering August heat, it had edges, finite definition—a daytime shadow against the pale blue sky, no longer blocking it completely, but still surrounding me. The dark silhouette loomed, but didn't swallow me. My inner landscape was changing. This was progress. This was hope.

38

Milestones

September, a gauntlet of family birthdays—Ollie's, my brother's, his twins', my aunt's, Jerry's sister's, and my own. And then there was our anniversary.

This September began with a wedding. Keith's father was marrying an elegant, compassionate woman. Both had been very kind to us, especially to Ollie, acting as an extended family, inviting him to stay overnight with them whenever he was in town. The ceremony took place at their house, on the lawn. When I arrived, I noted the small group of family and friends. Thank goodness, since I wasn't yet up to crowds. The day shone brilliant and warm, after the downpour of the previous one, which had caused a quick postponement. The bride glowed. The vows were personal and moving. I glanced around me, and didn't see any other single women, except the bride's mother, long-widowed. Witnessing our friends make their pledges of love, I felt fine, even relaxed.

Afterwards, though, during the extended cocktail hour, I began to feel unmoored. I chatted and circulated up and down the redwood deck, crammed with people, but except for Keith's family, I knew no one. I reminded myself that this was to be expected. Still, I grew uneasy. Every so often, Ollie checked on me, and then went back to his friends. My son had an effortlessly social personality, much like his father, who had been a true extrovert. I, on the other hand, was sociable, but not gregarious. My discomfort amidst this group of strangers, however, didn't come from introversion. The joy of the occasion had only highlighted my sorrow.

When we finally sat down to eat, I found myself at a table of young couples. I asked after their children, their jobs, where they lived. By this point, badly wanting to leave, I was anxious for the bride and groom to cut the cake. The bride and her mother approached the table.

"How are you doing?" the mother asked, with a knowing look.

"I'm okay," I lied.

The bride said how hard it was not to have her father there. "It will get easier," she said, and patted my shoulder. Her mother gave a tiny, almost imperceptible shrug, an involuntary disagreement with her newly married daughter, which revealed the truth. It would get easier, but it might not get *better.*

The newlyweds danced. Other couples joined them. I could hardly stand to watch so many husbands and wives enjoying themselves. This was worse than the Broadway matinee. I waited until everyone at our table had eaten their cake, then I excused myself, and asked Ollie to take me back to our house, though it was only a few blocks away.

Inside, on our family room couch, I bowed my head. Ollie wrapped his arms around me. "I didn't think it would be so hard to be surrounded by happiness," I said through sobs that I had been suppressing all afternoon.

"I know," he said.

I repeated what another friend, a widow who had remarried, said to me months earlier: weddings were the toughest. Then I said, "Our twenty-fifth anniversary was supposed to be three days from now."

Ollie nodded. "You were robbed."

And, true as that statement was, I snapped out of my sadness. I sat up. The last thing I wanted was for my son to feel sorry for me. I couldn't have him worried sick about me when he was going through his own profound mourning. I hated self-pity. When my writing coach had wondered aloud if I asked, "Why me?" I responded, "Why *not* me?" This was what I believed: life wasn't fair; death was random; no one was exempt, but life was also wondrous. Though I had a helluva time doing so, I believed I had no choice but to accept it all—the miracle of meeting Jerry, the tragedy of losing him. *The greater the love, the greater the loss.*

Ollie and I held each other tightly. I told him to go back to the party.

"I'll be okay," I said. And I was.

Two evenings later, at a local restaurant, seated at a circular table, surrounded by young men—Ollie's friends from high school and college—I couldn't have been happier. It was an old-fashioned Italian steak place, all dark wood, leather banquettes and male waiters—professionals who had been serving their whole adult lives, the kind of staff you didn't often find in Montclair—and it was Ollie's twenty-second birthday. It was fun to hold court, to be in the midst of so much boisterous health and testosterone. The boys—I should say young men—were funny, irreverent, and polite, much like my son. A couple of stragglers showed up mid-meal, having heard via text message that Mom was paying. Fine with me. I felt like splurging, living in the moment, suspending my day-to-day worries about money and the future. Ollie and I needed this party, a timeout for us both.

That night, I went into my study to look at the picture of our family taken exactly a year earlier on Ollie's twenty-first birth-day—a photograph I saw everyday, because it sat on my desk, the last picture of the three of us together. Our small nuclear family had had a rocky time that fall. Both Ollie and I had grown more and more concerned about Jerry.

The evening before, Jerry had come home drunk. The moment he walked through the door into our kitchen, I knew. He didn't have to open his mouth. His body listed to the right, his eyes drifted. The sight triggered disgust in me, desperation in Ollie. Jerry knew enough not to defend himself. He went outside to the backyard. I stayed inside, paralyzed with anger. Ollie followed. Then, after a few minutes, I went out, too. It wasn't our son's job to take care of his father.

As I walked down the deck steps, I heard Ollie half-pleading, half-lecturing. "Why are you doing this to yourself, Dad? You're going to lose everything." Ollie saw me, and swung his arm in my direction. "Look at her." Jerry couldn't. "How can you do this when you have this great woman?" Jerry said nothing, still hanging his head in shame. I was startled and moved by Ollie's question. But I knew that my "greatness," as Ollie saw it, had no real sway over Jerry's addiction. "It isn't real over there," Ollie went on, meaning Dubai. "This is." Again, he gestured towards me.

"Do you want to go back to rehab?" I asked. His two lives had collided, and it was his choice whether or not he wanted to change.

After a long pause, he refused. "I can't leave the job."

When I said, "You'll lose that, too," and repeated Ollie's warning, my husband walked deeper into the shadows.

Ollie shouted, "I'm afraid you're not going to be there to dance at my wedding." Slowly, a deflated Jerry came back inside.

After we put him to bed, Ollie and I stayed up late talking, frightened and frustrated. We knew from previous experience that there was little we could do. I urged Ollie to call Scott. And I was upset that Jerry had cast a pall over our son's big milestone. I knew that the next day my husband would be sober and contrite—and he was—but that didn't change the sick feeling I had preparing for our evening out.

When one of Ollie's friends showed up early to ride into New York with us for the birthday dinner, we asked him to take our picture. We stood in the backyard, arms entwined, me in the middle wearing a dress Jerry had surprised me with on our last island vacation, flanked by my guys, looking handsome and clear-eyed. The shot was so good we used it for our holiday card, along with pictures of Edgar and Tisbury in front of the corresponding Martha's Vineyard signs. When I looked at the photograph, I found solace. Somehow, despite illness and uncertainty, despite the dark night before, we were radiant, individually and as a family. Our resilience shone through, and our love.

September 9, 2008—the day I had nervously anticipated for so long—had arrived, and with it, our twenty-fifth wedding anniversary, an event I hadn't been able to picture ten months earlier. Usually Jerry and I made plans for such landmark dates far in advance. We loved the Caribbean. We'd taken our honeymoon on Virgin Gorda. Maybe we'd go back. Or to Peter Island, in honor of Pete. The idea made us laugh. Transporting our private game to his own special island would be a trip in more ways than one.

But when Jerry suggested to me early in January that it was time to make our reservations, I said, "No, let's not." His brow furrowed. Then I added, "I can't see that far ahead." Now I wish I hadn't given voice to my blankness. Jerry knew I was a great believer in visualization. If I could see an event, I could make it happen. "Let's just get through Ollie's graduation," I added, as if that would smooth things over.

"Okay," Jerry said, clearly disappointed, "whatever you want."

Three weeks later he was dead.

I realized these many months later, more fully than I had at the time, that his death had been a shock, but not a surprise. When you've been married for as long as we had been, you were both physically and psychically connected, even thousands of miles apart. I had strong radar for his moods. The stress of his work had become obvious, but I sensed something more bleak lurking. He kept repeating, "My head's going to explode," a phrase he hadn't used before, referring not to a headache—though that was the final symptom—but to his overloaded life. I had vowed that 2008 would be our final year apart, and I had the distinct sensation that I was preparing for something major. I projected only good: Ollie's graduation, Jerry's recovery, paying off the house, renovating the bathrooms, buying a vacation home for our retirement, the pub-lication of my novel, our twenty-fifth anniversary—celebration, health, fulfillment, the beginning of a more peaceful, more unified life together.

Throughout the summer, I had begun calling the upcoming first anniversary without Jerry "the un-iversary." I still felt mar-ried to my not-anymore-husband; I didn't really understand how much this was true until he was gone. Jerry was the one who knew me whole, the one I could be my crazy self with, my playmate. *Who would talk to Pete now? Vicky?* There would be no replacing such intimacy. Seven months in, Jerry was still my shadow self, who haunted my every breath. *How could I un-marry my soul from my soul-mate?* I couldn't, but I had to keep moving, bringing him with me, like Wali said.

When the day came, I got out of bed and put my new locket around my neck, trusting its magic. This talisman of our present and past, which rested on my solar plexus holding our rings within its plain gold oval, would make the day bearable. I drove to the cemetery, towards the graveyard's landmarks—the carillon tower in front of me and the magnificent oak up the hill, above and to the left, reaching out its strong branches to shade the headstones. I got out of the car, climbed the few feet to Jerry's plot, then turned around, looking past the sloping rows of markers to the skyline beyond. The leaves hadn't fallen yet, obscuring the winter view of New York City I had prized when I picked the spot. Nevertheless, I saw it: the city where we met, fell in love, and married. I turned back, knelt, and placed three red roses on the flat granite rectangle, for the family we made. Then I plucked grass blades from its edges and brushed the smooth red-brown surface etched with the words, *Beloved Husband and Father.*

September sixteenth, 7 a.m. I turned on the radio, and in my bleariness caught the phrase, "AIG liquidity crisis," which instantly sent me into emergency mode. The insurance company that still held my money in an interest-bearing checking account was going under. I took a deep breath and called the 800 number on the account book. I told myself to stay calm, reasoning the money was actually at State Street Bank, not AIG, then realized with rising terror that the insurance company backed the funds.

The man on the other end of the line said as much. "Your money is safe." His weary, apologetic manner indicated that he must have repeated this many times that morning to worried customers, grieving widows and widowers all. *Who else received insurance payouts?* All the fear and instability of the past several months roared back. My back tightened in the familiar clench, the muscle memory of panic. *What if I lost everything?*

I threw on my clothes and went straight to my local bank to speak to the young woman who had so patiently helped me months earlier. I needed to move the money out of that account immediately. She was well aware of the gravity of the situation, having spent the day before fielding calls from clients freaked out by the Lehman Brothers melt-down. I said I wanted to put the funds in safe instruments: treasuries, brokerage CDs, a money market fund. As I wrote the check, she said, "You will be okay. The money is already yours." Action helped, but a world-class failure cascading in my direction gave me pause. There was no safe place.

Bill must have been worried, too. He chastised me via email about continuing as the contact for our elusive deal—"Now, Roselee"—invoking Jasim, who he said often repeated, "Women run the household,"—and said that he, Bill, should take over negotiating the terms.

Once again, his tone infuriated me, and his impulse to negotiate was alarming. Not to mention his reversal; only a month earlier, he had wanted me to play the bereaved widow, and now he wanted me out of the way. I gathered myself, and shot back:

> *It's important that you realize that I am the primary contact, because Jerry was the original contact. Legally I represent Jerry's Estate as its Executor. One could say, that for the purposes of this deal, I am Jerry Mosier.*

> *We are equal partners. I do not have to have 'done deals' to understand the unchanging truth here: We have no leverage whatsoever, other than the honorable intentions of the Dubai principals. There is nothing to 'negotiate.' They can give us whatever they want, and we will say thank you, and be happy to receive it.*

> *When I spoke to Jasim at your behest, I was ready and able to do so. He volunteered that the deal would be honored. He was cordial, respectful of me, Oliver, and Jerry—no condescension whatsoever. Frankly, the only condescension I have been subjected to is yours.*

> *I agree that this is a long shot. If it comes to fruition, we will BOTH be the beneficiaries of my husband's good relationship with Jasim. Period.*

I cc'd my attorney. Jack agreed with my position, and said that he, too, was struck by Bill's condescension, but that I had handled him. Jerry would have been proud.

I did not want to spend my birthday at home in New Jersey. My Aunt Doris, who lived in Los Angeles, had invited Ollie and me to come for a dual celebration—her birthday was the day before mine. Ollie and I looked forward to getting away, and he could use the time to meet contacts in the film and television business.

I had an ulterior motive as well. My aunt's house was within walking distance of UCLA, and I wanted Ollie to consider its graduate film school. He was extremely resistant. "I want to work, Mom," he said. "I don't want to go to school and then be exactly where I am now in two years." I couldn't argue with this. A graduate degree in film was no guarantee of job prospects, though I did point out that he might make life-long contacts there. "I can do the same thing out in the world."

So we spent our time visiting with my aunt, whose career had spanned the entire last half of the twentieth century, and in her prime had acted on *I Love Lucy* as the bespectacled friend, Carolyn Appleby, chased around a sofa by Harpo Marx. On the telephone her ageless, musical voice sang.

When we rang the doorbell to her Westwood home, Doris answered, greeting us with warmth and hugs. Though she had lost an inch or two since I saw her last, at eighty-eight—no one would ever guess her age—she was still beautiful and glamorous in classic Hollywood style. Even the death six years earlier of her husband, my Uncle Charlie, hadn't diminished her buoyant spirit. Doris was the most positive person I knew—just the tonic Ollie and I needed.

In the kitchen, while my aunt and I chose appetizers for a formal cocktail hour, a reliable treat at her house, she turned to me. "We had the best," she said.

"We did." It cheered me that Doris recognized my husband's true nature. For all the problems, Jerry had been a loving and earnest partner. Unlike my parents, Doris and Charlie had wholly embraced Jerry from the moment they met. Jerry and my uncle instantly bonded. They had a lot in common: humor, tons of stories, a disgruntled view of the world, and politics at odds with their extended families. My aunt and uncle were fun, loving, and their acceptance helped us both heal.

Ollie, who aspired to follow in his great-uncle's footsteps as a comedy writer, had worshipped him, and loved getting his hilarious, typed letters. Charlie always addressed Ollie as his equal. My son couldn't get enough of the black and white photos in Charlie's office, chronicling his amazing career. Charlie Isaacs wrote for and with all the greats: Jimmy Durante, Groucho Marx, Johnny Carson. Sid Caesar, Carl Reiner, and Larry Gelbart had spoken at his memorial.

Once in the library, a retro-style man-cave complete with plaid couch, red chairs, wood paneling, and tiny mirrored bar, where Charlie's talking toy parrot still perched, I relaxed—though an echo of "Charlie Parrot's," the bar in Dubai across from Jerry's apartment building, where the men had gone for "beerhams"—reverberated in a distant corner of my consciousness. I banished it, and looked around. Nothing in the room had changed. A comfort. Doris, Ollie, and I drank, nibbled, laughed, and told stories, avoiding those about our missing men. I gazed through the shuttered windows at the kidney-shaped pool and the cabana draped with bougainvilleas, and felt secure. This was exactly where I wanted to be.

The next day Ollie and I drove Charlie's ancient BMW to Burbank for Ollie's first interview. The car had no air-conditioning, and to our surprise, once we got on the highway, no power steering. We arrived parched and sweating, and dragged ourselves into a convenience store for drinks. I waited by the car while Ollie entered one of the low-lying buildings. The street was deserted, a desolation that momentarily reminded me of Dubai. The meeting went well, but Ollie was already inclined not to move west for an internship or a production assistant job that didn't pay a living wage.

In the car on the way to meet a commercial director Jerry knew, we didn't give voice to what we were both thinking: this would have been so much easier, more fun, more exciting if Jerry/Dad were there. He would have done the driving, bitched about the car, the directions and the heat, laughed when Pete shrieked "road trip," and gotten a tremendous kick out of Ollie's first forays into the working world.

And I was reminded of the last time I had visited Doris, two years earlier. I had planned the trip around Jerry's schedule, but when his plans changed, I decided, with some guilt—we spent so little time together—to go to California anyway, leaving him to return from Dubai to an empty house. While I was gone, he held a private showing of his latest film, setting up chairs in our family room, providing the audience with lemonade and popcorn. That evening, he called me with a full report. They had been impressed with the seriousness of the subject—religious factions in Lebanon—and the quality. And everyone wanted to know where I was. After his death, a friend who had attended told me that Jerry had taken her aside and said, "I hope Roselee doesn't hate me." He had finally realized how hard it was to be the one left home alone.

September twenty-ninth: my birthday. Doris took us to Spago, Wolfgang Puck's famous restaurant in Beverly Hills, along with our cousin Olive, who had been living with Doris for the past few years. I was genuinely happy to be there, and grateful. I blew out a candle on my dessert, a chocolate confection. I tasted the rich, dark mousse. In the moment, only pleasure.

39

Messages

While Jerry traveled, I made lists of little factoids about my day, my week, Ollie, the dogs, for when we talked, as we did every day by phone or by iChat no matter where in the world he was. I could count on half a hand the number of days we didn't speak at all. No matter what he was doing, time difference be damned, we spoke. Now that he was gone, I became more and more aware of the special resonance given to any occurrence by telling my husband about it. And I had the sense that whatever happened without Jerry shouldn't have, and wasn't quite real unless I could share the experience with him. I didn't believe in angels. Except for a few crazed rants—"How could you do this to me?"—I didn't talk aloud to Jerry. Nevertheless, I found myself storing tidbits to tell him:

It's October. Time to carve the pumpkins, as you always told Ollie. He landed an internship with Tom Fontana in the most incredible way, just walking down the street in Greenwich Village with Jim, who was giving him advice. Jim pointed to an old library building, "Here's where you should go—Levinson Fontana. Walk in there right now and give them a résumé." Two days later Ollie got a call. How cool is that? Homicide, St Elsewhere, Oz. The writer of your favorite shows.

I bought Ollie an old Beemer for his birthday really cheap—150,000 miles on it, stick shift, of course. It needs a lot of work, but I knew it's what you would have done.

Edgar is healthy, though slowing down a lot. It's hard to see him grow old. He missed you. He jumped on the bed for the first couple of months to keep me company. Then he couldn't anymore.

Tizzie is a pain, but we love her. Honestly, had I known what was coming I wouldn't have agreed to another dog. She hasn't "replaced" you, but I'm glad she's here.

Leo's voice is changing. I didn't recognize it the last time I called.

I don't know what to do about the house. I don't know where I'm going. I don't know how to go on without you.

Ollie and I drove to Nonny's in western Pennsylvania, with Edgar in the back. The rolling hills, stripped of fall foliage, reminded us of countless trips with Jerry to see his grandmother, the woman who I considered to be my grandmother too, the only one I'd ever known. My father's parents died in Poland during World War II, and my mother's father, when she was nine. I never met her mother, either. Nonny had filled the void. She accepted and loved me unconditionally, as I did her. And for Ollie, she became a true grandmother as well, connecting emotionally when her daughter couldn't. Though Nonny had grown frail—she used a walker now—she could still crush your ribs in a bear hug. And she was as feisty and opinionated as ever. We took her to her usual lunch place for soup and sandwiches. The owner, who knew her well, greeted us effusively. We talked little about Jerry. We didn't have to. Then after tea and pie, at the end of the meal, Nonny grabbed my hand. "He worked too hard. He couldn't slow down. Didn't know how." All I could do was nod.

Closing Jerry's home office took me more than nine months. Each Sunday since February, before I put out the recycling, I spent an hour or two in the vast basement space that Jerry worked in when he was home. In the far corner of the room, Jerry had placed his '60s drum-set, electric blue with silver sparkles. On many a weekend afternoon, the house would reverberate with its heavy beat, while he pounded back-up for his favorite rock songs.

Behind the drums stood a cardboard cutout of John Kerry given to my registered Republican husband at his fiftieth birthday party, a presentation that had sent our guests into paroxysms of laughter. Kerry dominated the deserted space, commenting with an uncomfortable grin, his neck wreathed in multiple nametags and ID lanyards from my husbands' conference and film festival appearances. On Kerry's lapel was a letter from Bush and a Bush-Cheney pin. Jerry, like many Republicans, had grown disillusioned by the administration's incompetence, but he never quite went over to the other side. He did admit, however, that either Hillary or Obama would make a fine president. I wished he had lived to see his hero, John McCain, get the nomination, but I knew he would have been appalled by the Palin pick, and I venture to say, he would have defected, along with his compatriots, David Brooks and Christopher Buckley. But, of course, like other more personal mysteries, I would never know for sure.

I removed four large folding tables that comprised three-quarters of the office's work surfaces. The fourth quarter of the room housed a built-in work area/desk from the previous owner's tool and dye business. Jerry kept his big screen Mac there. I had yet to summon the strength to open its files.

Bolted-in metal shelves covered one entire wall, but they were never full. Jerry preferred to pack our crawl spaces and closets with old advertising posters, ads, and promotions. The previous fall, only months before his death, he had bought a couple dozen plastic bins, and filled them with hundreds of copies of his projects. I'd made it my business to clean out every bin, to know where everything was, to look at each piece of paper, no matter how trivial, no matter how painful. I saved one or two of every print ad or article he'd written, and placed the containers on the bare shelves, in plain sight, for my move—whenever I was ready—and because I needed a concrete grasp of what was left. Forty-five minutes was my limit. After that I had to come up for air.

There were things I couldn't bring myself to move—foremost, the evidence of his creative mind. On the wall nearest the office door was a floor-to-ceiling bulletin board where Jerry proudly assembled a collage of his vibrant, combative work, laminated, on poster board or glossy stock. There was a print ad showing an exploding doll, "The Toy that's Making a Lasting Impression on Thousands of Afghan Children," for the Afghan Relief Committee; "St Patrick's Day—the one day your body looks good to almost everyone," for the New York Sports Club; and framed editorial pieces for the *National Review,* the *Detroit News,* and his *Daily News* article, "Memo to New York: Drop Dead," as we were about to leave the city for the New Jersey suburbs, all hanging at odd angles. I didn't know how long I would or could stay at this address—every other day I wanted to bolt, or resolved to never leave—but I knew if I went, I would strip these walls last.

I kept the display case outside the office: Jerry's 1986 Addy, his many New Jersey Tellys and Jersey Awards, his newly received documentary awards from the Djerba TV Festival and the Medina Festival in the Middle East. Lined up next to each other, the sharp silhouettes in plexiglass, gold, and silver formed a New York skyline. Behind the awards, I placed the Little League plaque picturing Jerry and the team that Ollie and I had given him to commemorate his stint as coach. I had a hard time looking directly at the photograph, but I wanted it there, nevertheless.

Ollie, preparing for his own writing career, had begun to take over the office. He covered Jerry's whiteboard with ideas, deadlines, and plans. Our son liked having the memorabilia wall and the awards case to remind him of his dad's accomplishments, to spur him on, but now this was *his* lair, alive again.

By November, there wasn't much left in the room, but the denuded space still reflected my husband's mind and drive. Its stripped-down core, its closed containers, the pictures of him in Lebanon or his New York office, the exercise bike he didn't get to use, the silent drum set, and even, or maybe especially, the cardboard blow-up of Kerry both brought him back and proved he was gone like no other room in the house.

While I sat on the floor, sorting through the last category of papers, the most personal one—twenty-six plus years of valentines, birthday, and anniversary cards—I felt like Alice falling down a rabbit hole of the past.

I found Jerry's 1994 letter to the *New York Post*, a submission for "Best Love Stories:"

It was an unseasonable chilly night in May 1981. The place: the bus stop at 82ⁿᵈ St. and Second Avenue. It was midnight. A petite, attractive young woman dressed in a cowgirl outfit stepped inside the shelter. We were alone. We exchanged smiles. When the bus finally arrived we sat together. I was going as far as Tudor City. She was continuing on to Gramercy Park. We never exchanged names or phone numbers. At 43ʳᵈ Street I exited. But I couldn't stop thinking about her.

The next day I called the comedy club and said I had to get in touch with the cowgirl comic. As hard as it may be to believe in today's age of paranoia, they provided me her name. She admitted to me over the phone that she had been frantically trying to locate me, too.

On September 9, 1983 at that very spot where we had first met, we were married by the Yankee Pine Tar Judge, Orest V. Maresca. We had asked the TA for permission to rent a city bus, and then they turned on their PR machine. Our dozen guests were met at the bus stop by over a thousand uninvited New Yorkers. Plus every TV network and the local papers—even the New York Post (check your clip file.) It was the marriage of the century.

Ten years later, we're still married and we have a seven and a half year old son, a Yankee fan!

I gathered copies of the invitation to the October first wedding reception in our Park Slope apartment. No half measures here: Jerry had a cartoonist friend sketch the wedding scene. He captured Jerry—the broad grin, the locked knee posture—but he made me a tall, skinny slouching bride resembling Olive Oil.

I picked up a card for our ninth anniversary:

"To a wonderful wife, mother and friend! We've had a great nine years and I can think of no one else I'd like to spend the rest of my life with."

And from Dubai in 2005, a sonnet:

So, either by thy picture or my love,
Thyself away are resent still with me:
For thou not farther than my thoughts canst move
And I am still with them and they with thee

John Donne's words softened the residual sting left by the poem to an unknown woman that I had found on Jerry's flash drive nine months earlier. In fact, each message touched me more deeply than when I first received it. I stored the cards in folders, organized by occasion, placed them in bins alongside the records of his life's work and of our history, a repository of our time together, labeled and closed, but not forgotten.

Rereading Jerry's cards gave me the courage to look once more at the emails he wrote me from Dubai. I was glad I'd printed each one as I received it. On paper, they felt more like the love letters they were.

Tuesday, November 30, 2004, 3:48 p.m.

Roselee,
The only downside is that I have to be here so freaking long. I know we end up bitching at each other when we are together. I do miss you and I miss talking with you in person about my day. I know I don't say it very often but I do indeed love you and I don't know how I would have gotten this far without you. Thanks.

Love,
Jerry

Friday, September 16, 2005, 4:30 p.m.

...understand you are not a source of my anxiety. If anything you are the person that keeps me on an even keel. You know me better than anyone else. A Sheik asked me tonight who was the one person I could depend on. I immediately said my wife of 22 years and he said I was a blessed man to have someone who was my partner for life. He is one of the richest men in the world and he was envious of me. I am truly happy and blessed.

Wednesday, November 9, 2005

Had an iChat with Oliver this morning….He is the best thing that we did together. Thanks for being the great parent that you are. You talk about not succeeding at anything, but you are a great mother to our son and a great wife. I love you.

Monday, June 19, 2006, 4:10 p.m.

Dearest Roselee,

I know I have been distant and aloof in the recent past. Part has been my selfishness and self-centeredness that I thought was necessary to deal with my addiction issues. I know you have paid a heavy price to stay by my side. But I want you to know that there isn't any future I can imagine without you. This path has been painful, but I know in my heart that there is no one for me other than you. And yes, I see us growing old together and more in love, as long as I finally quit smoking. You are in my dreams tonight.

Xxxx,
Jerry

Friday, August 4, 2006, 7:30 p.m.

R,
Just woke up from a bad dream. Now awake just wanted to talk to you, yet know it is too late. Wanted you to know that I am still in love with you. I miss you dearly. And I wish you were next to me sans Edgar.

Love,
Jerry

And the last message, on Wednesday, Nov. 7, 2007 at 4: 59 p.m., the one I knew by heart:

R,

Been a long day and I miss you more than you can imagine. I want you to know that my love for you has not wavered in the past twenty-five years. My job sucks…but at the same time I think it will in the end give us the opportunity to be together even more. I know this separation is tough for you, as it is for me, but I BELIEVE that in the end it will benefit both of us. I made a very big deal tonight that might guarantee us future financial stability. I love you, and I appreciate the sacrifices you are making on a daily basis.

XXXX, J

It had been a year since I received that email from Jerry. I clung to it in Dubai—repeated it to myself after meeting Raine—held fast to the thought that he did indeed love me and always had, that this was the truth of our marriage. As I read it again, along with the other sure signs of his feelings, and of his struggle to reconcile work, his demons, and our life together, I wondered if he could have written this and been screwing around at the same time …*my love for you has not wavered in the past twenty-five years…*Yes, it was possible, even probable, given what I found in his apartment bathroom.

But how much did that matter? Did it outweigh our decades together? No. It didn't. I held the opposing thoughts in my head: he loved me, he betrayed me, he hurt me, he didn't want to lose me, he was desperate to find a way out, but not before he got what he came for—enough financial success to secure our future. He was profoundly stressed and conflicted. Not excuses, reasons.

Maybe Scott was right in the first place that day in Dubai, after he had seen the body off, when we sat together in Jerry's bedroom and I told him what I had found. *He loved you. It doesn't mean anything.*

I imagined my husband sitting on the edge of his bed, pants around his ankles, paralyzed with shame, because he knew what was right and what was wrong. Jerry had a strong moral compass, even when he went off course. This pathetic image was as close as I could come to playing out the unknowns. *Did it quash the permanent uncertainties left to me?* No. But it served an important purpose. In Dubai, faced with Raine, pills and packets, I automatically adopted the perspective that his loss superceded his missteps, essentially the same conclusion I had drawn after almost a year without him. The months of railing and questioning, of playing out scenarios had, if anything, solidified it. I understood that for all his worldly courage, which was considerable, my husband had been a coward where I was concerned. Jerry had told me he didn't want to hurt me, that he was protecting me, but he was really protecting himself. *I know in my heart that there is no one for me other than you.* He was terrified of losing me. If he never faced me, he didn't have to face himself and the consequences of his actions. Now I had done that alone. And even if he only drank, the consequences were cumulative. I couldn't trust him as completely as he had trusted me. His alcohol abuse was part and parcel with his possible infidelity, both evidence he was losing his bearings.

I took "for better or for worse" seriously—for me there had been *no* deal breakers—but years of seeing my husband deteriorate personally while soaring professionally had left me on the sidelines of my life. I had grown weary. I confronted it when I could, but towards the end, when my energy had all but run out, I stopped fighting, and only stated what I knew to be true: I couldn't see past Oliver's graduation from college; I couldn't picture our twenty-fifth anniversary trip; I was merely hanging on day to day; it was up to him not to lose *me*. In those last months, I faced the fact that I couldn't change him, that I had no control over his choices.

Then the unthinkable happened, and grief nullified his transgressions. The wounds, the causes known and unknown, painful, messy, disturbing, had less and less power to torment me. After the anger, the hurt, and the haunted questions, I sensed a shift, as if an intense storm had washed through me, leaving behind the truth: that only love and sorrow remained, and even the sorrow would one day fade. My own words echoed, the ones I left the mourners at Jerry's memorial: love never dies. I believed them now more than when I had spoken them.

And I believed the cards and the messages. My heart was broken in two places: one where what I found resided, one where I had lost him. Both gashes would heal, but his death would leave the bigger scar.

The early November sky was brilliant blue, the air crisp. In a few days I would have to pack up the summer furniture, empty the giant pots surrounding our patio, prepare the yard for winter. But on this late autumn day, I sat outside under the shade of a giant oak and typed the messages on the cards and emails into a single document. I wanted Jerry's words in one place. When I finished, I placed the printed emails downstairs in the card bin. I might not read them again. I might not have to. They had entered my body. They were part of me, like Jerry was. Understanding and acceptance were so much simpler than I had thought. We loved each other. Ours was a real marriage, not a perfect one. Jerry had his struggles. I had mine. Now I had to love myself enough to let the rest go.

40

New Year

For our two-person Christmas, Ollie and I sat in the living room and went through the motions, with Charlie Brown's familiar holiday music playing in the background. We opened gifts, took pictures of the dogs, praised the surprises, thanked each other, and smiled. Then I unwrapped Ollie's last gift to me: a framed picture with a dozen photograph openings filled with pictures of Jerry and me, in the early years before our son's birth. There was my husband in front of Edinburgh castle, and I with our first dog, Deco—the puppy that showed us we could love and care for a living being—and in the center, Pete on Jerry's shoulder, Pete with me in Bryce Canyon, and Jerry with his arm around Pete, who was wearing a Yankee's hat, both of them lolling on our black leather couch, our first purchase together, watching the game. I was overcome. Such a loving gesture.

That night in the car on the way home from dinner at our favorite Chinese restaurant, continuing our family's nod to Jewish tradition, we talked about last December, and the trip to Nonny's

that Ollie had taken with his father. Ollie repeated Jerry's directive: "Be good to your mother. She's having a really hard time with
me being away so much." Then he had said, "I really want it to
be over." And we recalled the previous year's Thanksgiving and
Christmas—how it had been just the three of us, though we usually spent at least one of those holidays with George's family.

"It's like we knew," I said.

Ollie kept his eyes on the road, hands firmly on the steering
wheel. "But we didn't, Mom. We didn't know." I sighed and looked
over at my son in admiration. Unlike me, he steadfastly refused the
crutch of magical thinking.

On New Year's Eve, Ollie and I clinked champagne flutes,
and toasted to a better year. *How could it not be?* Then he left for
Keith's to party with his friends, where he would spend the night.
I watched *Pride and Prejudice* on A & E, putting up with the com-
mercials—thankful for them, because they stretched the two-hour
movie into three-and-a-half, eating up the interminable evening.
I wept at the sweeping romance of Elizabeth and Mr. Darcy.
After the movie, I sat at the kitchen table, mesmerized by the minute hand on the wall clock above the sink as it ticked inexorably
towards midnight. I thought of where I had been the previous
New Year's Eve—in bed, in my husband's arms, making love for
the last time. "I feel so close to you," Jerry had said. We had never
been more one. *As if we knew.*

I grew more and more agitated, more and more desperate
to stop time. In 2008, he lived. When the minute hand reached
twelve, I put my head down on the table. In 2009, he would not.

41

Three Januarys

On January 4, 2008, Jerry's fifty-third birthday, he began individual therapy for the first time in years. Afterwards, we met for dinner at a local restaurant, and as soon as we sat down, I asked him how it had gone. I didn't expect details, just whether or not he liked the guy.

He didn't answer my question. Instead, he said, "I want you to know that no matter what, I'll always take care of you. You've got to get that homeless, living-in-a-box thing out of your head. I wouldn't abandon you, ever."

My husband's attempt to reassure me had the opposite effect. He really expected me to leave him. I wanted to get up and walk out, and told him as much.

"I'll be there if you're sick," he went on, "but if you decide…" He was hiding something, something he thought would force me to end the marriage if I knew. *That he was drinking out of control? That he was screwing around? Both?* I didn't know.

"What did your therapist say?"

He looked down at his plate. "It was time to grow up."

For the rest of the meal, I tried to swallow my rage along with the handmade ravioli. Tell me everything, or tell me nothing. I'd had quite enough of oblique statements. The earth shifted underneath me. I no longer knew where I stood.

A week later, Jerry was leaving again. I had been steaming for days. Usually, we stayed in the kitchen until his departure, waiting together for the car to pick him up and take him to the airport. This time, I couldn't. I sat in the family room and listened to him zipping and unzipping his bags, checking to make sure he hadn't forgotten anything. I had an overpowering sense that I was through with all this. Then, suddenly, I had a tremendous urge to reach him. I got up and walked into the kitchen. Jerry was wearing his travel uniform: black wool jacket, black sweater, black skullcap. He looked somber. I could see that he hated the impasse we were at as much as I did. I stood in front of my husband, took both his hands in mine, looked up into his eyes and without knowing what I was going to say spoke slowly and firmly, "You know how much I love you."

Jerry didn't move. He seemed frozen in fear and sadness. Then he nodded ever so slightly. He kissed my forehead and hugged me tightly. The car came. Jerry gave me a quick peck on the cheek, and was gone. I never saw him conscious again.

As the first anniversary of Jerry's death approached, I became impatient with The Widow. I wanted to evict her. I still mourned, but no longer needed external trappings. The doll would go the way of the flower arrangements, condolence cards, and candles I had stored or gotten rid of the previous winter. I had absorbed what she represented. I had accepted my widowhood. I didn't need her unchanging expression to remind me of what I had endured. I had planned to store the doll in the closet again, but chose instead to put her in a yellow donation bag. As disturbing as The Widow was, I couldn't bring myself to discard her. Perhaps someone else would need her. I tossed the bag in the garage to await the next pick-up.

Rosie would stay. The mischievous little girl in the red gown and feathered hat would remain, propped on her stand, boa askew. The girl with the self-satisfied smile and closed eyes imagining herself in new roles reminded me of who I was Before Jerry, and who I could be, now that it was After.

Not only was I fed up with The Widow, but also, and much more completely, with the stalled business deal, and the absurdly inaccessible bank account. I was sick of calling Jasim each month, only to be strung along. I understood the deal wasn't real—Bill and Raine were right about that—but I couldn't seem to let it go. The stress of hanging on to the illusion of a big payday had depleted me. I had witnessed Jerry's struggle to believe the vague promises, to have faith in ephemera. No wonder he had been falling apart.

I asked Jack to make the next contact, and, if possible, to meet with Ashar, who called the shots and whom he knew well. I needed to find out, once and for all, if this project was going anywhere. Big as the money might have been, I hoped that the deal could finally be declared over. Its invisible thread tied me to Dubai, kept me prisoner. As long as I was still on one end, stretched across the ocean to that disturbing city many time zones away, I lived there, at least psychically.

And the deal was a distraction from the more important problem. The bank account situation had worsened. I couldn't fathom why, after I became the corporate director of Jerry's company, the bank still refused to open the account. Just as I had been a year earlier, I was terrified that the branch manager's blank computer screen meant an empty account. I had paid tens of thousands in legal fees, and for what? Enough was enough. I was losing faith this would work out. The bureaucratic twists and turns seemed

nuts, schizophrenic, even. The moment my legal team and I fulfilled one demand, another contradictory one was made. I was
at my breaking point. I had just reduced my health insurance to
the bare bones variety, and had raised the deductibles on my car
and home insurance. It was all a gamble. Would I have to sell my
house, move who knows where? My future was at risk and on hold
until some UAE functionary sought fit to release it. *Would I actually
have to go back over there?*

The thought made me sick to my stomach.

The tax extension deadline of February twenty-seventh—
exactly thirteen months after Jerry's death—was little more than
a month away. I couldn't stand any more last-minute pressure, so I
decided to tell Jack I had to know immediately that the funds were
there, exactly as Jerry had left them. I reminded my attorney of
the amount. The bank must unfreeze the account. No excuses. I
was through being patient. This was *my* deadline, the only one that
mattered.

Shari invited me over for lunch to watch Barack Obama being
sworn in as President. She didn't want me to be alone on the anniversary of the phone call. We ate prime rib, and basked in the history-making day. Jerry would have been so excited.

January 27, 2009: one year. From now on, the first month of
the year would be Jerry's, book-ended by his birthday, and by the
day he died. I walked into the kitchen. Sun streamed from the skylight onto lilies and roses in a lush floral bouquet Vicky had sent,
an empathetic gesture that touched me. I fed and exercised Tizzie
and Edgar, and did my T'ai Chi Chih practice. Then I put on my
coat, hat, and gloves to go to the cemetery. I was just about to leave
when the phone rang. It was Jack's assistant in Dubai. She never
called. All of our contacts had been by email.

"Ms. Blooston? I wanted you to know that the account is open. All the money is there, just as you said."

Stunned, I laughed. The timing was unbelievable, and I told her as much. She said they would proceed with transferring the funds. All at once my shoulders let go, my whole body relaxed. I took a deep breath. I had been holding myself together by sheer will for twelve agonizing months, waiting for resolution, and it had come with striking exactitude.

I stood over the grave with yellow roses, which reminded me of the night we met—me in my ten gallon hat with the artificial yellow rose attached, Jerry in his yellow rain slicker. I gazed at the Manhattan skyline, and thought of Wali's words. I felt my husband's shadow presence beside me, no longer all around, no longer as big as the sky or the trees—still huge, yet human in scale—beside me now, a companion, neither dark, nor sad, nor overpowering. *Just as the man said.*

January, 2007. My husband and I were on a desert dune-busting trip with a dozen other tourists. By the time we reached the dinner site, where we sat on pillows under the stars to watch belly dancers and feast on an array of goodies, my stomach roiled from the jeep's wild trek up and down the dunes. The setting sun's orange brilliance cast a rust and gold veil over the sand, in stark contrast to the surreal city we had left behind. The elemental beauty of sky, sun, and sand gave me my first moment of serenity since I had arrived.

We lined up for one more event: a camel ride. I had my doubts. The animals reeked, and were a good deal taller than I had envisioned. I was afraid of heights, including one between two humps, where I would have to sit.

"Come on. It'll be fun. Great photo op," Jerry said. So up I went, gripping the saddle so tightly that my knuckles turned white.

Luckily, the ride wasn't much, once around the makeshift sandy parking lot.

"Smile," my husband said. Looking down at his beaming face and silly grin, how could I not?

Near midnight, in the bus on the way back to the city, Jerry whispered in my ear, "You're Penelope." He meant the long-suffering and faithful wife of Odysseus.

"Didn't she wait a decade for him to return?" I asked.

"Twenty years," he said.

I shook my head. "Don't think for one second I'm going to do any such thing. I told you four years was the limit, and I meant it." That early and somewhat arbitrary deadline felt like a biological clock ticking down the minutes until this separation would be over. As traditional a wife and mother as I was, once Jerry began traveling, I clung to my self-image as an independent person, at least in spirit—a label quickly affixed by my parents when, in elementary school, I rejected little girl cliques, and again later, among my peers, in my stubborn adherence to a creative path. But now in the midst of a long-distance marriage, I felt only my total, utter dependence.

"It might not be so easy to leave when you want me to. It might take a couple more years to wrap things up."

"I don't have a couple more years," I said, as if I knew his life would end, when what I really meant was that our life together might. The steadfastness of character that my husband compared to a mythic mate's came partly from my loyal, disciplined personality, and partly from inertia and fatigue.

I had once asked Jerry how he would characterize our marriage. "We're entwingled," he said. We laughed at the nonsense definition. It perfectly captured who and how we were together.

I couldn't laugh now. Jerry looked dead tired. I felt his untenable position, caught between my needs and his work. I stroked his hand, and kissed his cheek. I hated that I had given him an ultimatum. "So if I'm Penelope and you're Odysseus, who are the sirens?"

Jerry smiled. "They're out there. But don't worry. I'm lashed to the mast." Then he put his head on my shoulder and fell asleep.

During the first ten years of our marriage, I had been hard on Jerry. I expected him to prove my parents wrong by being everything I needed: emotional partner, lover, best friend, hands-on father to our child, provider. To his credit, he never treated my expectations as unfair. He wanted what was best for me, for Ollie, for our family. On our tenth anniversary, with my mother dying of cancer, I realized that I had to stop pushing him, judging him. He had passed the test the very day he first loved me. It was time for me to accept him as fully as he had me. But as soon as I let up, he began pushing himself hard enough for both of us.

I couldn't know what I would have done had Jerry lived, had we been able to confront all that had been held back in those last days. I do know that my story was about more than faith in each other, faith in marriage against difficult odds. In the beginning, I asked everything of him; in the end, he asked the same of me. I believe that, had Jerry lived, his life in Dubai would have come crashing down—another bout of severe depression, public drunkenness, legal trouble, job loss, and then home to rehab. Nothing good. He was in too deep. He was too fragile, still the baby in the incubator.

What Shari said in those first vulnerable days after Jerry's death—that I would always know what love is—was true. Being loved was not as important as having loved. When Jerry and I met, I saw him whole, in a pure flash of connection, which had yet to be tried. Through marriage and mourning, I learned to embrace my husband's entire self—even the aspects that couldn't be fully known—with mind, heart, soul, body, being. It was an important lesson, though the price was high. I'm grateful I got up from my chair and walked into the kitchen that last day. In the end, I made sure he knew how I felt. No matter how disappointed, enraged, or frustrated I was, no matter how sad, hurt or scared, I never stopped loving my husband.

42

Fifteen Days, Thirteen Months

In February, the Dubai bank account was finally transferred to the New Jersey estate. I thought that once the frozen account had been opened, the money would be released. But it wasn't. The branch manager still dragged his feet, asking for more documentation. I had to send yet another notarized and attested permission document from my local bank. It seemed like purgatory. Though my accountant informed me that the money didn't actually have to be stateside to file, I didn't care. I was sick of trusting anyone else with my best interests. I told my lawyer that the funds had to be in my possession by the twenty-fifth, since the tax-filing was due on the twenty-seventh. There couldn't be another extension. *Why had I not done this months sooner, in September, before the original deadline?* I suppose I wasn't ready. I wasn't fed-up enough.

No sooner had I given my attorney the order, than the money was moved to the law office's escrow account. Two days later, the wire transfer happened. I checked the account online, repeatedly. It seemed unreal. After so much time, money, effort, fear, and frustration, I had difficulty believing this lengthy episode was really done.

Perhaps because it wasn't quite. One loose end dangled: the phantom business deal. At my request, Jack met with Ashar. Ashar professed no knowledge of an agreement with Jerry, confirming my suspicion—and Bill's—that Jasim couldn't say no to a widow, and was stringing me along. By this time, I didn't want the money. I wanted to be out of Dubai, and finally, I was. Throughout the year, I had been steeling myself for the possibility, however remote, that I would have to return. The slog through my husband's complex life in Dubai was finally over. I would never have to go back, either on a plane or in my mind. It was all over. I had survived, and I would be okay.

Thank goodness Jerry had died with his illusions intact. He wouldn't know that the ship wasn't coming in, that there was no ship. His relationships with these UAE businessmen weren't genuine. At least my husband was spared a disappointment, which surely would have crushed him. Now that the world economy had come crashing down, taking Dubai's massive construction projects with it, I saw that even if these men had been serious about doing business with Jerry, it would have come to nothing. In November, Dubai's markets had sunk, and by February, the building boom had halted.

My husband had grand dreams. *I made a very big deal tonight that might guarantee us future financial stability.* Like so many, he gambled with his life and ours for a win that would never have happened. *I BELIEVE that in the end it will benefit both of us.* The capitalization was heartbreaking. He was trying to convince himself. Jerry had been operating on faith and fumes.

My husband died in Dubai, but he could have died anywhere. The aneurysm could have burst at home in New Jersey, or while driving down a highway, here or there, taking others with him. As it was, it took him and me and our son into an overblown land, a city on steroids pumped up by millions of ex-pat dreams of fortune, like his own. The fifteen traumatic days that Ollie and

I spent in Dubai weighed on us almost as heavily as the thirteen months following. The wrenching external journey traversing alien medical care, government bureaucracy, and tribal law informed my year of mourning, an inner journey every bit as foreign.

In a sense, I too, died in Dubai—the self that was forged and defined by our marriage, the self that, despite our difficulties, saw the future he wrote about as the truth of who we were together, as life itself. That life died with him, and so did that self. I knew this intuitively on the return flight. *We would be different people now.* The experience of those two life-altering weeks blocked out any sense of a future. I did not know then that I could live anew, without my role as Jerry Mosier's wife, without my anchor, with only my son and myself. But the following year proved my resilience. I surrendered. I grew. I would have given anything not to know what I was capable of, but a terrible thing happened, and a new, stronger version of myself emerged.

Only days after the money and business issues were settled, I got a call from one of Jerry's colleague's—a man whom my husband admired, whom I had never met. "I don't know if you realize," he said, "but I want you to know how respected Jerry was by everyone who worked with him. He did great things. He was a star. I hope he knew." I told the man Jerry did know, that he had felt valued by his colleagues, more than ever before. Jerry was proud of his work at the station, and of his films. His success was real, even if the world in which it manifested itself was illusory. The man, unlike other friends of Jerry's, didn't offer to help me. That was fine. I had gotten the help I needed, and I had helped myself. I thanked him. We both knew we wouldn't speak again. Though I would continue to associate my husband's exploding brain with the extraordinary demands of his life in the Middle East, it was gratifying to hear that the work my husband had paid with his life for had been appreciated.

Jerry's undershirt, wadded under my pillow, rarely washed the entire year, had stayed in place until the end of February, when I realized I didn't need a security blanket anymore. I washed it one last time, folded it, and put the threadbare material inside the cedar chest at the foot of my bed, the chest that contained my wedding dress and our son's baby clothes. I wasn't sure if I would take it out again, but I knew it belonged there, tucked away, safe and close.

Friends and acquaintances still asked regularly, "How are you?"

I would say, "I'm coping," though "okay" and "fine" were waiting on my tongue. I saw my widow's walk as a slog with pebbles in my shoes and the earth quaking under my feet, but it led me to more solid, smoother ground. When I stumbled, I told myself to walk through it—the pain, the fear, the wretchedness—walk through it all. Sometimes the walk felt more like a free fall, a solo flight with no controls and nowhere to land. Sometimes the trek was an uphill struggle, under constant pressure from inside and out. Sometimes a friend or family member took my hand, listened, and walked with me. But for the most part, my widow's walk was mine alone. Widow. Just another fact. With each step forward, I was preparing a place inside myself to carry my loved one the rest of the way.

Epilogue

July 3, 2013 – Red Hook, New York

I sit on the top step of my sunroom, looking up through skylights at gray blue. Then I look down through a wall of glass windows and doors at a pond that can only be described as a Monet—complete with lily pads, intermittent sunlight dappling the water in prismatic bursts, and reflected shades of green from leaves, grass, and bushes that I cannot yet name. Its serenity envelopes me, and I am overjoyed at possessing it after such a fraught journey, yesterday and forever ago. But this present could not be mine without the past. It took everything I had physically, emotionally, and financially to get here, not to mention luck and my husband's dream advice one year ago.

I am in the hallway bathroom I just refurbished. The newly painted tile gleams white. Jerry is there. I mention moving in 2012, after he decides whether or not he wants to live with someone else. He turns to me, and I get a clear look at him. He is older, sixty-ish, gaunt, but entirely himself, the man he might have become if he'd lived and gotten well. I see his face, his short white hair, and his body dressed all in white. His glasses magnify his green eyes. "I'm not going to do that," he says, slowly, calmly—meaning he's not going to leave me. Then I reiterate the 2012 deadline I'd imposed on myself, and am transported to the living room, kneeling in front of the picture window, packing suitcases. Jerry lifts me up by both hands, the way I held his that last time. He says, "or 2013, or 2014," giving me permission, time to stay where I am as long as I need. His voice is loving, secure, sensible. When I awake, I realize that this is what I missed most—Jerry's ability to give me the best possible advice—and how much I crave his guidance about the subject that has nagged at me: where to live. This has become my mantra: "2013, 2014." And though the *move* would be mine alone, he has said that he wouldn't leave me. And he hasn't.

I took my time and slowly un-married myself from the setting of our life together. I wore Jerry's sweaters and pajama tops. I learned how to be in the world without my partner. Mostly, I was in a good place. Much had healed. Much had settled. Well-being returned. Gradually I began to trust my evident survival, and to envision a future without Jerry.

The house was transformed from tormenter—memories on every wall—to a source of comfort, for the same reason. Jerry kayaking in New York Harbor, the Twin Towers in the background; swimming with Edgar; carrying Ollie in a backpack; holding his hand, while he takes his first steps in the Bronx Zoo; our family in a Dubai souk; Jerry and I arm in arm, standing in front of a city bus, the words "Just Married" on its monitor; a black and white family portrait, my head touching Jerry's as we held our laughing three year old—the pictures, flashcards of our life together, which could only be understood in its entirety, the difficulties indivisible from the joys. Love and adversity, just like my brother said.

There has been another adversity, another shadow big as the world. George died of tongue cancer in August 2011, the day after I put down our beloved fourteen-year-old Edgar, of whom the vet said, "he'd had extra innings." But not my brother. George was only fifty-five, a couple of years older than Jerry had been. Two of my three men gone, two of the three who loved me unconditionally, who shared my history, understood and bore witness, whom I loved. Because George was being treated at Memorial Sloan Kettering in New York City, he had spent a great deal of his last year living with me, in Montclair. As unhappy as I was about the reason, I was grateful to have had time with him. After his death, Ollie and I had the surreal experience of once again delivering eulogies before hundreds. *Unbelievable...what it is.*

My work life expanded. I wrote magazine articles, coached writers privately, and finished the novel. I also received my T'ai Chi Chih teaching accreditation. To fulfill the requirements, I gave a presentation to a hypothetical class. I had intended to speak to writers about the practice's creative benefits. But the night before the presentation, I couldn't shake the sense that there were others I needed to address. I lay in bed, mentally revising what I would tell this audience, a group I had been a member of for almost two years at that point: the bereaved.

The next morning I told my fellow teachers-in-training, who stood in for the designated group, about my epiphany in Dubai— the flash of benign lightning, which had shot through me like never before or since. "I needed energy, and I received it." I told them how, on good days and bad, I did my practice. As I spoke, I heard sniffling. Two of the teacher trainers fled, overcome. I continued, "When you don't know how to go on, let go. When loss robs you of your identity, put your attention on the soles of your feet, shift your weight and flow from the center. Chi will carry you forward, and you will remember who and what you are, a human being, able to experience sorrow and joy, and above all, a still vital force." The room dissolved into sobs. Not me. In the telling, I had transcended my own story.

Moving presented an existential dilemma. I wasn't moving for a job or a relationship. I was moving for me, the new me, the After Jerry me. Years of walking in and out of New Jersey open houses, of not feeling "right" about anything I saw, led to an epiphany when I drove into Rhinebeck, parked on its main street, and said to my son, "This is it. This is where I'm going to be in a year." It was another love-at-first-sight attraction, primed by my Before Jerry self—the one who went to college nearby—and by the wife who gazed for years at the Montclair Art Museum's Hudson Valley paintings, which rendered its mountains, water, green, and light—a light as soft as Dubai's was harsh—familiar and singularly compelling. Finally, a new place I could call home.

In preparation, I threw myself a sixtieth birthday party—equal parts milestone celebration, goodbye to my Montclair home, and thank you to the community of family and friends that had supported me. Then I packed, sorted, kept what counted and tossed the rest, simultaneously releasing the past, and embracing the future. I kept every inscribed book, including *Man Against Himself*, which predated me, and was signed, "J. Mosier, To Himself."

I watched twenty-five years of home movies that I had finally transferred to DVD. Only once the moving date was set—a hard deadline—could I listen to Jerry's voice again, or look at his animated face and body on screen. I knew if I didn't do so while still in Montclair, I probably never would. Surrounded by boxes, I watched one a day, writing their contents on the covers, taking breaks to plow through *Gilmore Girls* and *The Wire*, both of which Jerry had recommended. I listened to Jerry's arguments for the organization US English, and for advocacy advertising, on network talk shows from the '90s, his resonant voice, intelligence, and passion on full display—as was the contrast between his youth and his poise. I watched our wedding video in each of its NYC local news versions; our Christmas mornings in apartment, first house, second house, Jerry showing Ollie his Lego castle, train set, kayak, and the sweet embarrassment on our faces as we took turns holding our gifts up to the camera while being "interviewed" for our responses; vacations on the Vineyard; Thanksgivings with George's family; Little League games Jerry coached; Ollie's graduations from pre-school, middle school, and high school; his cello concerts; the Fourth of July parades. And the last tape: Jerry's fiftieth birthday party, where he paraphrased his grandmother's advice, "We're long-lived in this family, so you better deal with your shit," and everyone laughed and applauded. Watching our history, our personal traditions, made me laugh, too, and weep. We had a full cycle together. I'm glad I have this record of our marriage, but I doubt I'll look at it again. I won't need to. It's inside me now.

There have been times, during the past few years, when I have wondered what might have happened to us if I had vetoed the work in Dubai. But I could no more have stood in Jerry's way than he could have stood in mine. We gave each other the freedom to be ourselves. Almost thirty years ago I took a chance, fell in love, and continued throughout our marriage to take chances with my chosen man. Implicit in this was an abiding faith, often counter to reason, in him, in us, in myself. Jerry expanded and shaped my life. He delighted, infuriated, and challenged me. I am who I am because I was married to Jerry Michael Mosier. The widow who said I'd become more like my husband than I ever thought possible was right. I'm more gregarious, chatting up every new person I meet, just as Jerry would have done. I knew I would be a different person after his death; I didn't know who or how. It seems that facing loss opened me up, and I like who I've become.

I wait for the movers, all of my possessions in their truck. The house is empty, though warm and inviting. I am filled with something I didn't think possible: joy. I did it. I moved on. I'm happy and at peace. Happiness plus peace equals joy.

I can't wait for Ollie to arrive. I think back to last summer, one

Saturday night at a New York comedy club, as I sat waiting to see my son perform. He was a natural. I knew it all along. Like his dad, Ollie's been funny his entire life. Though he'd run material by me over the past few months, he didn't want me to see him perform live until the show was suitably professional. This was it, his first weekend booking. When Ollie took the stage, wearing a black Neil Young shirt and jeans, long curls flying, I saw before me a young man with attitude, wit, Jerry's gruff charm, and a point of view all his own. Ollie grabbed the audience and held us, not with the usual riff on dating, jobs and family drama, but with his interests—history, philosophy, human behavior—which his father had cultivated and passed on. How Jerry would have loved Ollie's take on dinosaurs, dictators, the rapture, and Dr. Seuss. As soon as Ollie was done, the booker offered him another gig the following week.

My friend Lily, who accompanied me to the show, who attended my wedding and held my baby on his first day, said, "What did you expect with you and Jerry as parents?"

She was right. He had my performance chops, and his father's brainy irreverence. What a kick that two people who had met at a bus stop after one of them had performed at a comedy club produced such an original, confident young man, and that Ollie was exactly Jerry's age then—full circle, and a revolution beyond.

Just as the movers finish in my new home, Ollie arrives with Tizzie. She spins and jumps, wild with happiness at seeing me. We've been apart for a week, the longest separation since the trip to Dubai. I've missed her. I've stopped resenting her for being the dog Jerry had so pointedly said would "replace" him. I had bristled at the word, but now I understand. Maybe he knew, like I did, that something more would separate us. Perhaps we all carry our entire trajectory on a cellular level, our whole life story imprinted within us from the day we are born.

Ollie looks around, bowled over by the beauty of the place. "It's your answer to the Vineyard, Mom." We take a walk around the lake. We talk about the thrill of being here, the great good fortune. I feel twenty years younger, unburdened. I have survived, and now I can thrive.

It seems Ollie is thriving, too. He announces that he has just sent out a slew of résumés. I assume this is for work with production companies, like his previous jobs.

"No, Mom. Advertising."

I am floored. I had tried over the past few years, ever so gingerly, to nudge him in that direction. After all, it was a way for a writer to make a living, and Ollie was nothing if not a writer. Dad did it, I'd say. Still, our son resisted. Now he had decided, on his own, to follow his father. I am pleased and proud.

The next morning, Ollie leaves early to host his own Fourth of July celebration. I kiss his cheek goodbye. "Happy Independence Day, Mom."

Happy independence day.

I don't believe in closure. I know how contradictory that sounds in light of writing about the cataclysm of Jerry's death, which I have diligently worked at precisely because I didn't know how else to handle it, precisely because I needed closure. It turns out, for me, there is no closure but the absence itself, which gives none of the resolution that the idea promises. Nevertheless, I dredge through the sediment of my past with my husband, doing what I have always done, making art of my personal challenges—a practice I believe in more than religion or therapy to heal and transform. I take what churns inside me, put words on the page, order the chaos, name the pain. I trust the result will be something tangible to move on *from*.

I've been using Jerry's laptop to write this book. Every time I write "Jerry," "Mosier" appears on the screen. The writing of this memoir, among other acts, re-balances me, takes me through mourning, my unanswerable questions—opens me to life again, altered as it is, and I am grateful. For all my protestations that I would never return to Dubai, I do, over and over, in draft after draft, flashing back to the plane, the ICU, the apartment, the police stations, the dunes—not to mention whenever a promotional plug for Emirates Airlines interrupts my favorite programs on WNYC, or *60 Minutes* does a piece on the Arab city's building bust, or the *New York Times* runs a travel article on its luxuries. In the process, I relive the experience of being there, and defuse the grief and anger I had layered onto Dubai. I still don't want to go back. Ever. But I no longer resist its power. It simply has nothing to do with my life. *I'm not Penelope anymore.*

I often think about a day early in that first winter, when Ollie and I discussed our shattered world. I had said how much harder even the most mundane task was without his father, and how difficult it was to imagine ever getting past his loss. Ollie told me that he thought of his grief as an infant. It needed everything. It took every ounce of energy, but would grow and change, and one day leave. I said I hoped that by the time it went to school, some form of regular life would return, and I wouldn't have to wait until it entered college. He smiled and nodded. Such a wise young man. My son gave me this living image of grief, a way of seeing the dark, new territory we had entered as less barren, as a passage that would mature and one day free itself, and us. I use it often. My grief is in kindergarten now, and my life is indeed freer and more whole.

Of course, Wali's words have stayed with me, too. I carry Jerry deep inside. Both images mark how far I've come.

And I *have* come far.

Now when someone asks how I am, I answer, "Fine." And mean it.

Acknowledgments

I would like to thank director and publisher Kevin Atticks, program assistant Amanda Berning, project coordinator Karl Dehmelt, designer Ashley Nicholson, marketing advisor Itzayana Osorio, editorial consultant Lorena Perez, and the entire publishing team at Apprentice House Press for making this book a reality. I am eternally grateful to you all.

This memoir began in short essays, which became the basis for Part Two. Those essays were developed in Alice Elliott Dark's 2008 summer workshop. I wish to express my thanks to Alice and to the workshop participants for their perceptive comments and encouragement. In the summer of 2010, I joined three members of that workshop—Patricia Berry, Lynne Cusack, and Cindy Handler—to continue sharing our work on our own. I could not have written the first draft of Part One without them. Having astute and sensitive readers willing to look at such raw material, made re-creating the events in Dubai bearable, and helped me envision what the memoir could become. Thank you.

I would also like to thank the editors who weighed in on full drafts of the memoir. Lynne Cusack offered her considerable insight, and the book is better for it. Nicole Bokat gave important developmental guidance, for which I am extremely grateful. My appreciation extends to Claire Gerus for her professional suggestions, and I am deeply indebted to Cindy Handler for her meticulous line editing of the final draft.

A short essay from an early version of the book appeared in the *Vital Force*, the journal of the T'ai Chi Chih community, in 2010—my thanks to Kim Grant for making that possible. Editors

Jacqueline Lapidus and Lise Menn chose another short selection for their 2014 anthology, *The Widows' Handbook* (Kent State University Press). Their on-going support has meant a great deal. Both publications showed me that my story had an audience, and gave me the confidence to take the project all the way.

My love and thanks go out to my sister-in-law Jeanne Fountain, for allowing me to use my brother George's words in the text, and for her expertise on the publication process, to my brother-in-law Scott Mosier, for helping clarify the sequence of events in Dubai, and to Shari Coronis, a reader and dear friend, whose steadfast support on this long journey has been invaluable. To all the family and friends who cheered me on, I send a heartfelt thank you. Publicist Jennifer Prost and web designers Sandra Arias and Paul Tsang deserve special thanks for helping me to get the word out.

Finally, I want to thank my son, Oliver Mosier, who read, proofed, and re-framed various sections of the book, who allowed me to use his writings in it, and who, over the past eight years, gave his unstinting support when I needed it most. I love you, Ollie.

About the Author

Roselee Blooston is an award-winning writer whose plays have been produced in New York, across the country, at the Edinburgh Festival, and over Voice of America. Publications include articles in *AARP The Magazine, the Vital Force,* and *Montclair Magazine,* fiction in *Moxie, Pulse Literary Journal,* and in an e-anthology from Release, Netherlands, as well as essays for Burning Bush Publications and *The Widows' Handbook,* an anthology published by The Kent State University Press. She was founding director of the non-profit Tunnel Vision Writers' Project Inc., and taught in university programs. Roselee lives in New York's Hudson Valley, and can be reached at roseleeblooston.com.

Apprentice House is the country's only campus-based, student-staffed book publishing company. Directed by professors and industry professionals, it is a nonprofit activity of the Communication Department at Loyola University Maryland.

Using state-of-the-art technology and an experiential learning model of education, Apprentice House publishes books in untraditional ways. This dual responsibility as publishers and educators creates an unprecedented collaborative environment among faculty and students, while teaching tomorrow's editors, designers, and marketers.

Outside of class, progress on book projects is carried forth by the AH Book Publishing Club, a co-curricular campus organization supported by Loyola University Maryland's Office of Student Activities.

Eclectic and provocative, Apprentice House titles intend to entertain as well as spark dialogue on a variety of topics. Financial contributions to sustain the press's work are welcomed. Contributions are tax deductible to the fullest extent allowed by the IRS.

To learn more about Apprentice House books or to obtain submission guidelines, please visit www.apprenticehouse.com.

Apprentice House
Communication Department
Loyola University Maryland
4501 N. Charles Street
Baltimore, MD 21210
Ph: 410-617-5265 • Fax: 410-617-2198
info@apprenticehouse.com • www.apprenticehouse.com.